IDEAL HOME

The Plant Guide

IDEAL HOME

The Plant Guide

SUCCESSFUL PLANTS FOR EVERY GARDEN

David Joyce

Photographs by Jerry Harpur

CONRAN OCTOPUS

To Graham

First published in 1995 by Conran Octopus Limited
37 Shelton Street, London WC2H 9HN

Text copyright © David Joyce 1995
Design and layout copyright © Conran Octopus Limited 1995
Photography copyright © Jerry Harpur 1995

A catalogue record for this book is available from the British
Library.

ISBN 1 85029 670 7

Commissioning Editor Sarah Pearce
Project Editor   Helen Ridge
Art Editors   Ruth Prentice
                      Alistair Plumb
Picture Research   Jessica Walton
Production   Jill Macey

Printed and bound by Butler & Tanner, Somerset.

FRONT JACKET A summer medley of alliums, a dark-flowered pink (*Dianthus*) and larkspur (*Consolida ambigua*).

BACK JACKET A mixed border fronted by pinks (*Dianthus*) and diascias, backed by roses, lilies and a blue-flowered geranium among shrubs.

PAGE 1 The golden form of creeping jenny (*Lysimachia nummularia* 'Aurea') weaving among the woolly leaves of lamb's ears (*Stachys byzantina*).

PAGE 2 The golden-leaved hop *Humulus lupulus* 'Aureus' climbs through the grey-leaved *Rosa glauca*.

RIGHT 'Apeldoorn', one of the showiest of the mid-season tulips, with the variegated honesty *Lunaria annua* 'Alba Variegata'.

Contents

Introduction

The superb photographs illustrating this book are an inspirational reminder that those who garden in temperate parts of the world are fortunate in the number of beautiful and useful plants from which they can choose. How, though, is one to select from the bewilderingly wide range of plants available to make the most of one's own suburban plot, country garden or town courtyard?

The role of my contribution to this book is to make it easier to select plants that are beautiful, useful and likely to do well in the growing conditions available. Five chapters cover the principal components of the garden, special conditions, such as highly alkaline soils, the creation of cottage gardens and other styles or effects, and gardening for outdoor rooms, including planting in containers. Each chapter includes suggestions for planting that are precisely focused to meet specific requirements or to suit particular conditions. To convey the maximum amount of information succinctly the suggestions are presented in the form of charts. There are slight variations from chart to chart in the way information is organized but the core information includes dimensions (these must be treated as approximations), season of interest and, in the form of a brief description, the distinctive features that justify a plant's inclusion. No symbols have been used but there are some self-explanatory abbreviations. Ornamentals are listed throughout by their botanical names (common names being added if they are widely used and they are included in the index), while fruit, vegetables and herbs are listed under their common name. Botanical names may at first sight seem cumbersome and forbidding to those who are unfamiliar with them. They are, however, the only reliable way of identifying plants accurately and they are, therefore, the names by which plants are labelled in nurseries and garden centres.

I frankly admit that the selection process has proved difficult for me. A good many plants could be included on several lists and there is intentionally some repetition. However, my preference throughout has been to nominate a single cultivar when there is a range available but to avoid as much as possible giving the same cultivar in more than one chart. Using the index in conjunction with the charts will help gardeners to broaden the range of options open to them.

In early summer the garden often seems to stall; the great flourish of spring is over and many plants are just getting geared up for the spectacular display of high summer. The columbines are among the loveliest flowers for this tentative season. The common columbine (*Aquilegia vulgaris*) and its hybrids are available in a range of colours that includes violet, pink, crimson, plum and a very beautiful white. The granny's bonnets dance above blue-green foliage which is itself very beautiful. Although plants are generally not long-lived, they self-seed in an inoffensive way. Here a vivid *Centaurea* makes a showy foreground while the spikes of *Euphorbia characias characias* form a dense phalanx behind.

The Framework

W hen the broad lines of a garden are being established, planting and design must go hand in hand. It is for this reason that the first chapter of this book looks at ways of planting a garden's boundaries and divisions.

Among the planting options considered are hedges and screens as well as plants that can be used to dress the vertical surfaces which define all areas within a garden. It deals, too, with trees and large shrubs, for which, in a small or medium-sized garden, there may only be room for one or two; these must, therefore, be chosen and placed with care.

This chapter also deals with broad areas of planting which are often used instead of or to counterbalance areas of hard surface. Grass, whether grown as a fine lawn or combined with other plants to make a flowery turf or meadow, is the most commonly used form of ground cover but there are alternatives.

Few plants can create living architecture as effectively as yew (*Taxus baccata*). Piercing by portals and windows only accentuates its massive solidity, and it is easily shaped to represent buttresses, pilasters and columns, as well as balls and more fanciful flourishes. Its close-textured surface can be maintained by a single trim in the growing season and provides a sober background that flatters the more transient beauties of the garden.

Hedges & windbreaks

The usefulness of hedges as components of a garden's framework is matched by their considerable ornamental value. Whether planted to define the boundaries of a garden or to mark divisions within it, one of their chief values is in providing shelter. They have an advantage in this over solid walls and fences in that they present a porous surface, filtering wind and cutting its force without creating turbulence. They are also versatile, capable of creating intimate private areas while blocking out unwanted views of eyesores. They are increasingly taking on another role, too, for they help to deaden noise and therefore provide some defence against the sound of traffic.

When planning your garden, rather than having to choose between the austere beauty of a formal hedge or the softness and seasonal charm of an informal one, it is certainly worth considering whether both types of hedge can be accommodated, for they complement each other admirably.

Formal hedges

Resilient trees or shrubs that respond to regular trimming by forming a dense, even surface are needed for formal hedges. Because they provide year-round leaf cover, evergreens are often chosen in preference to deciduous trees or shrubs. However, beech and hornbeam are two deciduous trees, much used for hedging in the past, that retain their russet leaves well into winter and make a very pleasing contrast to hedges of more sombre hue.

Preference is also very often given to fast-growing plants which will quickly reach the desired height. Regrettably, fast-growing plants do not change their nature once a hedge has attained its mature form and may need to be trimmed up to three or four times in the

Evergreens are frequently the first choice for formal hedging but there are several deciduous trees and shrubs that are also suitable. Hornbeam (*Carpinus betulus*) and beech (*Fagus sylvatica*), for example, both hold their russet leaves through the winter months. Here, an arch in a hornbeam hedge frames a specimen of *Cornus controversa* 'Variegata'.

PLANTS FOR FORMAL HEDGES

Name	planting distance	height at 5 years	clip	description
EVERGREEN				
Buxus sempervirens common box	45cm/18in	1.2-1.5m 4-5ft	x1 late sum. to early aut.	slow but versatile; dense, glossy, dark green foliage
Buxus sempervirens 'Suffruticosa' common dwarf box	15cm/6in	15-25cm 6-10in	x1 late sum. to early aut.	miniature version of box
Chamaecyparis lawsoniana 'Green Hedger'	60cm/2ft	1.8-2.5m 6-8ft	x2 late spr. to late sum.	one of numerous fast-growing forms; good green foliage but rather coarse
Cotoneaster lacteus	75cm/2½ft	1.8-2.5m 6-8ft	x1 early to late sum.	moderate growth; leathery leaves; long-lasting berries
Euonymus japonicus spindleberry tree	45cm/18in	1.5-2.2m 5-7ft	x2 late spr. to early aut.	moderate growth; glossy, dark green leaves; good for seaside but not cold districts
Ilex aquifolium holly	60cm/2ft	1.5-2.2m 5-7ft	x1 mid- to late sum.	slow-growing; many forms, with variegated or dark green, glossy foliage, most prickly; females berry if a male plant nearby
Ligustrum ovalifolium privet	45cm/18in	1.2-1.8m 4-6ft	x3 late spr. to early aut.	fast-growing; dark green foliage may be semi-evergreen
Lonicera nitida	25cm/10in	90-150cm 3-5ft	x2 late spr. to early aut.	fast-growing; dense and dark green; shade-tolerant
Lonicera nitida 'Baggesen's Gold'	25cm/10in	90-150cm 3-5ft	x2 late spr. to early aut.	gold-leaved form needing full sun
Prunus lusitanica Portugal laurel	75cm/2½ft	1.5-2.2m 5-7ft	x1 mid- to late spr.	slow-growing; glossy, dark green leaves on red stalks
Taxus baccata yew	60cm/2ft	1.2-1.8m 4-6ft	x1 late spr. to early sum.	slow-growing; dark green, dense hedge; a classic
Thuja plicata western red cedar	60cm/2ft	1.8-2.5m 6-8ft	x2 late spr. to early aut.	moderate growth; dense, pineapple-scented foliage
Tsuga heterophylla western hemlock	60cm/2ft	1.8-2.5m 6-8ft	x1 late spr. to early sum.	moderate growth; on moist soils a vigorous, dense, dark green hedge
DECIDUOUS				
Carpinus betulus hornbeam	45cm/18in	1.2-1.8m 4-6ft	x1 late sum. to early aut.	moderate growth; dense foliage; prominently veined leaves are russet in winter
Crataegus monogyna hawthorn	30cm/12in	1.2-1.8m 4-6ft	x1 late sum. to early aut.	moderate growth and thorny; white flowers in late spring; colourful haws in autumn
Fagus sylvatica beech	45cm/18in	1.8-2.5m 6-8ft	x1 late sum. to early aut.	moderate growth; makes superior hedge; brown leaves retained in winter
Fagus sylvatica Purpurea Group	45cm/18in	1.8-2.5m 6-8ft	x1 late sum. to early aut.	purple-leaved plants, useful for contrast
Hippophae rhamnoides sea buckthorn	60cm/2ft	1.5-2.2m 5-7ft	x1 late sum. to early aut.	moderate growth; spiny with silver foliage; females bear orange berries if a male plant nearby
Prunus cerasifera myrobalan plum	45cm/18in	1.5-2.5m 5-8ft	x1 mid-spr.	moderate, dense growth; white spring blossom

PLANTS FOR INFORMAL HEDGES

Name	planting distance	height at 5 years	clip	description
EVERGREEN				
Berberis darwinii	45cm/18in	1.5-2.2m 5-7ft	x1 early sum.	yellow flowers in mid-spring; blue berries
Berberis x **stenophylla**	45cm/18in	1.5-2.2m 5-7ft	x1 early sum.	arching shrub; yellow flowers in mid-spring
Cotoneaster franchetii	30cm/12in	1.5-2.2m 5-7ft	x1 mid- to late sum.	arching shrub; grey-green leaves; red fruits
Escallonia 'Donard Seedling'	45cm/18in	1.5-2.2m 5-7ft	x1 late spr., x1 late sum.	pink flowers in summer; hardy hybrid
Fargesia murieliae **(Arundinaria murieliae)** bamboo	75cm/2½ft	1.8-3m 6-10ft	none	clumps of canes with arching foliage
Lavandula x **intermedia** lavender	30cm/12in	75-90cm 2½-3ft	x1 early to mid-spr.	one of several suitable lavenders; aromatic flowers mid- to late summer
Olearia x **haastii**	90cm/3ft	1.5-2.2m 5-7ft	x1 mid-spr.	white, daisy flowers mid- to late summer
Pyracantha 'Teton'	60cm/2ft	1.8-2.5m 6-8ft	x1 late spr.	yellow-orange berries
Rosmarinus officinalis 'Miss Jessopp's Upright' rosemary	45cm/18in	1.2-1.5m 4-5ft	x1 late spr.	aromatic shrub of narrowly erect growth; blue flowers in mid-spring
Santolina **chamaecyparissus** cotton lavender	25cm/10in	30-45cm 12-18in	x1 mid-spr., x1 late sum.	aromatic leaves of felted grey
Viburnum tinus laurustinus	75cm/2½ft	1.2-1.8m 4-6ft	x1 early sum.	white flowers late autumn to late spring
DECIDUOUS				
Berberis thunbergii **atropurpurea**	45cm/18in	1.2-1.8m 4-6ft	x1 late sum. to early aut.	purple foliage; scarlet berries
Chaenomeles x **superba** 'Rowallane'	75cm/2½ft	1.2-1.8m 4-6ft	x1 late spr. to early sum.	red flowers late winter to mid-spring
Forsythia x **intermedia** 'Lynwood Variety'	60cm/2ft	1.2-1.8m 4-6ft	x1 mid- to late spr.	yellow flowers early to mid-spring
Fuchsia 'Riccartonii'	45cm/18in	1.2-1.8m 4-6ft	x1 late win. to early spr.	red/purple flowers mid-summer to autumn
Prunus cerasifera 'Nigra'	60cm/2ft	1.5-2.2m 5-7ft	x1 early sum.	dark leaves; pink flowers in early spring
Prunus spinosa blackthorn, sloe	60cm/2ft	1.5-2.2m 5-7ft	x1 early sum.	white flowers in early spring
Rosa 'Cornelia'	60cm/2ft	1.2-1.8m 4-6ft	x1 late win.	pink flowers in summer
Rosa rugosa 'Alba'	60cm/2ft	1.5-2.5m 5-8ft	x1 late win.	white flowers in summer; large red hips
Symphoricarpos x **doorenbosii** 'White Hedge' snowberry	45cm/18in	1.5-2.2m 5-7ft	x2 early to mid-sum.	white berries
Syringa vulgaris lilac	1.5m/5ft	1.5-2.5m 5-8ft	x1 early to late win.	lilac, white or pink flowers in late spring

TREES AND SHRUBS FOR WINDBREAKS

Name	planting distance	height at 10 years	description
BROAD-LEAVED PLANTS			
Elaeagnus x **ebbingei**	75cm/2½ft	3-4.5m 10-15ft	leathery and silvered evergreen leaves
Griselinia littoralis	75cm/2½ft	4.5-6m 15-20ft	shiny evergreen leaves; good for seaside gardens
Hippophae rhamnoides sea buckthorn	1.2m/4ft	3-6m 10-20ft	deciduous silvery leaves; orange berries; good for seaside gardens
Populus nigra italica Lombardy poplar	2.5m/8ft	6-9m 20-30ft	deciduous tree with a columnar shape
Prunus laurocerasus cherry laurel, common laurel	90cm/3ft	3-4.5m 10-15ft	shiny, evergreen leaves; white flowers in mid-spring; black berries
Rhododendron ponticum	60cm/2ft	3-4.5m 10-15ft	evergreen leaves; purple flowers in early summer
Tamarix parviflora	75cm/2½ft	3.7-5.5m 12-18ft	fine, deciduous leaves; feathery, pink flowers in early summer
CONIFEROUS EVERGREEN TREES			
x **Cupressocyparis** **leylandii** Leyland cypress	2.5m/8ft	4.5-9m 15-30ft	columnar shape with a dense crown
Cupressus macrocarpa Monterey cypress	2.5m/8ft	4.5-9m 15-30ft	columnar shape when young; good for seaside gardens
Pinus contorta lodgepole pine	1.8m/6ft	4.5-7.5m 15-25ft	narrow crown; good for seaside gardens
Thuja plicata western red cedar	1.8m/6ft	4.5-7.5m 15-25ft	narrow cone shape when young

growing season. The implications for long-term maintenance and the quality of the mature hedge need to be considered when choosing hedging material. For fine texture, yew is unbeatable and it is faster growing than is often imagined. It is, however, poisonous and should never be planted next to grazing land.

Formal hedges are frequently treated as simple cubes, with a straight top and vertical sides. Giving a slight batter to the sides, so that the hedge is broader at the base than at the top, has the advantage of allowing the whole surface of the hedge to be more evenly exposed to light, encouraging uniform growth. The dense growth of plants such as yew makes it possible to create hedges of ambitious architecture. They can have buttresses and pilasters, curved or crenellated tops and finials, and they can be pierced with archways and windows. These variations are not difficult to create but they make cutting hedges a much slower business, often requiring the use of hand shears.

An interesting variation is the hedge on stilts, where the hedging plants, usually hornbeam, are grown on a bare stem to a height of about 1.8m/6ft with the hedge proper formed above

this height. As a screen it is an alternative to pleaching in which trees, typically limes (*Tilia*), that make flexible growth have all branches removed except the chosen horizontal and vertical ones which are trained on wire supports.

Mechanical trimmers considerably reduce the labour involved in maintaining hedges. When using them it is essential to work from a firm base and to follow the safety precautions recommended by the manufacturer. Although experienced gardeners may have no difficulty trimming without the aid of levels, if you are lacking in confidence it is worth fixing a line in advance that provides a guide to the trim height.

The number of times a hedge needs to be trimmed in a season depends very much on growing conditions. In a warm summer with plenty of rain hedges will put on much more growth than during a hot, dry season. The number of trims suggested in the chart on page 11 is the minimum required.

Informal hedges

A wide range of plants can be used for informal hedges, among them far more roses than the two examples given. Although the soft outline

of an informal hedge is part of its appeal, some trimming is frequently necessary to keep growth within bounds. A balance usually has to be struck so that checking over-exuberance does not mean drastic loss of attractive natural shape (for example, *Berberis x stenophylla*), of flowers (for example, forsythia) or of berries (for example, pyracantha). Pruning at the right season can be of critical importance.

Windbreaks

In very exposed positions establishing a dense belt of wind-tolerant trees and shrubs that filters the prevailing wind is usually the only way to create a microclimate in which less robust plants can grow. Windbreaks can be composed of a mixture of plants, with the fastest growing making up the outer defences. It may even be possible to remove the less attractive of these when the inner ranks are well established. However, gaps can easily funnel winds into a garden that will tear out its heart.

When planting shrubs or trees as windbreaks, fix hessian or mesh screens around them to give some protection from the desiccating power of wind until they become established.

FAR LEFT The tamarisks (*Tamarix*) are remarkably wind-resistant and even tolerate salt-laden sea breezes. Although they have slender branches and light foliage, they make useful windbreaks. The pink plumes of *T. parviflora* are borne in profusion in early summer. Prune immediately after flowering to keep compact.

LEFT The lavenders (*Lavandula*), easily propagated from cuttings, are useful for making low, informal hedges to flank paths or to create divisions within a garden. The deep-coloured *L. angustifolia* 'Hidcote' is typical in its preference for full sun and well-drained soil. Clip lavenders in spring to keep them compact.

Fences, screens & walls

CLIMBERS FOR SHADE

Except where indicated, the following climbers are deciduous.

Name	height	description
Clematis see pages 22-5		
Hedera see page 21 ivy		
Hydrangea anomala petiolaris	7.5-9m 25-30ft	self-clinging giant with flat clusters of white flowers in early summer
Lapageria rosea Chilean bellflower	3.7-4.5m 12-15ft	evergreen; choosy and rather tender twiner for lime-free soil; superb waxy, pink flowers in summer and early autumn
Schizophragma integrifolium	7.5-9m 25-30ft	self-clinging and very vigorous; broad heads of long-lasting, white flowers in mid-summer
Tropaeolum speciosum flame nasturtium	3-4.5m 10-15ft	herbaceous; best when its vivid orange-red flowers show from mid-summer to early autumn against dark foliage

WALL SHRUBS FOR SHADE

Except where indicated, the following shrubs are deciduous.

Name	height	description
Berberidopsis corallina coral plant	3.7-4.3m 12-14ft	lax and needs support; globular red flowers hang in clusters in summer and early autumn
Chaenomeles speciosa 'Moerloosei'	1.8-2.5m 6-8ft	an example among many, with apple-blossom, white-and-pink flowers from early to late spring
Chaenomeles x **superba** 'Knap Hill Scarlet'	90-180cm 3-6ft	a colourful example of these hybrids, with brilliant red flowers from early spring to early summer
Cotoneaster horizontalis	1.2-1.8m 4-6ft	remarkable for its herringbone growth; bright red berries follow the small, pink-and-white flowers
Jasminum nudiflorum winter jasmine	3-3.7m 10-12ft	very lax; invaluable for yellow flowers produced from early winter to early spring
Pyracantha 'Mohave' firethorn	4.5-5.5m 15-18ft	evergreen; white flowers followed by large crops of orange-red berries from late summer

Although it may seem to falter in its early stages, *Hydrangea anomala petiolaris* is a very vigorous, self-clinging climber that does well in shade or sun. It can be trained into trees as well as on walls but needs a sturdy giant to support it.

The rich blue of the evergreen *Ceanothus impressus* is an unusual colour in shrubs and makes this species a magnificent feature of the spring garden. Like other *Ceanothus*, it needs a sunny position with well-drained soil and is suitable for training against a warm wall.

The architectural features of a garden's framework usually benefit from being draped with living material. Fortunately, the climbing fraternity that is particularly suited to the task includes some of the most valuable of garden ornamentals. Depending on their nature, they can streak or slowly clamber up house walls, garden walls, fences and screens. Pergolas and arches, too, can make highly attractive architectural features; they have the great advantage of creating vertical components within gardens that can be clothed with vegetation much more quickly than a tree could grow to a comparable height.

Climbing plants

Among the climbers are two outstanding groups of flowering plants: those roses that produce long flexible stems and clematis. Both categories are of such importance as garden ornamentals that they are treated separately (for climbing and rambling roses see pages 18-20; clematis see pages 22-5). The ivies, the most

CLIMBERS FOR SUNNY WALLS

Name	height	description
DECIDUOUS		
Actinidia kolomikta Kolomikta vine	3.7-4.5m 12-15ft	twining climber, its heart-shaped leaves with startling pink-and-white variegation at the tips
Akebia quinata	6-7.5m 20-25ft	semi-deciduous; twining vivid green leaves, fragrant flowers in late spring
Aristolochia durior (A. macrophylla) Dutchman's pipe	6-7.5m 20-25ft	twiner with heart-shaped leaves and unusual, brownish flowers
Campsis grandiflora	7.5-9m 25-30ft	vigorous and self-clinging; deep orange, trumpet-shaped flowers in late summer; needs warmth
Campsis radicans trumpet vine	9-12m 30-40ft	vigorous and self-clinging; scarlet, trumpet-shaped flowers from late summer to early autumn
Campsis x **tagliabuana** 'Madame Galen'	7.5-9m 25-30ft	vigorous, self-clinging hybrid; salmon-red trumpets produced freely from late summer to early autumn
Clematis see pages 22-5		
Jasminum officinale	5-7.5m 15-25ft	vigorous twiner with sweetly fragrant, white flowers in summer and autumn
Lonicera periclymenum	6-9m 20-30ft	ubiquitous, fragrant twiner; 'Belgica' (early Dutch) has purplish-red flowers, fading to yellow-pink in early to mid-summer; 'Serotina' (late Dutch), with darker purple flowers, follows and continues into autumn
Schisandra rubrifolia	6-9m 20-30ft	vigorous twiner with toothed leaves; crimson flowers in early summer followed by red fruits
Wisteria floribunda Japanese wisteria	6-9m 20-30ft	very vigorous twiner, with racemes of fragrant, violet flowers from late spring to early summer
Wisteria sinensis Chinese wisteria	18-25m 60-80ft	classic giant twiner with drooping racemes of fragrant, mauve flowers from late spring to early summer
Wisteria venusta	7.5-9m 25-30ft	very vigorous twiner; racemes of fragrant, white flowers from late spring to early summer
EVERGREEN		
Lonicera x **brownii** honeysuckle	3.7-4.5m 2-15ft	semi-evergreen; unscented but magnificent twiner; scarlet flowers from early summer to early autumn
Lonicera sempervirens	3-4.5m 10-15ft	semi-evergreen twiner with heads of tubular orange-red flowers, yellow inside, in summer; superb visually but unscented
Passiflora caerulea common passion flower	4.5-6m 15-20ft	semi-evergreen twiner with unusual purple-and-white flowers through summer, sometimes followed by large, orange fruit
Trachelospermum jasminoides	3.7-4.5m 12-15ft	twiner with jasmine-like, creamy flowers against glossy leaves from mid- to late summer; less vigorous is T. jasminoides 'Variegatum', with white-edged leaves

WALL SHRUBS FOR SUN

All the following plants benefit from the shelter of a warm wall and many are best trained on supports.

Name	height	description
DECIDUOUS		
Aloysia triphylla lemon-scented verbena	1.2-1.8m 4-6ft	flowers of little consequence but the leaves are deliciously lemon-scented when crushed
Ceanothus x **delileanus** 'Gloire de Versailles'	1.8-2.5m 6-8ft	puffs of pale blue, fragrant flowers over a long season from early summer to early autumn
Cytisus battandieri	3.7-4.5m 12-15ft	silvery leaves and pineapple-scented, yellow flowers from late spring to early summer
Forsythia suspensa	3-3.7m 10-12ft	lax shrub, graceful when well trained, with clusters of yellow flowers from early to mid-spring
Ribes speciosum	2.5-3m 8-10ft	bright red flowers dangle from arching stems from mid-spring to early summer; somewhat tender
EVERGREEN		
Abutilon megapotamicum	1.8-2.5m 6-8ft	semi-evergreen; slender and best wall-trained; dangling, red-and-yellow flowers through summer into autumn
Abutilon x **suntense** 'Jermyns'	2.5-3.7m 8-12ft	semi-evergreen; saucer-shaped flowers of deep mauve from late spring to early summer
Abutilon vitifolium	2.5-3.7m 8-12ft	semi-evergreen; vine-like leaves and mauve flowers late spring to early autumn
Carpenteria californica	2.5-3m 8-10ft	scented, white flowers with yellow stamens for zest in early to mid-summer
Ceanothus 'Burkwoodii'	3-3.7m 10-12ft	very beautiful, rich blue flowers in mid-summer and early autumn; on the tender side
Ceanothus impressus	2.5-3m 8-10ft	deep green leaves and rich blue flowers mid-spring to early autumn
Clianthus puniceus parrot's bill	3-3.7m 10-12ft	lax and worth training; dangling clusters of crimson, claw-shaped flowers in late spring and early summer
Fremontodendron 'Californian Glory'	4.5-6m 15-20ft	fast-growing, producing masses of cupped lemon-yellow flowers from early to late summer
Garrya elliptica 'James Roof'	2.5-4.5m 8-15ft	mournful shrub except for its long, dangling catkins of grey and purple in late winter and early spring
Myrtus communis common myrtle	2.5-3m 8-10ft	glossy, aromatic leaves brightened by white flowers with prominent stamens from mid- to late summer
Piptanthus laburnifolius	2.5-3.7m 8-12ft	semi-evergreen; very dark green leaves and yellow, pea flowers in late spring
Prostanthera rotundifolia mint bush	1.2-2.5m 4-8ft	deliciously aromatic foliage and purple flowers in mid- to late spring
Solanum crispum 'Glasnevin' Chilean potato tree	3-3.7m 10-12ft	semi-evergreen; although lax and untidy, desirable for the starry, purple flowers, lit by orange centres, produced freely from late spring to mid-summer
Solanum jasminoides 'Album'	3.7-4.5m 12-15ft	rambler for a choice, sheltered position; starry, white flowers through summer to early autumn

CLIMBERS WITH ORNAMENTAL FOLIAGE

The following plants are deciduous, except where indicated. For *Hedera* (ivy) see page 21.

Name	height	description
Actinidia kolomikta Kolomikta vine	3.7-4.5m 12-15ft	twiner with green, heart-shaped leaves tipped green and pink
Ampelopsis glandulosa brevipedunculata	6-9m 20-30ft	lush, hop-like leaves; blue berries
Humulus lupulus 'Aureus' golden-leaved hop	4.5-6m 15-20ft	twining, herbaceous perennial; attractive leaves flushed golden yellow
Lonicera japonica 'Aureoreticulata'	7.5-9m 25-30ft	evergreen twiner; yellow-veined leaves; cream flowers summer to early autumn
Parthenocissus henryana Chinese Virginia creeper	7.5-9m 25-30ft	self-clinging; leaves have 3-5 leaflets with white veins; good autumn colour
Parthenocissus quinquefolia Virginia creeper	15-22m 50-70ft	self-clinging; leaves have 3-5 leaflets; brilliant autumn colour
Parthenocissus tricuspidata	12-15m 40-50ft	self-clinging; 3-lobed mature leaves, vivid crimson in autumn
Trachelospermum jasminoides 'Variegatum'	3-3.7m 10-12ft	evergreen twiner; creamy white margins to the leaves
Vitis coignetiae crimson glory vine	18-25m 60-80ft	climbs with tendrils; large leaves, usually 5-lobed; magnificent display of autumn colours
Vitis vinifera 'Incana'	3.7-6m 12-20ft	tendrils; handsome leaves covered with grey down
Vitis vinifera 'Purpurea' claret vine	3.7-6m 12-20ft	tendrils; handsome purple leaves, red in autumn

FAST-GROWING CLIMBERS

Name	height	description
Cobaea scandens cup and saucer plant	3.7-6m 12-20ft	half-hardy perennial with tendrils, grown as an annual; green and purple flowers early summer to early autumn
Cucurbita pepo ornamental gourds	3.7-4.5m 12-15ft	half-hardy annual; smooth or knobbly gourds in various colours in late summer
Eccremocarpus scaber Chilean glory vine	2.5-3m 8-10ft	half-hardy perennial with tendrils, grown as an annual; tubular, scarlet flowers mid-summer to early autumn
Humulus lupulus 'Aureus' golden-leaved hop	4.5-6m 15-20ft	hardy twining perennial with yellow-green divided leaves; does not flower freely
Ipomoea tricolor morning glory	2.5-3m 8-10ft	half-hardy twining perennial, grown as an annual; large purple to blue flowers mid-summer to frost
Lathyrus latifolius 'White Pearl'	1.8-3m 6-10ft	hardy perennial with tendrils; white, pea flowers mid-summer to early autumn
Lathyrus odoratus sweet pea	2.5-3m 8-10ft	hardy annual with tendrils; fragrant, pea flowers in various colours in summer
Rhodochiton atrosanguineus	2.5-3m 8-10ft	half-hardy twining perennial, grown as an annual; pendulous, deep purple flowers late summer to early autumn
Tropaeolum peregrinum canary creeper	3-3.7m 10-12ft	perennial, grown as an annual; fringed yellow flowers mid-summer to early autumn
Tropaeolum speciosum flame creeper	3-4.5m 10-15ft	hardy perennial, best grown through a supporting shrub; scarlet flowers mid-summer to early autumn

important group of climbing foliage plants, also warrant special treatment (see page 21).

Even without these specialized categories, there are many climbers to choose from, some with ornamental flowers, others with ornamental foliage, many with woody stems but also some that are herbaceous perennials and yet others fast-growing but short-lived. To these can be added a group of plants often loosely referred to as 'wall shrubs'. These do not necessarily have to be grown against a support but their nature is, on the whole, rather lax and they lend themselves to training.

There are other plants that benefit from the special conditions close to the base of sunny walls. These may not be fully hardy but cosseted in such a choice site, usually warmer than the rest of the garden, they will often perform magnificently and survive from year to year. Some, including certain *Ceanothus*, can be trained while others, such as the common myrtle, are better left to form a natural shape.

Planting

The soil at the base of walls and fences is usually much drier than in other parts of the garden. Before planting a climber in such a location, incorporate generous quantities of organic matter such as garden compost. Plant 15-30cm/6-12in out from the support and, whenever possible, with the roots of the plants fanned out away from it.

Training

Climbers use various means to lift themselves to the light. Many, including the honeysuckles and wisterias, have twining stems. Especially among perennials and annual climbers, there are some, like the sweet pea, that use tendrils. Other climbers are self-clinging, that is they are equipped with aerial roots or pads by which they attach themselves to surfaces.

If you are growing plants that are not self-clinging, it is essential to provide a suitable support. Panels of wooden latticework or trellis can be fixed to walls as can plastic or plastic-coated metal mesh. Unfortunately, many of the purpose-made materials do not blend easily into a garden. The least conspicuous and probably most satisfactory form of support is that provided by galvanized wires attached to walls by vine eyes and strained taut. Wires are normally fixed horizontally and spaced about 50cm/20in apart, starting approximately 30cm/12in from ground level.

Many plants that will eventually find their own way up supports need tying in when they are first planted, and lax shrubs that are trained against walls will need to be tied in throughout their lives. It is important to check ties on a regular basis to ensure that they are sound and not so tight that stems are being strangled.

Some climbers are plants of phenomenal vigour that can easily overwhelm an ill-matched support. They are often best grown away from buildings and come into their own where they can romp over a well-built pergola.

VIGOROUS CLIMBERS FOR PERGOLAS

The following climbers are deciduous, except where indicated.

Name	height	description
Actinidia deliciosa (A. chinensis) kiwi fruit	9-12m 30-40ft	twiner with hairy, heart-shaped leaves; cream flowers and edible fruit
Clematis montana	9-12m 30-40ft	twiner giving a prodigious display in spring of pink or white flowers
Fallopia baldschuanica (F. aubertii)	9-12m 30-40ft	twiner of astonishing vigour; frothy, white flowers in late summer
Hedera colchica 'Dentata Variegata'	6-9m 20-30ft	evergreen and self-clinging; one of the hardiest large-leaved ivies, with showy cream variegation
Schisandra rubriflora	6-9m 20-30ft	twiner with bold foliage and conspicuous red flowers in early summer
Vitis coignetiae crimson glory vine	18-25m 60-80ft	a magnificent giant, with very large leaves outstanding for their rich autumn colour; small, black grapes; climbs with tendrils
Vitis vinifera 'Purpurea' claret vine	6-7.5m 20-25ft	purple foliage that catches fire in autumn; blue-black grapes; tendrils
Wisteria floribunda 'Multijuga'	6-9m 20-30ft	twiner, remarkable for the racemes of violet-blue flowers, 90cm/3ft or more long
Wisteria sinensis 'Prolific'	18-25m 60-80ft	twiner, freely producing long racemes of mauve flowers

Few plants provide more brilliant autumn colour than the Virginia creeper (*Parthenocissus quinquefolia*). Here it weaves its way through an open tapestry of climbers, which include ivies and *Clematis armandii*, with handsome leaves divided into threes. When this flowers in spring the young leaves are copper-tinted.

ABOVE Two scented climbers, *Clematis montana* 'Elizabeth' and the honeysuckle *Lonicera periclymenum* 'Belgica', make a magnificent early summer pairing.

LEFT The golden-leaved hop (*Humulus lupulus* 'Aureus') is a herbaceous perennial grown for its foliage.

Roses for walls

Its profusion of medium-sized, silvery pink flowers in early summer makes 'New Dawn' one of the outstanding climbing roses for soft colour schemes. Although the flowers are not powerfully fragrant, this is a nicely scented rose. It is generally classified as recurrent and often proves so but is not absolutely reliable on this score.

For billowing and fragrant beauty the climbing and rambling roses have few equals among plants that are suitable for training up walls and other supports. The distinction between them is not absolutely clearcut, but the typical rambler each year throws out vigorous new shoots from or near its base, whereas on climbers the new shoots may be produced almost anywhere. Ramblers usually flower prolifically in one burst, carrying numerous clusters of small, often single, flowers. In size and shape the flowers of climbers are more akin to those of the bush roses, and many are simply climbing sports of these. Although not all the climbers have more than one flush of flower, many do.

At planting the roots of climbing and rambling roses should be trained away from supporting walls and fences. For general information on planting roses see page 66.

Climbing roses

There are many opportunities for growing climbing roses, even in small gardens where the so-called pillar roses, rarely growing taller than 3m/10ft, come into their own. The most common way of supporting them is on wires or trellis attached to walls or fencing, and on arches or pergolas. To give height to borders, they can be trained over tripods of wooden poles, tree trunks with the branches cut back to short stubs (gruesomely gaunt in winter) or purpose-made metal stands with the roses trained up through the centre and cascading over the sides. Whatever the support, the main stems need to be tied in, an operation normally carried out when the roses are pruned.

The colour range available in climbing roses provides plenty of scope for sophisticated combinations with other climbers and also

CLIMBING ROSES (ROSA)

Name	height	flowering season	description
BLUSH TO DEEP PINK			
R. 'Aloha'	2.5-3m 8-10ft	sum. to early aut.	slow climber or large shrub with fragrant, peach-pink flowers
R. 'Bantry Bay'	2.5-3m 8-10ft	sum. to early aut.	little scent but yellow stamens light up the semi-double, bright pink flowers
R. 'Blairii Number Two'	3-3.7m 10-12ft	early sum.	good scent and double flowers in subtle shades of pink
R. 'Cécile Brünner, Climbing'	6-7.5m 20-25ft	early sum.; few later blooms	blush buds open to small, loose, lightly scented blooms
R. 'Madame Grégoire Staechelin'	4.5-6m 15-20ft	early sum.	semi-double, fragrant flowers with wavy petals, pink with carmine stains
R. 'New Dawn'	4.5-6m 15-20ft	mid-sum. to early aut.	refined double, sweetly scented flowers of silvery pink
R. 'Pink Perpétue'	3.7-4.5m 12-15ft	early sum. & later flush	two-tone, deep pink flowers with little scent are borne freely
R. 'Zéphirine Drouhin'	2.5-3m 8-10ft	early sum. to early aut.	fragrant, semi-double, pink flowers; nearly thornless but mildew-prone
RED OR SCARLET			
R. 'Allen Chandler'	4.5-7.5m 15-25ft	sum. to early aut.	semi-double, well-shaped, lightly scented flowers of vivid red
R. 'Altissimo'	2.5-3m 8-10ft	sum. to early aut.	arresting blood-red, single flowers but with little scent
R. 'Danse du Feu'	3-3.7m 10-12ft	sum. to early aut.	double flowers of vibrant orange-scarlet but with little scent
R. 'Guinée'	3.7-4.5m 12-15ft	early sum.; few later blooms	double, velvety, deep scarlet flowers with a rich scent
R. 'Parade'	3.7-4.5m 12-15ft	early sum. & later flush	double, carmine flowers, with pink lights; lightly scented
CREAM, YELLOW OR APRICOT			
R. 'Gloire de Dijon'	3.7-4.5m 12-15ft	late spr. to early aut.	buff buds open to lightly scented, double flowers of soft apricot-pink
R. 'Golden Showers'	2.5-3m 8-10ft	sum. to early aut.	fragrant, double, yellow flowers are borne freely; a good pillar rose
R. 'Leverkusen'	3-3.7m 10-12ft	sum. to early aut.	semi-double, pale yellow flowers with a light scent
R. 'Madame Alfred Carrière'	4.5-6m 15-20ft	early sum.; some later blooms	a light blush touches the creamy white, fragrant flowers; possible on shady walls
R. 'Maigold'	2.5-3m 8-10ft	early sum.; few later blooms	semi-double, yellow flowers darkening to bronze; fragrant
R. 'Meg'	3-3.7m 10-12ft	early to mid-sum.	fragrant, semi-double flowers with wavy petals blend pinks and apricot
R. 'Mermaid'	7.5-9m 25-30ft	mid-sum. to early aut.	large, single, pale yellow flowers with a light scent; stiff-stemmed climber
R. 'Schoolgirl'	3-3.7m 10-12ft	early sum. to early aut.	sweetly scented, double flowers of deep apricot
BI-COLOURED			
R. 'Handel'	3-3.7m 10-12ft	sum. to early aut.	double, lightly scented flowers are an ice-cream sundae of cream and pink

BELOW 'Madame Grégoire Staechelin' produces only one flush of flowers, in early summer, but in magnificence it outclasses many roses that are recurrent. It is well scented and the wavy petals add distinction to the beautifully shaped flowers. This rose thrives in full sun but will even do well on a shady wall.

LEFT A short-growing climber with glossy leaves and among the best of the so-called pillar roses, 'Golden Showers' repeats reliably throughout the summer. It has clusters of large, double flowers of bright yellow, which are well scented.

Some of the ramblers are extremely vigorous roses, needing the support of a large tree or well-built pergola. 'Goldfinch' is a useful short-growing example, with a single flush of fragrant flowers in mid-summer.

RAMBLING ROSES (ROSA)

Name	height	flowering season	description
WHITE OR BLUSH			
R. 'Aimée Vibert'	4.5-6m 15-20ft	mid-sum. to mid-aut.	clusters of small, double flowers, pink in bud, then white, with a light scent; best on a warm wall
R. 'Felicité et Perpétue'	3.7-4.5m 12-15ft	mid- to late sum.	small, double, white flowers, stained crimson in bud; little scent; suitable for a shady wall
R. 'The Garland'	3.7-4.5m 12-15ft	early to mid-sum.	semi-double flowers, blush-pink in bud, then white; fruity scent
PINK			
R. 'Albertine'	4.5-6m 15-20ft	early sum.	fairly large but loose, semi-double flowers of salmon-pink, richly scented; mildew-prone and best on open supports such as trellis
R. 'Dorothy Perkins'	4.5-6m 15-20ft	late sum.	clusters of double, brash pink flowers with little scent; mildew-prone and best on open supports
R. 'Paul's Himalayan Musk'	9-12m 30-40ft	mid-sum.	small, neatly double, soft pink, fragrant flowers; a charmer but vigorous enough to climb large trees
CREAM OR YELLOW			
R. 'Albéric Barbier'	4.5-6m 15-20ft	early sum.; few later blooms	yellow buds open to creamy, sweetly scented flowers; foliage often partly evergreen
R. 'Bobbie James'	7.5-9m 25-30ft	early to mid-sum.	large clusters of semi-double, nearly white, fragrant flowers; good for training into trees
R. filipes 'Kiftsgate'	9-12m 30-40ft	mid-sum.	large, loose clusters of single, creamy white flowers with a scent that carries; will clamber into a large tree with prodigious vigour
R. 'Goldfinch'	2.5-3.7m 8-12ft	mid-sum.	clusters of small, semi-double, fragrant flowers that turn from soft yellow to cream
R. 'Phyllis Bide'	3-3.7m 10-12ft	early to late sum.	clusters of double, lightly scented flowers that are yellow, flushed pink
R. 'Rambling Rector'	4.5-6m 15-20ft	early to mid-sum.	numerous clusters of semi-double, off-white, fragrant flowers with golden stamens
R. 'Wedding Day'	7.5-9m 25-30ft	mid-sum.	many clusters of yellow buds open to fragrant, cream flowers; tender and best on a warm wall

with shrubs and perennials planted in close proximity. Well-timed coincidences or sequences of roses and clematis are especially beautiful. Climbing roses that flower only once, such as the delectable and fragrant 'Madame Grégoire Staechelin', with wavy-edged petals in shades of pink, could be followed by a late-flowering clematis such as the velvety, deep purple 'Royal Velours'.

The way a rose is trained will depend largely on the nature of the support and on the space available. If at all possible, train stems at or near the horizontal, for this will encourage flower production along their length and not just at their tips. Roses on tripods can be spiralled round their support rather than simply allowed to grow vertically.

Prune climbing roses between mid-autumn and mid-spring, late in this period where the climate is particularly harsh. After cutting out dead and diseased stems and any that have been injured, for example by rubbing, cut back flowered laterals to about 15cm/6in. A proportion of old stems can be removed if there are new ones to replace them.

Rambling roses

Caution is called for when planting some of the most vigorous rambling roses; a giant such as 'Kiftsgate' has it in its power to swamp a small bungalow. It is a pity, however, to grow them in a way that curtails their careless charm. Furthermore, they are less prone to disease when grown in a relatively open position.

The vigorous kinds are naturals for training on pergolas and even better when allowed to work their way up into trees. In cottage gardens popular ramblers such as 'Albertine' are often simply allowed to lounge over a fence and they seem to fare none the worse for this casual approach to their cultivation. However, ramblers flower most prolifically on vigorous canes produced in the previous year. In an ideal pruning regime, all or most of the canes that have produced flowers in summer should be cut out in late summer or autumn and the new canes then trained in.

Versatile ivies

The numerous cultivars of the common ivy (*Hedera helix*) make very adaptable, self-clinging, evergreen climbers, most doing well in sun or shade. Many are also useful as ground cover or as trailing plants for containers. In a well-lit position the leaves of 'Buttercup' are completely yellow but in full sun they may scorch and in shade they turn green.

CLIMBING AND GROUND-COVER IVIES (*HEDERA*)

Name	height	description
COMMON IVY (cultivars of *Hedera helix*)		
'Atropurpurea'	3-9m 10-30ft	familiar ivy leaves become dark purple in winter
'Buttercup'	3-9m 10-30ft	cheerful golden green when grown in an open position but scorches in bright sun
'Cavendishii'	3-9m 10-30ft	irregular, pale yellow margin, flushed pink in winter, sets off the mid-green leaves
'Congesta'	45-60cm 1½-2ft	non-climbing form with narrow leaves arranged in ranks along erect stems
'Erecta'	60-90cm 2-3ft	non-climbing form; a beefier version of 'Congesta'
'Glacier'	3-9m 10-30ft	leaves a cool combination of grey-green, silver and cream
'Ivalace'	3-9m 10-30ft	wavy-edged leaves with pale veins take on copper tones in winter
'Oro di Bogliasco' ('Goldheart')	3-9m 10-30ft	pink stems, later brown, carry dark green leaves splashed bright gold
'Pedata'	3-9m 10-30ft	bird's-foot leaves with a long central 'toe' are dark green with pale veins
LARGE-LEAVED IVIES		
Hedera algeriensis 'Gloire de Marengo'	4.5-6m 15-20ft	reddish stems carry broad, dark green leaves with grey to cream margins
Hedera colchica 'Sulphur Heart'	6-9m 20-30ft	heart-shaped, dark green leaves magnificently splashed with gold

There are few plants more tolerant of such a wide range of soils and positions than ivies and, furthermore, they are very little troubled by pests and diseases.

The common ivy (*Hedera helix*) has a knack of presenting itself in many uncommon guises. Admittedly, among the many named ivies there are some that are difficult to tell apart, but there are plenty of distinctive character, marked out from others by their leaf size, shape or coloration. The intrinsic beauty of their patterning is a good reason for growing some of the variegated kinds, but they are also among the best plants to light up dingy corners with their cool or sunny colouring.

Ivies as climbers

The large-leaved ivies, as well as the various forms of the common ivy, need no support, working their way up a surface by clinging with little aerial roots. To hasten their often slow start, it may be worth tying young shoots close to the surface they are to climb. Ivies will take almost any surface in their stride and are unlikely to do harm to a brick or stone wall that is sound. However, they can accelerate the decay of a wall that is in a bad state of repair and their aerial roots will mark paintwork.

Some trimming may occasionally be needed, especially if there is a risk of vigorous growths getting under the eaves of a house. Ivies left unchecked will eventually develop flowering stems with no aerial roots, but it is an easy matter to cut back plants to maintain them at their juvenile stage.

Other uses

As well as being among the most versatile of evergreen climbers, ivies make superb ground cover. Furthermore, the common ivy provides an invaluable range of trailing plants for containers and a couple of upright forms that make curious shrubs for borders. The small-leaved climbing kinds can also be used in a novel way to form 'topiary' shapes, the shoots being trained on to wire frames.

Clematis

Clematis are an exceptionally versatile group of flowering climbers. They include rollicking ramblers and gentle twiners, plants with flowers of subtle refinement and hybrids of sumptuous splendour. Clematis flower with reckless freedom, and there are examples for most seasons. The most widely grown are the large-flowered hybrids with new cultivars steadily being added to an already long list of old favourites. The species and numerous hybrids with small flowers often make up for the size of individual blooms by flowering with great prodigality and in some cases the seedheads that follow are highly ornamental.

Planting

Although the flowering stems need to be in the sun, clematis like to have a cool, shaded root run, so should be planted where the base of the plant is in shade, such as next to or behind a suitable shrub. Alternatively, you can place tiles or paving slabs around the base of the plant.

Clematis do not need lime but thrive in alkaline and other soils where there is an adequate supply of moisture. In early spring give an application of a slow-release fertilizer and, as the ground warms, apply an organic mulch. Clematis have shallow roots so avoid working soil around the base of plants. Container-grown clematis can be planted at any time of the year but preferably during mild weather between autumn and early spring.

Training & pruning

Clematis obligingly hoist themselves up by twining their leaf stalks round man-made supports, such as netting, or other plants. Training is rarely needed except to give direction to plants at an early stage.

Many clematis will flower freely with no

Clematis are particularly effective at stiching together the various layers of a garden. They are at their most winning when, trailing through trees, shrubs and other climbers, their own flowering adds a second season of vivacity once the plants supporting them are out of flower. The large-flowered 'Perle d'Azur' blooms in the second half of summer.

The progeny of *Clematis viticella*, native of southern Europe, all flower in the second half of summer and often into autumn. The small-flowered 'Etoile Violette' is one of the first of this group to come into bloom and is an exceptionally vigorous and free-flowering example, in which the dark purple is lit by creamy stamens. Cut back hard in spring.

Well-timed sequences and coincidences are very telling in the garden. Clematis are ideal for running in tandem with roses, their joint flowering creating an effect of dreamy artlessness. The rose 'Climbing Iceberg' and the large-flowered clematis 'Henryi' make subtle variations in near white that highlight the differences of flower form.

LARGE-FLOWERED HYBRID CLEMATIS

All of the clematis listed below are deciduous.

Name	height	description
FLOWERING EARLY SUMMER		
C. 'Barbara Jackman'	3-4m/10-13ft	single purple flowers with magenta bar
C. 'Countess of Lovelace'	3-4m/10-13ft	very double, lilac-blue flowers with white stamens
C. 'Duchess of Edinburgh'	2.5-3m/8-10ft	double, white flowers with a green tinge
C. 'Edith'	4-5m/13-16ft	single, white flowers with red anthers
C. 'Empress of India'	4-5m/13-16ft	single, violet-purple flowers with deeper bar
C. 'Henryi'	2.5-3m/8-10ft	single, white flowers with chocolate anthers
C. 'General Sikorski'	2-2.5m/6-8ft	reddish base but otherwise single flowers of a good blue
C. 'Lady Londesborough'	2.5-3m/8-10ft	prolific display of pale mauve, single flowers with dark stamens
C. 'Miss Bateman'	3-4m/10-13ft	white, semi-double flowers with a bold centre of reddish anthers
C. 'Rouge Cardinal'	2.5-3m/8-10ft	single, magenta flowers of velvety texture
FLOWERING EARLY SUMMER, REPEATING LATE SUMMER OR AUTUMN		
C. 'Beauty of Worcester'	2-2.5m/6-8ft	rich blue flowers with creamy stamens; early flowering double, later single
C. 'Elsa Späth'	2.5-3m/8-10ft	lavender-blue, single flowers with reddish anthers, the later crop smaller
C. 'Ernest Markham'	2-2.5m/6-8ft	single, magenta flowers; late main display
C. 'Lady Caroline Nevill'	2.5-3m/8-10ft	single, pale lavender-blue flowers
C. 'Lasurstern'	3-4m/10-13ft	single flowers, with a wavy edge, fade from purple-blue to grey-blue; cream stamens
C. 'Marie Boisselet'	4-5m/13-16ft	single, white flowers with creamy stamens open from pink-tinged buds
C. 'Mrs Cholmondeley'	4-5m/13-16ft	single, violet-blue flowers, prone to bleach
C. 'The President'	3-4m/10-13ft	single, purple flowers, with a paler reverse and reddish anthers
C. 'Ville de Lyon'	3-4m/10-13ft	single flowers, paling from carmine to mauve; creamy stamens
FLOWERING LATE SUMMER AND AUTUMN		
C. 'Belle Nantaise'	2.5-3m/8-10ft	near white stamens stand out in pale lavender flowers
C. 'Comtesse de Bouchard'	2.5-3m/8-10ft	freely produces single, mauve-pink flowers with cream stamens
C. 'Gipsy Queen'	3-4m/10-13ft	single, purple flowers with reddish anthers
C. 'Hagley Hybrid'	2-2.5m/6-8ft	prolific display of single, mauve-pink flowers with purplish anthers
C. 'Huldine'	3-4m/10-13ft	single, white flowers with pale mauve reverse
C. 'Jackmanii'	3-4m/10-13ft	single flowers of vibrant bluish-purple
C. 'Lady Betty Balfour'	4-5m/13-16ft	single, rich purple flowers with a white bar on the reverse and cream stamens
C. 'Niobe'	3-4m/10-13ft	single, deep red flowers with green stamens
C. 'Perle d'Azur'	3-4m/10-13ft	single, blue flowers, tinged mauve at the centre, with greenish anthers

regular pruning, and when plants are growing through trees any pruning other than the judicious cutting out of old wood may prove impracticable. Indeed, the plants are often such a tangle of fragile stems that pruning can be a daunting task in any situation, and great care must be taken not to damage young shoots as you pull away old wood. However, where regular pruning is possible, it will certainly increase the full flowering potential.

The small-flowered clematis that flower in late winter and spring can be left unpruned, unless a lack of space, or an unsightly tangle, demands otherwise. If so, cut them back to new buds after flowering. The very vigorous C. montana can be sheared over in early summer.

Large-flowered hybrids that bloom once in early summer should be pruned immediately after flowering. Cut out flowered stems, and trim back other stems by about 30cm/12in, cutting to a pair of buds.

The large- and small-flowered clematis that bloom between mid-summer and autumn benefit from hard pruning once a year. Prune this group, which includes the exceptionally vigorous C. orientalis and C. tangutica, in late winter or early spring, or as soon as young green shoots appear, by cutting all growths back to a pair of buds about 90cm/3ft or less from ground level.

Prune large-flowered hybrids that bloom in early summer and again in late summer or autumn by cutting back only a proportion of stems in late winter or early spring. Prune these

The large-flowered hybrid clematis create some of the most spectacular floral effects of summer. The standard advice is to plant with the roots in shade and the flowers in sun but many clematis, including 'Perle d'Azur', may be bleached by exposure to sunlight all day.

to a pair of buds about 90cm/3ft from ground level. Cutting back all stems sacrifices the early display but enhances the second.

General care

Clematis wilt is a serious fungal disease, causing sudden die-back, but which can be controlled to an extent by systemic fungicides. Powdery mildew, which disfigures foliage and weakens plants, also responds to fungicides.

Although individual blooms of the forms and hybrids of *Clematis viticella* are considerably smaller than those of the large-flowered clematis, they are borne in great profusion and this group is not troubled by the disease clematis wilt. 'Abundance' is vigorous and bears its semi-nodding, richly coloured flowers freely in sun or light shade.

SMALL-FLOWERED CLEMATIS

Unless otherwise stated, the clematis listed below are deciduous.

Name	height	description
FLOWERING LATE WINTER OR SPRING		
C. alpina 'Burford White'	1.5-1.8m/5-6ft	single, elegant white flowers
C. alpina 'Frances Rivis'	1.5-1.8m/5-6ft	deep blue, nodding flowers
C. alpina 'Rosy Pagoda'	1.5-1.8m/5-6ft	single flowers of gentle pink
C. alpina sibirica 'White Moth'	1.5-1.8m/5-6ft	hovering, white, double flowers
C. armandii	5-6m/16-20ft	vigorous evergreen with fragrant, white, single flowers
C. cirrhosa 'Freckles'	2.5-3m/8-10ft	maroon-spotted, nodding flowers, followed by silky seedheads
C. macropetala 'Maidwell Hall'	3-4m/10-13ft	nodding, double, blue flowers
C. macropetala 'Markham's Pink'	3-4m/10-13ft	bell-like, rose-pink, single flowers
C. montana	9-12m/30-40ft	rampant, with a profusion of single, fragrant, pink or white flowers
C. montana 'Elizabeth'	9-12m/30-40ft	very vigorous; pale pink, single, scented flowers
C. montana rubens	9-12m/30-40ft	very vigorous; foliage bronzy purple, especially when young; single flowers that are mauve-pink and fragrant
FLOWERING LATE SUMMER OR AUTUMN		
C. 'Abundance'	3-4m/10-13ft	free-flowering; single, crimson-red blooms
C. 'Alba Luxurians'	3-4m/10-13ft	single, green-tipped, white flowers with a contrasting dark eye
C. 'Bill Mackenzie'	4.5-6m/15-20ft	single, nodding, yellow flowers and silky seedheads
C. 'Etoile Rose'	3-4m/10-13ft	single, bell-like flowers of pale pink with a purple centre
C. 'Etoile Violette'	4-5m/13-16ft	cream eye to single, purple flowers
C. 'Kermesina'	4-5m/13-16ft	single flowers, deep crimson with a white base
C. 'Minuet'	3-4m/10-13ft	erect, off-white flowers, with a deep mauve margin
C. 'Pagoda'	3-4m/10-13ft	pink-mauve flowers with a faint bar; recurved sepals
C. 'Royal Velours'	3-4m/10-13ft	single flowers of velvety purple
C. tibetana vernayi 'Orange Peel'	4.5-6m/15-20ft	thick-petalled, yellow flowers and silky seedheads
C. viticella 'Purpurea Plena Elegans'	3-4m/10-13ft	double flowers of soft purple

Trees & large shrubs

Trees and large shrubs deserve to be chosen with particular care. By virtue of their size and in many cases their superb ornamental value, they will eventually become major features of a garden, adding to it the weight of living architecture. They tend to be expensive to buy and are relatively slow growing so it is important to make a well-considered choice at the outset.

The distinction between trees and shrubs is often enough ignored by the plants themselves. A tree has a single main stem supporting a head of branches while a shrub produces several stems more or less equal in size from ground level or just above. With the numerous woody plants that can be grown in either form it is a matter of formative training whether a plant has a single stem or is grown as a shrub.

Feathered trees have lateral branches growing from the main stem down to ground level. Ornamental trees are frequently trained as standards, that is with a bare stem to a height of about 1.8m/6ft. Standards create a more open effect than feathered trees and it is much easier to plant close to the trunk. Most trees that are suitable for small or medium-sized gardens are grown with a branched head and they are often sold with the central leader cut back to encourage the formation of side branches.

Few gardens can accommodate even a single specimen of forest trees such as oaks (*Quercus*) and beeches (*Fagus*). It is on account of their ultimate size rather than any inherent faults that some of the most splendid of all plants are

Magnolia x soulangeana ranks high in a genus warranting many superlatives. It makes a large shrub or small tree that presents with unforced elegance its beautifully shaped flowers in mid-spring. There may also be a few blooms at intervals in summer.

The early summer display of the calico bush or mountain laurel (*Kalmia latifolia*) makes it one of the finest evergreens for gardens on acid soils. The sheer mass of bloom is in itself impressive but, in addition, the individual flowers are exquisitely shaped and the dark tints give their pink the quality of superior confectionery. All forms are worth growing.

OUTSTANDING TREES AND LARGE SHRUBS

Name	height	growing requirements	description
EVERGREEN			
Abies koreana Korean fir	3.7-4.5m 12-15ft	sun; shelter; best on moist, acid soil	neat conifer; white underside to the leaves; violet-purple cones
Arbutus x **andrachnoides**	2.5-3m 8-10ft	sun; shelter; lime-free soil	reddish bark; white flowers in early to mid-spring
Camellia x **williamsii** 'J. C. Williams'	1.8-3m 6-10ft	sun or shade; lime-free soil; shelter	single pink flowers with golden stamens from late autumn to early spring
Cryptomeria japonica 'Elegans'	3.7-4.5m 12-15ft	sun; shelter; best on moist soil	conifer with blue-green foliage in summer, bronze or purple in winter
Eucryphia x **nymansensis**	4.5-6m 15-20ft	sun or shade; shelter; cool root-run	cream flowers borne freely late summer to early autumn
Ilex x **altaclerensis** 'Golden King'	6-9m 20-30ft	sun; very adaptable	female holly; yellow margin to nearly spineless leaves
Kalmia latifolia calico bush, mountain laurel	1.8-3m 6-10ft	light shade; moist, lime-free soil	clusters of cup-shaped, pink flowers in early summer
Photinia x **fraseri**	1.8-3m 6-10ft	sun; shelter; lime-tolerant	mature leaves are dark green, brilliant red when young
Prunus lusitanica Portugal laurel	3.7-4.5m 12-15ft	sun or light shade; ordinary soil	lustrous dark-green leaves on reddish stalks
DECIDUOUS			
Acer griseum	4.5-6m 15-20ft	sun or light shade; best on moist soil	bark peels to reveal an orange-brown layer; good autumn colour
Aesculus parviflora	2.5-3.7m 8-12ft	sun; ordinary soil	suckering shrub; handsome foliage and candles of white flowers mid-to late summer
Betula pendula 'Youngii' Young's weeping birch	6-7.5m 20-25ft	sun or light shade; ordinary soil	dome-shaped weeping tree with white bark
Cornus alternifolia 'Argentea'	5.5-7.5m 18-25ft	sun; ordinary soil	grown for the silvery effect of white variegated leaves on horizontal branches
Crataegus persimilis 'Prunifolia'	4.5-6m 15-20ft	sun; ordinary soil	white flowers in early summer; crimson haws; good autumn foliage colour
Genista aetnensis Mount Etna broom	4.5-6m 15-20ft	sun; well-drained soil	airy growth with few leaves; yellow, pea flowers mid- to late summer
Magnolia x **soulangeana** 'Alexandrina'	3-4.5m 10-15ft	sun; shelter; well-drained soil	erect, white, chalice flowers, with a claret stain at the base, in mid-spring
Malus 'John Downie' crab apple	7.5-9m 25-30ft	sun; ordinary soil	white apple blossom in late spring; yellow and scarlet fruit
Prunus x **subhirtella** 'Autumnalis Rosea'	6-9m 20-30ft	sun; ordinary soil	semi-double, pink flowers in late autumn to early spring
Sorbus aria 'Lutescens' whitebeam	4.5-6m 15-20ft	sun; ordinary soil	downy underside to the leaves that turn from cream when young to grey; autumn berries
Sorbus aucuparia rowan, mountain ash	4.5-7.5m 15-25ft	very adaptable; short-lived on chalk	attractive leaves with good autumn colour; orange-red berries

FLOWERING TREES AND LARGE SHRUBS

The following trees and shrubs are deciduous, except where indicated.

Name	height	description
SPRING-FLOWERING		
Aesculus x carnea 'Briotii'	4.5-6m 15-20ft	horse chestnut with deep pink flowers from late spring
Amelanchier lamarckii	4.5-7.5m 15-25ft	masses of white flowers in mid-spring with copper-tinted young leaves; rich autumn colours
Berberis darwinii	2.5-3m 8-10ft	evergreen; in mid- to late spring masses of small, orange-yellow flowers; blue-black berries follow
Cercis siliquastrum Judas tree	4.5-6m 15-20ft	purplish-pink, pea flowers on bare stems in late spring; seed pods redden when ripe
Cornus mas cornelian cherry	2.5-3.7m 8-12ft	clusters of small, golden flowers cover bare stems from late winter to mid-spring
Crataegus laevigata 'Paul's Scarlet' hawthorn, may	4.5-6m 15-20ft	masses of double, scarlet flowers make an impressive display in late spring
Davidia involucrata dove tree, pocket handkerchief tree	6-9m 20-30ft	insignificant flowers but paired creamy white bracts of uneven size are arresting in late spring
Laburnum x watereri 'Vossii'	4.5-6m 15-20ft	dangling chains of golden, pea flowers in late spring
Magnolia campbelli mollicomata	12-15m 40-50ft	sensational large flowers, pink or purple, in late winter; may take 12 or more years to flower
Magnolia x loebneri 'Merrill'	4.5-6m 15-20ft	many large, starry flowers, white and fragrant in early to mid-spring
Magnolia x soulangeana 'Lennei'	3-4.5m 10-15ft	superb rose-purple flowers, white inside, in mid-spring and some later
Magnolia stellata	2.5-3m 8-10ft	grey-green buds open to starry, fragrant, white flowers in early to mid-spring; slow-growing but flowers when young
Malus coronaria 'Charlottae'	4.5-6m 15-20ft	semi-double, shell-pink and lightly fragrant flowers in late spring; leaves colour well in autumn
Malus floribunda	3.7-4.5m 12-15ft	in late spring bright pink buds open to single, pale pink flowers; yellow fruit
Malus sieboldii	2.5-3m 8-10ft	semi-weeping with white flowers opening from pink buds in mid-spring; orange-yellow or red crabs
Prunus 'Amanogawa' Japanese cherry	6-7.5m 20-25ft	profusion of lightly fragrant, soft pink, semi-double flowers on a columnar tree
Prunus 'Kiku-shidare-zakura' Cheal's weeping cherry	6-7.5m 20-25ft	double, deep pink flowers on a weeping tree in early to mid-spring; bronze new growth
Prunus 'Shirotae' Japanese cherry	4.5-7.5m 15-25ft	dangling clusters of fragrant, single or semi-double, pure white flowers in mid- to late spring
Rhododendron see page 132		
Salix caprea 'Kilmarnock'	2.5-3m 8-10ft	weeping (female) 'goat willow' with silver catkins in early spring
Stachyurus praecox	2.5-3m 8-10ft	elegant, drooping racemes of small, pale yellow cups, sometimes opening in late winter
Syringa vulgaris common lilac	2.5-3.7m 8-12ft	fragrant flowers in pyramid-shaped heads from late spring to early summer; numerous cultivars, single and double, in purple, lilac or white
Viburnum plicatum 'Mariesii'	2.5-3m 8-10ft	in late spring tiered growth laden with heads of sterile, white flowers

Name	height	description
SUMMER-FLOWERING		
Buddleja alternifolia	4.5-6m 15-20ft	in early summer arching branches wreathed in fragrant, lavender flowers
Buddleja davidii butterfly bush	2.5-4.5m 8-15ft	dense plumes of fragrant flowers attract butterflies from mid-summer; numerous cultivars in lilac, purple or white
Caragana arborescens	3-4.5m 10-15ft	yellow, pea flowers in early summer
Catalpa bignonioides Indian bean tree	4.5-6m 15-20ft	elegant, open heads of frilled, white flowers with purple and yellow markings; handsome, large leaves and 'beans'
Cornus kousa	2.5-3m 8-10ft	tiered branches; tiny flowers in early summer with showy bracts, changing from greenish-white to cream before taking on a pink tinge; ornamental fruits and autumn colour
Cornus nuttallii Pacific dogwood	4.5-6m 15-20ft	showy display in early summer of white, later pink-tinged, bracts around modest flowers
Eucryphia x nymansensis 'Nymansay'	4.5-6m 15-20ft	evergreen; prodigal display of creamy flowers with prominent stamens from late summer into autumn
Genista aetnensis Mount Etna broom	4.5-6m 15-20ft	airy profusion of golden flowers in mid- to late summer
Hibiscus syriacus 'Woodbridge'	1.8-3m 6-10ft	masses of rose-pink flowers, darker at the centre, from mid-summer into autumn
Hoheria lyallii	3-4.5m 10-15ft	numerous fragrant, white flowers in late summer
Itea ilicifolia	1.8-3m 6-10ft	evergreen; drooping, catkin-like strands of fragrant, yellow-green flowers in late summer
Koelreuteria paniculata golden-rain tree	7.5-10m 25-33ft	large heads of small, yellow flowers from mid-summer; bladder-like fruits
Olearia x macrodonta	2.5-3.7m 8-12ft	evergreen; masses of small, white, daisy flowers among holly-like leaves
Philadelphus 'Belle Etoile'	2.5-3m 8-10ft	richly fragrant, white flowers, stained purple at the base, in early to mid-summer
Philadelphus 'Virginal'	2.5-3m 8-10ft	heavy clusters of double, white, fragrant flowers in early to mid-summer
Spartium junceum Spanish broom	2.5-3m 8-10ft	almost leafless bush brightened by fragrant, golden, pea flowers through summer
AUTUMN- AND WINTER-FLOWERING		
Hamamelis x intermedia 'Jelena' witch hazel	2.5-3.7m 8-12ft	clusters of fragrant, spidery, yellow flowers with copper tones; rich autumn colours
Hamamelis x intermedia 'Pallida' witch hazel	2.5-3.7m 8-12ft	fragrant flowers of luminous pale yellow; leaves yellow in autumn
Mahonia x meadia 'Lionel Fortescue'	2.5-3.7m 8-12ft	evergreen with clustered upright spikes of yellow flowers; this and the hybrids 'Charity' and 'Buckland' flower over a long season in winter
Prunus incisa 'Praecox'	3-4.5m 10-15ft	in late winter bare stems smothered with single, white flowers that are pink in bud
Prunus x subhirtella 'Autumnalis'	4.5-7.5m 15-25ft	intermittent but welcome small, semi-double, white flowers from late autumn to early spring
Viburnum x bodnantense 'Dawn'	2.5-3.7m 8-12ft	clusters of fragrant, white flowers with a pink tinge in succession through winter
Viburnum farreri	2.5-3.7m 8-12ft	outstanding over a long winter season for fragrant, blushing white flowers

excluded from the charts in this section. Some categories of trees and shrubs are dealt with elsewhere in the book. The maples (*Acer*), which include some of the finest foliage trees and shrubs for temperate gardens, are discussed on pages 132-3. The evergreen and deciduous rhododendrons, outstanding among flowering shrubs, are also covered on these pages. Charts of small and medium-sized shrubs particularly suitable for mixed borders are featured on pages 55-63. In addition, there are charts of trees and shrubs to suit particular growing conditions and to achieve special effects.

Size & siting

It is hazardous to be firm about the growth rate of many trees. Climatic factors and soil conditions combine with variability in vigour to produce a wide range of results. The heights and spreads in the charts give very rough average dimensions for reasonably mature specimens about 20-25 years of age.

Size is a major factor to take into account when deciding where to plant trees and large shrubs, not only because of a plant's eventual bulk above ground but also because the diameter of the canopy indicates the area of root spread. Trees and large shrubs crowding round buildings can be oppressive and the shade they cast unwelcome; more alarming in reality is the way their roots can destabilize foundations or work their way into drains. Most of the trees and shrubs in these charts will look their best with space around them or planted as the dominant feature in a small group of woody plants. Specimen planting, that is in isolation, preferably at well-sited focal points, allows the full ornamental beauty of a tree or shrub to be appreciated.

Buying and planting

Deciduous trees and shrubs are traditionally sold in the dormant season as bare-root specimens or root-balled, that is with the roots and some of the soil lifted with them wrapped in netting or hessian. Evergreens are usually sold as root-balled specimens but not bare-root.

The mock oranges (*Philadelphus*) are, admittedly, somewhat indifferent shrubs when out of flower but their heavily fragrant, white blossom marks a high point in summer. 'Virginal', a double, is one of the taller-growing cultivars but there are several suitable for small gardens. All are easily grown in a wide range of conditions.

TREES AND LARGE SHRUBS FOR AUTUMN COLOUR

All of the following trees and shrubs are deciduous.

Name	height	description
Acer (see page 132)		
Amelanchier lamarckii	4.5-7.5m 15-25ft	glowing red autumn leaves as well as masses of white flowers in spring
Betula papyrifera paper birch, canoe birch	6-9m 20-30ft	in autumn triangular leaves turn soft yellow; peeling, white bark
Crataegus persimilis 'Prunifolia'	6-7.5m 20-25ft	orange and scarlet autumn foliage with eye-catching and persistent red haws
Liquidambar styraciflua sweet gum	6-9m 20-30ft	large tree with prettily fingered leaves, brilliant orange and scarlet in autumn
Malus tschonoskii	6-10m 20-33ft	leaves with an irregular margin are splendidly coloured in autumn; spring apple blossom and yellow fruits tinged purple
Nyssa sylvatica tupelo	6-9m 20-30ft	large tree with lustrous leaves turning reds and oranges in autumn
Parrotia persica	6-9m 20-30ft	autumn leaves in browns, yellows and reds; attractive bark and crimson spring flowers
Prunus sargentii	6-7.5m 20-25ft	leaves turn orange and red in early autumn; pink flowers in mid-spring
Sorbus commixta	4.5-6m 15-20ft	lovely autumn foliage colours combine with the orange-red berries
Sorbus 'Joseph Rock'	4.5-7.5m 15-25ft	rich mixture of autumn foliage colour sets off the yellow of the berries

Trees and shrubs that are strikingly ornamental in more than one season are especially valuable in small or medium-sized gardens. The crab apples, such as *Malus floribunda*, wreathed in blossom in spring and later hung with colourful fruit, fall into this category.

Most deciduous trees and shrubs can be planted at any time between mid-autumn and mid-spring, provided the weather is mild. Evergreens can be planted in mid-autumn or mid- to late spring. Autumn planting is in general advisable where the summers tend to be droughty. Where winters are harsh, spring planting is preferable.

It is increasingly common for both deciduous and evergreen trees and shrubs to be sold as container-grown specimens. In theory, container-grown specimens can be planted at any time of the year but the quality of stock management at garden centres and other outlets is so variable (container-grown specimens are often root-bound or watered

only irregularly) that it is safer to keep to conventional methods and times for planting. Setting aside the matter of price, it is tempting to buy specimens that are large enough to give a garden a mature look. As a general rule, however, young trees and shrubs are quicker to get established than older specimens, catching up with them in a year or two.

Trees and large shrubs should be planted in ground that has been well-prepared in advance, with plenty of organic matter incorporated in the planting hole. To give stability in the first year or two, use a stake with a height above ground that is not more than one-third the height of the tree, tying with a broad, flexible strap just below the top of the stake. Ties need to be checked regularly to ensure that they are not constricting growth or working loose. Bracing at a low level is an alternative to staking and is often more practicable with large shrubs. In exposed positions a shield of mesh or netting will cut considerably the force of wind

and reduce water loss. Anti-desiccant sprays will also provide some degree of protection to newly planted evergreens.

Pruning & training

Many mature trees and shrubs require little or no annual pruning; if they do, it often means that a poor choice has been made for a given site. Some formative pruning may be necessary, however, and should be carried out during the dormant period. As a first step all dead, diseased and damaged wood should be removed. Other pruning should aim at creating an open framework of branches. If a tree is to be grown as a branched-head standard and the leader has not been cut back, this should be done in its third year, the cut being made immediately above a strong bud or lateral.

Major tree surgery is potentially dangerous. A qualified member of a professional body of tree surgeons should be employed for the felling of trees and the removal of large limbs.

TREES AND LARGE SHRUBS WITH ORNAMENTAL FRUIT

Name	height	description
DECIDUOUS		
Catalpa bignonioides Indian bean tree	4.5-6m 15-20ft	ornamental for its large leaves, foxglove-like flowers in summer and the long beans that follow
Clerodendrum trichotomum fargesii	3-4.5m 10-15ft	scented pink-and-white flowers in late summer leave red calyces, among which blue berries stand out
Cornus kousa	2.5-3m 8-10ft	flowers in early summer, made showy by white bracts, followed in early autumn by strawberry-like fruits
Crataegus persimilis 'Prunifolia'	4.5-6m 15-20ft	white flower clusters in early summer followed by long-lasting, red haws; excellent foliage colour in autumn
Decaisnea fargesii	2.5-3.7m 8-12ft	steel-blue 'broad bean' pods in autumn follow greenish-yellow flowers in early summer
Euonymus latifolius	3-4.5m 10-15ft	pendulous rosy fruits persist from late summer, splitting to show orange seeds; brilliant autumn foliage
Hippophae rhamnoides sea buckthorn	2.5-3m 8-10ft	on female plants, which need a male to set fruit, branches are thickly clustered with bright orange berries in autumn and winter
Malus 'John Downie'	7.5-9m 25-30ft	white blossom in late spring and crab apples of yellow and bright crimson in autumn
Malus x **zumi** 'Golden Hornet'	4.5-6m 15-20ft	long-lasting, yellow crab apples in autumn and winter; white blossom in late spring
Mespilus germanica medlar	6-7.5m 20-25ft	edible fruits like large, brown rose hips in autumn; white or pink blossom in late spring
Sorbus aucuparia rowan, mountain ash	4.5-7.5m 15-25ft	white flowers in late spring followed by large clusters of orange-red berries; good foliage colour in autumn
Sorbus 'Joseph Rock'	4.5-7.5m 15-25ft	dense bunches of yellow fruits ripen before leaves turn bright red in autumn; creamy flowers in late spring
EVERGREEN		
Arbutus unedo Killarney strawberry tree	4.5-6m 15-20ft	picturesque tree with dark leaves and clusters of urn-shaped, white flowers in autumn coinciding with strawberry-like fruits
Cotoneaster frigidus 'Cornubia'	6-7.5m 20-25ft	semi-evergreen; white flowers in early summer and heavy bunches of long-lasting, red berries
Cotoneaster salicifolius 'Rothschildianus'	2.5-3.7m 8-12ft	semi-evergreen; clusters of pale yellow berries in autumn after white flowers in early summer
Ilex aquifolium 'J. C. van Tol'	4.5-7.5m 15-25ft	lustrous leaves with few spines and red berries in abundance if a male plant nearby
Ilex aquifolium 'Pyramidalis' holly	4.5-6m 15-20ft	dark green leaves, some spiny, and heavy crops of red berries if a male plant nearby
Photinia davidiana (**Stransvaesia davidiana**)	3.7-6m 12-20ft	clusters of crimson berries start to ripen in late summer after white flowers in early summer
Pyracantha 'Mohave' firethorn	3-4.5m 10-15ft	thick crops of orange-red berries in autumn; white flowers in early summer
Pyracantha rogersiana firethorn	3-4.5m 10-15ft	after fragrant, white flowers in early summer red (or in *P. rogersiana flava*, yellow) berries in autumn

TREES AND LARGE SHRUBS WITH ORNAMENTAL BARK AND TWIGS

Name	height	description
DECIDUOUS		
Acer griseum	4.5-6m 15-20ft	thin, buff bark curls back to show orange-brown new bark; brilliant autumn colour
Acer palmatum 'Sango-kaku' (**A. palmatum** 'Senkaki')	3-4.5m 10-15ft	young branches are a startling coral-red; yellow leaves in autumn
Acer pensylvanicum snake bark maple	4.5-6m 15-20ft	young green bark handsomely striped white and light green; yellow leaves in autumn
Betula utilis jacquemontii	6-7.5m 20-25ft	peeling bark with stems of flashing white; many other *Betula* have attractive white stems
Parrotia persica	6-9m 20-30ft	flaking bark makes a pretty patchwork of green, greys and browns; excellent autumn colour and crimson flowers in early spring
Prunus serrula	6-7.5m 20-25ft	old bark peels away in strips to reveal burnished red-brown new bark
Salix alba vitellina 'Britzensis'	9-12m 30-40ft	young shoots are a striking orange, especially in winter; suitable for pollarding
Salix daphnoides violet willow	4.5-8m 15-26ft	violet-purple shoots are softened by white bloom, especially when hard-pruned; catkins in early spring
EVERGREEN		
Arbutus x **andrachnoides**	3-3.7m 10-12ft	rich red-brown bark; white flowers in winter to early spring
Eucalyptus pauciflora niphophila	6-7.5m 20-25ft	shedding bark creates a mottled effect of red-brown and grey on cream; young growths have a blue-white bloom

The combination of blue berries and red calyces makes *Clerodendrum trichotomum* and *C. trichotomum fargesii* startling small trees or shrubs in autumn. The fragrant flowers, borne in late summer, are pink and white.

TREES AND LARGE SHRUBS WITH ORNAMENTAL FOLIAGE

Name	height	description

GREY, SILVER OR BLUE FOLIAGE

DECIDUOUS

Buddleja fallowiana alba	1.8-3m 6-10ft	grey leaves with silver backing that complement white flowers from mid-summer
Elaeagnus angustifolia Caspica Group oleaster	3-4.5m 10-15ft	narrow, silvery leaves; fragrant flowers in early summer
Hippophae rhamnoides sea buckthorn	2.5-3m 8-10ft	narrow silvery leaves on spiny stems; long-lasting orange berries
Pyrus salicifolia 'Pendula'	3-4.5m 10-15ft	small, silver-leaved, weeping tree; creamy white flowers in mid-spring

EVERGREEN

Cedrus libani atlantica 'Glauca Pendula' weeping blue Atlas cedar	6-9m 20-30ft	weeping conifer with blue-grey foliage and bluish cones
Chamaecyparis lawsoniana 'Pembury Blue'	6-9m 20-30ft	conifer with foliage of conspicuous silvery blue
Eucalyptus gunnii cider gum	9-15m 30-50ft	rounded juvenile foliage blue-green or silvery, mature leaves long and darker green; can be maintained as juvenile
Olearia x **macrodonta** New Zealand holly	2.5-3.7m 8-12ft	holly-like greyish leaves, felted and white on the underside; daisy flowers in mid- to late summer
Picea pungens 'Koster' Colorado spruce	6-7.5m 20-25ft	conifer with stiff, prickly leaves of intense silver-blue

COPPER, RED OR PURPLE FOLIAGE

DECIDUOUS

Cercis canadensis 'Forest Pansy'	3-4.5m 10-15ft	rounded leaves of rich plum-purple
Corylus maxima 'Purpurea'	2.5-3m 8-10ft	an ornamental filbert with large leaves of rich purple
Cotinus coggygria 'Notcutt's Variety' smoke bush	2.5-3.7m 8-12ft	dark purple leaves attractively tinted in autumn; feathery heads of purple flowers in mid-summer
Euonymus europaeus 'Atropurpurea' spindle tree	1.8-3m 6-10ft	purple leaves brighten to cheerful red in autumn
Fagus sylvatica 'Riversii' purple beech	6-10m 20-33ft	large tree with leaves of sombre deep purple
Malus x **gloriosa** 'Oekonomierat Echtermeyer' **(M.** 'Echtermeyer')	4.5-6m 15-20ft	weeping branches form a cascade of mid-green flushed with purple; pink flowers in late spring and purple fruit
Prunus x **blireana**	3.7-6m 12-20ft	purple leaves with copper tones; pink flowers in mid-spring
Prunus cerasifera 'Pissardii' cherry plum	6-7.5m 20-25ft	dark red leaves turn deep purple; white flowers from pink buds in late winter and early spring
Prunus spinosa 'Purpurea' blackthorn, sloe	3-4.5m 10-15ft	small, purple-brown leaves; masses of white flowers in early spring

EVERGREEN

Photinia x **fraseri** 'Red Robin'	2.5-3.7m 8-12ft	glossy, leathery leaves that are bright red when young, then dark green

YELLOW OR GOLD FOLIAGE

DECIDUOUS

Catalpa bignonioides 'Aurea' golden Indian bean tree	4.5-6m 15-20ft	large, soft yellow leaves; 'foxglove' flowers in mid-summer, followed by bean-like fruit
Gleditsia triacanthos 'Sunburst' honey locust	6-9m 20-30ft	frond-like leaves, bright gold when young
Philadelphus coronarius 'Aureus'	1.8-3m 6-10ft	young leaves bright yellow, becoming greener as summer advances
Sambucus racemosa 'Plumosa Aurea'	2.5-3.7m 8-12ft	leaves finely cut and radiantly golden in a well-lit position, otherwise lime-green
Taxus baccata 'Standishii' yew	2.5-4.5m 8-15ft	slow-growing conifer with dense, upright growth and yellow foliage

EVERGREEN

Ilex aquifolium 'Flavescens' moonlight holly	4.5-7.5m 15-25ft	leaves in shades of yellow; produces berries when there is a male plant nearby
Juniperus chinensis 'Aurea' Chinese juniper	3-4.5m 10-15ft	slow-growing conifer making a narrow column of golden foliage

VARIEGATED FOLIAGE

DECIDUOUS

Acer see page 132

Aralia elata 'Aureovariegata'	4.5-6m 15-20ft	huge leaves divided into leaflets edged and splashed yellow, paling to cream
Aralia elata 'Variegata'	4.5-6m 15-20ft	similar to above but cream fading to white
Buddleja davidii 'Harlequin'	2.5-3m 8-10ft	creamy variegation on grey-green foliage; red-purple flowers from mid-summer
Cornus controversa 'Variegata'	4.5-6m 15-20ft	silver variegated leaves on tiered branches; cream flowers in late spring

EVERGREEN

Aucuba japonica 'Crotonifolia' spotted laurel	1.8-3.7m 6-12ft	the common form, *A. japonica* 'Variegata', can look sickly, unlike this example which has broad leaves with bold yellow markings and red berries
Elaeagnus x **ebbingei** 'Gilt Edge'	3-4.5m 10-15ft	showy yellow margins to leaves; scented flowers in autumn
Elaeagnus pungens 'Maculata'	2.5-3.7m 8-12ft	bold yellow splashes on dark green leaves
Ilex x **altaclerensis** 'Golden King'	4.5-7.5m 15-25ft	female holly with broad leaves margined or wholly yellow
Ilex aquifolium 'Handsworth New Silver'	4.5-7.5m 15-25ft	long, prickly leaves with a creamy edge and grey markings; female plant that berries freely
Ilex aquifolium 'Silver Queen'	4.5-6m 15-20ft	dark green, prickly leaves with a cream edge; perversely this is a male plant and produces no berries
Ligustrum ovalifolium 'Aureum'	3-3.7m 10-12ft	semi-evergreen; oval leaves with yellow margin
Pittosporum tenuifolium 'Irene Paterson'	2.5-3.7m 8-12ft	wavy-edged white leaves, heavily mottled green and grey

TOP The young leaves of *Photinia x fraseri* 'Red Robin' are as vividly coloured as many flowers. Unlike the red-leaved *Pieris*, it does not need acid soil.

BOTTOM The privets, easy shrubs to please, tend to be underrated as ornamentals. Several forms of *Ligustrum lucidum*, including 'Aureomarginatum', have variegated foliage.

EVERGREEN SHADE-TOLERANT TREES AND LARGE SHRUBS

Name	height	description
Aucuba japonica 'Crotonifolia' spotted laurel	1.8-3.7m 6-12ft	large leaves blotched gold; no fruit produced as this is a male plant; other cultivars are also suitable
Camellia japonica 'Adolphe Audusson'	1.8-3.7m 6-12ft	blood-red flowers and yellow stamens; one of many cultivars with glossy leaves and showy flowers from mid-winter to spring
Camellia x williamsii 'J. C. Williams'	1.8-3m 6-10ft	pink flowers; one of many cultivars with good foliage and white, pink or red flowers from late autumn to spring
Elaeagnus pungens 'Maculata'	2.5-3.7m 8-12ft	dark green leaves boldly splashed yellow; one of several good cultivars
Fatsia japonica	2.5-4.5m 8-15ft	large, glossy, fingered leaves; white flowers in mid-autumn
Ilex x altaclerensis 'Camelliifolia' holly	4.5-9m 15-30ft	glossy, almost spineless, dark green leaves; female plant that fruits well provided a male nearby; other non-variegated cultivars are also suitable
Ilex aquifolium 'Myrtifolia' holly	4.5-9m 15-30ft	small, glossy leaves; a male plant so no fruit is produced; other non-variegated cultivars are also suitable
Prunus laurocerasus cherry laurel	4.5-6m 15-20ft	very tolerant shrub with lustrous, leathery leaves; white flowers in spring
Prunus lusitanica Portugal laurel	4.5-6m 15-20ft	glossy, dark green leaves on reddish stems; fragrant, cream flowers in early summer
Taxus baccata yew	4.5-6m 15-20ft	very resilient conifer, densely clothed with dark green, narrow leaves

DECIDUOUS TREES AND LARGE SHRUBS CASTING LIGHT SHADE

Name	height	description
Betula pendula 'Laciniata' Swedish birch	6-9m 20-30ft	slender tree with deeply cut leaves on pendulous branches; silvery bark
Crataegus monogyna 'Stricta' hawthorn, may	4.5-6m 15-20ft	erect branches make a columnar shape; white flowers in late spring, followed by haws in autumn
Elaeagnus angustifolia oleaster	3-4.5m 10-15ft	spreading tree with narrow, silvery leaves; fragrant flowers in early summer
Genista aetnensis Mount Etna broom	4.5-6m 15-20ft	almost leafless; yellow flowers in mid- to late summer
Malus 'Van Eseltine'	3.7-4.5m 12-15ft	stiff, upright growth; scarlet buds then pink flowers in mid- to late spring; yellow fruit
Sorbus aucuparia 'Beissneri' mountain ash, rowan	4.5-7.5m 15-25ft	upright growth and deeply divided leaves; warm-coloured bark and orange-red fruit
Sorbus vilmorinii	2.5-3.7m 8-12ft	ferny foliage with good autumn colour; drooping clusters of rose to white berries
Tamarix pentandra tamarisk	3.7-4.5m 12-15ft	slender branches and feathery, blue-grey foliage; pink flowers in late summer

Lawns & ground cover

For centuries, grasses that tolerate regular trimming have been used to provide a specialized ground cover that is at once pleasing to the eye, a foil for other plants and garden features and a soft and springy carpet on which to walk. A lawn is either sown or laid as turf. Whatever the method, a lawn consists of a mixture of grasses which can be selected for the quality of lawn you require and the conditions in which you garden.

The perfectionist's lawn

The perfectionist's lawn, a velvety bowling green with clean outlines, consists of a selection of fine-leaved and compact bents and fescues. Pleasing though it may be to the eye, it is a feature that is only maintained in prime condition at the cost of considerable labour and it will not take heavy wear.

Unless a high-quality lawn is mown frequently and the mowings removed, coarser grasses and weeds will eventually take over. A cylinder mower with a back roller will give the neat, striped finish that the perfectionist is looking for. You will need to begin mowing as soon as growth starts in spring, with two or even three cuts per week once the grass starts growing vigorously. The first few cuts of the season should be light but you can then lower the mower blades; the closest cut should not be less than 1cm/½in. In summer, one or two cuts a week will be sufficient, the number being reduced further in autumn. An occasional light cut may be necessary in a mild winter if there is growth. To maintain the crisp finish of a high-quality lawn, it will be necessary to trim the edges regularly.

For a high-quality lawn to stay in peak condition, it needs to be aerated and scarified (an operation to remove thatch and dead moss)

BELOW LEFT For those who find the obligations of maintaining a conventional lawn a tyranny, there are other options. A meadow effect can be achieved by mowing grass only twice during the growing season. This can be adjusted to take account of the flowering and seeding timetables of plants such as spring-flowering bulbs that are mixed with the grasses.

BELOW A high-quality lawn – level, even textured and springy underfoot – can be created only by using fine-leaved grasses on carefully prepared ground. It must be cut at frequent and regular intervals during the growing season, watered during dry spells and fed annually. Moss and weed growth must be controlled and the edges trimmed to maintain a neat finish.

in autumn, treated to control moss in spring and autumn and weeds in summer, rolled in spring, fertilized in spring, summer and autumn, and top-dressed and cleared of fallen leaves in autumn.

Utilitarian lawns

Mixtures for utilitarian lawns contain some bents and fescues but the meadow grasses and ryegrass that dominate are much harder wearing. With this kind of lawn you can adopt a much more relaxed approach to mowing. Once a week or even less will usually be enough during the growing season and a rotary mower will give a perfectly adequate finish. After the initial light cuts in spring the blades can be set at a height of about 2.5cm/1in. Light mowings can be allowed to lie to return goodness to the soil. Treatment for moss and weeds will be beneficial, as will aeration and the addition of fertilizer.

Flowers & grass

Grass makes the ideal background for many spring- and autumn-flowering bulbs, and drifts of them can be planted in areas of utilitarian lawn (never high-quality lawn). Planted areas should not be mown for six weeks after flowering has finished to allow the leaves to die down naturally.

Meadow or cornfield effects, with wild and other flowers growing among grass, are beguiling options and in tune with ecological concerns. The best results are generally achieved on poor soils where the ground is first cleared and then planted with a mixture of grasses and flower seed, or where suitable plants are first raised from seed and then planted out in prepared ground. Summer-flowering bulbs can also be used.

WILD ANNUALS AND BIENNIALS FOR NATURALIZING

Name	height	growing requirements	description
Agrostemma githago corncockle	60-75cm 2-2½ft	well-drained, poor soil; sun	annual; purple-pink flowers in early to late summer
Centaurea cyanus cornflower	60-75cm 2-2½ft	well-drained, poor soil; sun	annual; frilled, blue flowers in early to late summer
Chrysanthemum segetum corn marigold	45-50cm 18-20in	well-drained soil; sun	annual; single, yellow, daisy flowers from mid- to late summer
Dipsacus fullonum teasel	90-180cm 3-6ft	well-drained soil; sun	biennial; thistle-like heads of purple flowers in mid- to late summer
Echium vulgare viper's bugloss	50-60cm 20-24in	well-drained, poor soil; sun	biennial; tubular flowers of violet-blue from early to late summer
Myosotis alpestris alpine forget-me-not	10-25cm 4-10in	most soils; sun or shade	biennial; masses of bright blue flowers from mid-spring to early summer
Oenothera biennis evening primrose	60-90cm 2-3ft	well-drained soil; sun	biennial; floppy, yellow flowers from early summer to early autumn
Papaver rhoeas field poppy	50-60cm 20-24in	well-drained, poor soil; sun	annual; floppy, scarlet flowers on slender stems from early to late summer

DAFFODILS (*NARCISSUS*) FOR NATURALIZING

Name	height	growing requirements	description
N. 'Actaea'	35-45cm 14-18in	most soils; sun or light shade	glistening white petals and small yellow cup with a red edge in mid-to late spring
N. bulbocodium conspicuus hoop petticoat daffodil	5-10cm 2-4in	moist soil; sun	pretty, open petticoat of deep yellow in late winter to early spring
N. 'Carlton'	35-50cm 14-20in	most soils; sun or light shade	yellow, hefty and large-cupped, flowering early to mid-spring
N. cyclamineus	15-20cm 6-8in	moist soil; sun or light shade	deep yellow, hanging flowers with swept-back petals in late winter to early spring
N. 'February Gold'	25-30cm 10-12in	most soils; sun or light shade	poised, yellow, trumpet daffodil in late winter or early spring
N. 'Golden Harvest'	35-50cm 14-20in	most soils; sun or light shade	large yellow trumpets in mid-spring
N. 'Jack Snipe'	20-25cm 8-10in	most soils; sun or light shade	well-matched primrose trumpets with off-white petals in early spring
N. 'Mount Hood'	35-50cm 14-20in	most soils; sun or light shade	large solid trumpets of ivory-white in mid-spring
N. 'Peeping Tom'	30-40cm 12-16in	most soils; sun or light shade	nosy, long trumpets of deep yellow in early to mid-spring
N. pseudonarcissus Tenby daffodil, Lent lily	20-30cm 8-12in	most soils; sun or light shade	pale yellow trumpet daffodil, unassumingly beautiful in mid-spring

OTHER SPRING BULBS FOR NATURALIZING

Name	height	growing requirements	description
Anemone blanda	10-15cm 4-6in	most soils; sun or light shade	blue flowers (also mauve and white) late winter to mid-spring
Crocus tommasinianus	10-15cm 4-6in	most soils; sun	flowers in mauve and lilac in late winter and early spring
Eranthis hyemalis winter aconite	8-10cm 3-4in	most soils; sun or light shade	lemon-yellow flowers with a green ruff in late winter
Fritillaria meleagris snake's-head fritillary	23-38cm 9-15in	moist soil; sun	chequered, hanging flowers, purple or greenish-white, in mid- to late spring
Galanthus nivalis snowdrop	8-20cm 3-8in	most soils; sun or shade	dangling white flowers with green inner markings from late winter to early spring
Hyacinthoides non-scripta English bluebell	20-30cm 8-12in	most soils; sun or shade	violet-blue bells from mid- to late spring
Muscari armeniacum grape hyacinth	20-25cm 8-10in	most soils; sun or light shade	heads of densely packed, dark blue flowers with a white rim in mid- to late spring
Ornithogalum umbellatum star of Bethlehem	25-30cm 10-12in	most soils; sun or light shade	numerous starry, white flowers with green stripes in mid- to late spring
Scilla siberica	10-15cm 4-6in	most soils; sun or light shade	sprays of small but brilliant blue flowers in early spring
Tulipa sprengeri	35-45cm 14-18in	most soils; sun or light shade	bright scarlet flowers in late spring

SUMMER AND AUTUMN BULBS FOR NATURALIZING

Name	height	growing requirements	description
Camassia leichtlinii	90-120cm 3-4ft	moist soil; sun	spires of starry, white or blue flowers in mid- to late summer
Colchicum speciosum	15-20cm 6-8in	most soils; sun or light shade	goblet flowers in shades of mauve during autumn
Crocus speciosus	10-15cm 4-6in	most soils; sun	lilac-blue flowers in mid-autumn
Cyclamen hederifolium	10-15cm 4-6in	most soils; shade or sun	pink or white flowers in autumn over variegated leaves
Gladiolus communis byzantinus	45-60cm 1½-2ft	well-drained soil; sun	spikes of wine-red flowers in early summer
Lilium martagon turk's-cap lily	90-150cm 3-5ft	most soils; sun or light shade	stems of 6-9 purplish flowers with darker spots in mid-summer

Bulbs are the most obliging plants to add interest to areas of mown grass. The common snowdrop (*Galanthus nivalis*) depicted here and its various close relatives, all showing a close family resemblance, are perfectly happy planted in grass under trees.

PERENNIAL WILD FLOWERS FOR MEADOWS

Name	height	growing requirements	description
Campanula glomerata clustered bellflower	15-45cm 6-18in	well-drained soil; sun	dense heads of purple-blue flowers from mid-summer to early autumn
Cardamine pratense cuckoo flower, lady's smock	30-60cm 1-2ft	moist soil; sun or light shade	pale pink flowers from mid-spring to early summer
Filipendula ulmaria meadowsweet	60-90cm 2-3ft	moist soil; sun or light shade	frothy plumes of fragrant, cream flowers from early to late summer
Geranium pratense meadow crane's-bill	45-75cm 1½-2½ft	prefers alkaline soil; sun	purple-blue flowers with dark veins from mid-summer to early autumn
Leucanthemum vulgare ox-eye daisy	60-75cm 2-2½ft	most soils; sun	white daisies from late spring to late summer
Lychnis flos-cuculi ragged robin	45-60cm 1½-2ft	moist soil; sun or light shade	tattered pink flowers in late spring and early summer
Primula veris cowslip	20-25cm 8-10in	prefers well-drained, alkaline soil	heads of yellow flowers in mid-to late spring
Primula vulgaris primrose	10-15cm 4-6in	most soils; sun or light shade	soft yellow flowers above leaf rosettes in early to mid-spring
Silene dioica red campion	60-90cm 2-3ft	prefers alkaline soils	showy, carmine flowers from late spring to early autumn
Trollius europaeus globe flower	45-60cm 1½-2ft	moist soil; sun or light shade	yellow, globular flowers from early to mid-summer

BELOW LEFT The ideal plants for naturalizing are, like the primrose (*Primula vulgaris*), well behaved, not rampageous like the lesser celandine (*Ranunculus ficaria*), which here keeps it company.

BELOW The late-flowering *Tulipa sprengeri* is easily naturalized with ox-eye daisies (*Leucanthemum vulgare*).

Meadow mixtures should not be cut until the second half of summer and again in autumn, a strimmer or scythe generally being more useful for the job than a rotary mower. Leaving seedheads and cut grass to lie before raking them up will encourage self-seeding. Cornfield annuals do best if the ground is cleared and lightly forked in autumn.

Suitable ground-cover plants

Bare soil is an open invitation to weeds so the best way of thwarting them is to cover the ground with plants that are pleasing to you. In an obvious sense all plants are ground covering but some are particularly valuable for creating a dense mantle of attractive foliage that deters weeds and, incidentally, may help to retain moisture in the soil.

Among the most useful of these plants are moderately vigorous evergreens that root as they go. Ivies (*Hedera*) are outstanding examples of these, fairly speedily covering ground in almost any conditions and available in a tremendous range of colour, leaf size and shape (see page 21). Clump formers that increase at a fairly rapid rate, such as the bergenias, are almost as valuable, as are a number of deciduous perennials and shrubs.

Some deciduous perennials and shrubs make their growth early enough in the year to steal a march on weeds and others, among them the hostas, have such dense roots that weeds have a job to get going before the plants' leaves unfurl. With deciduous ground cover, it is always worth using a weed-suppressing mulch as well. This is especially true with the so-called ground-cover roses. Without a mulch, precocious weeds can get away in springtime, and the thorniness of the roses makes for extremely uncomfortable weeding.

All the ground-cover plants listed here are perennials or shrubs. In new beds or borders, however, temporary fillers that are leafy enough to prevent weeds getting away can be very helpful. Nasturtiums (*Tropaeolum majus*) and busy lizzies (*Impatiens*) are the sort of annuals that defeat most weeds.

GROUND-COVER ROSES (*ROSA*)

The measurements given are for plants making average growth in 4 years.

Name	height/spread	flowering season	description
R. 'Avon'	30/90cm 1/3ft	early sum. to early aut.	pink buds open to semi-double, white flowers
R. 'Flower Carpet'	75/120cm 2½/4ft	mid-sum. to mid-aut.	smothering of bright pink, double flowers
R. 'Grouse'	45/300cm 1½/10ft	mid- to late sum.	rapid spreader with scented, single, pink flowers
R. 'Gwent'	20/90cm 8/36in	early sum. to early aut.	double, lemon-yellow flowers over dark foliage
R. 'Nozomi'	1.5/1.5m 5/5ft	mid- to late sum.	large clusters of pale pink, single, flowers
R. 'Partridge'	60/300cm 2/10ft	mid- to late sum.	fragrant, white, single flowers
R. 'Pink Bells'	75/150cm 2½/5ft	mid- to late sum.	large clusters of soft pink flowers
R. 'Red Blanket'	75/120cm 2½/4ft	early sum. to mid-aut.	fragrant, semi-double, red flowers with a paler centre
R. 'Suffolk'	45/90cm 1½/3ft	early sum. to mid-aut.	golden stamens; single, scarlet flowers; hips
R. 'Surrey'	75/120cm 2½/4ft	early sum. to mid-aut.	semi-double, deckle-edged pink flowers
R. 'Sussex'	60/90cm 2/3ft	early sum. to mid-aut.	double flowers of soft apricot over bronze-tinted foliage
R. 'The Fairy'	60/90cm 2/3ft	early sum. to mid-aut.	large clusters of small, pink flowers

The so-called ground-cover roses are in reality prostrate or mounding shrub roses that make dense, leafy growth in summer. They cannot be relied upon fully as ground cover but are nevertheless attractive and low-growing. R. 'Surrey' bears prettily shaped pink flowers over a long season.

DECIDUOUS GROUND COVER FOR SUN

Unless stated otherwise, all of the following plants are herbaceous perennials that thrive in ordinary soils.

Name	height/spread	description
Acanthus mollis Latifolius Group	90/90cm 3/3ft	handsome clump with large, glossy leaves and spikes of purplish flowers in summer
Alchemilla mollis lady's mantle	45/60cm 18/24in	obliging and beautiful with clumps of velvety leaves and frothy, greenish flowers in summer
Geranium endressii 'Wargrave Pink'	60/75cm 2/2½ft	clump of attractive, pale green leaves and in summer a long succession of pink flowers
Geranium x oxonianum 'Claridge Druce'	60/90cm 2/3ft	dense cover of lovely, soft green leaves and a long season of pink flowers in summer
Nepeta 'Six Hills Giant'	45/45cm 18/18in	aromatic clump of grey-green leaves and sprays of lavender-blue flowers in summer
Pennisetum vilosum	45/45cm 18/18in	clump-forming grass; attractive winter foliage; hairy flower spikes in late summer
Persicaria affinis (Polygonum affine) 'Darjeeling Red'	30/60cm 1/2ft	makes a dense carpet of narrow leaves, russet in winter; softly hairy flower spikes in late summer or autumn
Phlomis russeliana	90/60cm 3/2ft	good cover of heart-shaped, hairy leaves below stems of yellow flowers in summer
Potentilla 'Elizabeth'	90/120cm 3/4ft	dense shrub with bright green leaves and yellow flowers throughout summer
Rheum palmatum 'Atrosanguineum'	1.8/1.8m 6/6ft	in moist soil an impressive base of large leaves, reddish on the reverse, and spikes of small, crimson flowers in summer
Sedum 'Herbstfreude' **(S.** 'Autumn Joy')	60/60cm 2/2ft	clumps of fleshy, grey-green leaves and in late summer heads of pink to red flowers

EVERGREEN GROUND COVER FOR SUN

Unless stated otherwise, all of the following plants are herbaceous perennials that thrive in ordinary soils.

Name	height/spread	description
Brachyglottis 'Sunshine'	1.2/2.2m 4/7ft	shrub densely clothed with grey-green leaves, white and woolly on the reverse; yellow daisies in summer
Calluna vulgaris 'Robert Chapman'	60/45cm 2/1½ft	richly coloured foliage and purple flowers in late summer; this and other compact heathers make dense clumps in lime-free soils
Cotoneaster dammeri	10/60cm 4/24in	carpeting shrub with dark green leaves; white flowers in summer followed by red berries
Erica carnea 'Springwood White' heath, heather	20/60cm 8/24in	one of many heaths making dense carpets; this has white flowers in winter
Erica x darleyensis 'Arthur Johnson'	60/60cm 2/2ft	hybrid heath making dense hummocks and carrying spikes of pink flowers in winter
Helianthemum 'Wisley Primrose'	30/60cm 1/2ft	shrub for well-drained soils, with grey-green leaves and yellow flowers in summer
Heuchera micrantha diversifolia 'Palace Purple'	60/45cm 2/1½ft	makes a fine clump of bronze-red leaves topped in summer by plumes of tiny, white flowers
Hypericum calycinum rose of Sharon	45/90cm 1½/3ft	vigorous spreading shrub to treat with caution but in the right place, for example a steep bank, it is highly effective; lovely yellow flowers in summer
Iberis sempervirens 'Schneeflocke' ('Snowflake')	25/60cm 10/24in	in well-drained soils mats of dark green leaves covered with white, candytuft flowers in late spring and early summer
Juniperus communis 'Hornibrookii'	30/150cm 1/5ft	prostrate and fast-growing, grey-green conifer
Juniperus horizontalis	30/180cm 1/6ft	mat-forming conifer with blue-green foliage; several named forms of bluer colouring
Juniperus sabina 'Tamariscifolia'	60/120cm 1/4ft	fairly slow-growing conifer but with dense, blue-green foliage on horizontal stems
Liriope muscari	45/30cm 18/12in	in well-drained soils clumps of grassy leaves and spikes of purple-blue flowers in autumn
Salvia officinalis sage	45/60cm 1½/2ft	shrubby, aromatic herb with grey-green leaves and lavender flowers in summer
Santolina chamaecyparissus cotton lavender	45/60cm 1½/2ft	on well-drained soils makes a dense hummock of aromatic, grey, filigree leaves; yellow button flowers in summer
Stachys byzantina 'Silver Carpet'	15/45cm 6/18in	makes a carpet of woolly, grey leaves in dry soil; non-flowering
Thymus 'Doone Valley' thyme	10/30cm 4/12in	prostrate shrub making an aromatic, dark green mat blotched gold; mauve flowers in late summer

For ground cover to be effective it must be planted densely and even then it will need to be weeded regularly until individual plants knit together closely. The clump-forming *Sedum spectabile* and hybrids such as S. 'Herbstfreude' make an unusual but effective weed-smothering colony.

Some plants that undoubtedly make very effective ground cover are so aggressively invasive that they should only be introduced where they can brawl away without posing a threat to better behaved plants. Winter heliotrope (*Petasites fragrans*) and variegated yellow archangel (*Lamium galeobdolon* 'Florentinum', syn. *Galeobdolon argentatum*) come into this category and warrant a place only at the further reaches of large gardens.

Appropriate sites for ground cover

Ground-cover plants come into their own where it is difficult to use other kinds of planting. They are a particularly useful alternative to grass on steep slopes that need dense cover to prevent erosion but where mowing could be difficult and dangerous. Ground cover is also a good alternative to grass on soft, moist ground, where operating machinery can be problematic and where, because of inadequate light or poor soil, grass is unlikely to do well. Dry shade at the base of trees, hedges or buildings is another area where ground-cover plants can be very useful.

Preparation & planting

Autumn planting has the advantage of giving ground-cover plants a good start over weeds in spring but in mild weather planting can be carried out any time between autumn and mid-spring. In general, it is better to plant small, young plants at fairly close intervals rather than larger specimens further apart.

Good ground preparation is crucial. Eradicate all perennial weeds, dig the ground over and incorporate humus-rich material such as garden compost. A heavy mulch, such as bark chippings, will reduce the chances of weeds colonizing earth that is still bare and will help to conserve moisture during the critical early stages. Some hand weeding will probably be necessary until plants knit together.

Grasses are invaluable for extensive planting schemes. Here the caterpillar-like heads of *Pennisetum vilosum* make a soft band in front of the oat-like *Stipa gigantea*.

GROUND COVER FOR SHADE

Name	height/spread	description
EVERGREEN		
Bergenia cordifolia 'Purpurea'	30/35cm 12/14in	clumps of large, rounded leaves turning from dark green to purple in winter; vivid purple-pink flowers in spring
Epimedium perralderianum	30/35cm 12/14in	glossy leaves with bronze or copper markings in spring and autumn; sprays of yellow flowers in spring; spreads steadily
Euonymus fortunei 'Emerald Gaiety'	30/60cm 1/2ft	hummock-forming shrub with pretty silver variegation
Hedera helix common ivy	15/90cm 6/36in	numerous named forms (see page 21) with green or variegated leaves, most of which make good spreading cover
Hedera hibernica Irish ivy	30/150cm 1/5ft	dense growth of large, dark green leaves; surface-rooting, spreading vigorously
Lamium maculatum 'White Nancy'	20/90cm 8/36in	one of several good forms; semi-evergreen with white frosting on green leaves; white hooded flowers in spring and summer
Mahonia aquifolium Oregon grape	90/90cm 3/3ft	shrub with leathery leaves and scented, yellow flowers in spring followed by almost black berries; spreads slowly by suckering
Pachysandra terminalis	30/45cm 12/18in	spreading subshrub with dense growth of toothed leaves; small, scented flowers in spring
Polystichum setiferum soft shield fern	90/90cm 3/3ft	mid-green, lacy leaves, even lacier in some of the named forms
Prunus laurocerasus 'Zabeliana' cherry laurel	1.2/1.8m 4/6ft	shining, dark green leaves on a spreading shrub; white flowers in spring
Pulmonaria saccharata	25/45cm 10/18in	silvery clump of marbled grey-green leaves; blue and pink flowers in spring
Skimmia japonica 'Rubella'	90/90cm 3/3ft	hummock-forming shrub with dark green leaves; showy, reddish buds in winter open to cream flowers in spring
Tiarella cordifolia foam flower	15/35cm 6/14in	dense cover of maple-like leaves and runners; creamy flower plumes in spring
Vinca major 'Variegata' greater periwinkle	35/90cm 14/36in	shoots of dark green leaves with cream variegation root as they grow; blue flowers in spring
Vinca minor 'La Grave'	15/60cm 6/24in	dark green leaves on runners that root; large, blue flowers in spring
Viola riviniana Purpurea Group **(V. labradorica purpurea)**	15/45cm 6/18in	semi-evergreen; vigorous spreader with purple leaves and small, deep mauve flowers in early to mid-spring
DECIDUOUS		
Epimedium x **versicolor** 'Sulphureum'	30/30cm 12/12in	steady spreader with copper tints to the foliage in spring and pale yellow flowers
Geranium macrorrhizum 'Ingwersen's Variety'	35/45cm 14/18in	aromatic, light green leaves; pink flowers in late spring
Hosta sieboldiana elegans	90/90cm 3/3ft	magnificent clump of heavily veined, blue-grey leaves; pale mauve flowers in summer
Hosta undulata albomarginata (**H**. 'Thomas Hogg')	75/90cm 2½/3ft	white edge to dark green leaves makes a striking clump; pale lilac flowers in summer

TOP One of the prettiest deadnettles, *Lamium maculatum* 'White Nancy', makes a lovely frosted filler with variegated hostas.

BOTTOM Lily-of-the-valley (*Convallaria majalis*) and the purple-leaved *Viola riviniana* Purpurea Group are rapid colonizers in shade and lovely companions for ferns.

Beds & Borders

Beds and borders are clearly defined areas of the garden that are planted up with ornamentals. The distinction between the terms is somewhat blurred. A conventional bed is usually devoted to large-scale planting of a single plant such as roses, or a succession of plants, for example spring bulbs followed by summer-flowering annuals that, like petunias, are colourful for a long period. The classic border, however, is planted with a mixture of herbaceous perennials to give three or four months of beauty in summer.

In grand gardens you can still find large-scale bedding schemes and herbacous borders maintained on traditional lines but the cost and labour involved make this sort of gardening more and more impracticable. In any case, in a small or medium-sized garden you do not want a bed or border to be an empty blank for a good part of the year. While beds and borders remain the prime ornamental features of most gardens, increasingly they are planted with combinations of shrubs, roses, perennials, bulbs and short-lived plants to give a display that is sustained throughout the year.

When staging a border it is usual to place the lowest plants in the front and the tallest at the back so that all can be seen to best advantage. In an island bed the tallest plants are placed towards the centre. Whatever the shape of the bed, it is necessary to plant in interlocking drifts, with some taller perennials or shrubs brought forward, to avoid a rigidly tiered effect. This warm scheme in yellow, orange and brick-red includes crocosmias, golden rod (*Solidago*), heleniums and achilleas.

Classic herbaceous perennials

It is difficult to overstate the qualities found in this very large category of non-woody plants with a medium to long life span. The representatives from many corners of the world that clamour for a place in the garden include flowering plants for almost every month of the year in a wide range of forms and in a palette so minutely graduated that it makes every bold and subtle colour scheme an exciting possibility. Some perennials rank among the finest of foliage plants. Many have fragrant flowers or aromatic foliage (see pages 121 and 125). In addition, most are remarkably trouble-free.

As well as conveying the idea of a plant being reasonably long lived, the term 'herbaceous perennial' indicates that it goes through an annual cycle of active growth followed by a dormant phase when the foliage dies down. There are, however, a number of perennials with evergreen foliage, such as bergenias, that are usually included with those that are herbaceous. Conversely, bulbous and rhizomatous plants, which in the strict sense belong with fibrous-rooted herbaceous plants, are distinctive enough to justify the general practice of making them a group on their own (see pages 72-9).

Sometimes the plants referred to in this section (pages 44-53) are described as 'hardy herbaceous perennials' to indicate that they will survive winters outdoors in cool temperate regions. Their hardiness is a major factor in their usefulness as garden plants but it has to be remembered that 'hardiness' is a relative term.

The herbaceous perennials discussed here generally grow well in open positions where the soil is reasonably fertile and well drained but where there is a good supply of moisture during the growing season. Others that tolerate shade, dry soils and moist conditions, as well as those

Summer is the prime season for the classic perennials that once featured in herbaceous borders. There are some valuable off-season perennials, however, such as the choice and undemanding Lenten roses (*Helleborus orientalis*), with a colour range extending from greenish-white to deepest plum.

WINTER- AND SPRING-FLOWERING PERENNIALS

The bergenias are tolerant of a wide range of conditions, including dry shade.

Name	height/spread	flowering season	description
SHORT			
Ajuga pyramidalis	20/15cm 8/6in	late spr.	short spires of vivid, gentian-blue flowers over evergreen foliage
Bergenia 'Baby Doll'	25/30cm 10/12in	mid- to late spr.	heads of soft pink flowers over rounded, evergreen leaves
Bergenia 'Bressingham White'	35/45cm 14/18in	mid- to late spr.	heads with short, arching sprays of white flowers; evergreen
Bergenia 'Rosi Klose'	30/30cm 12/12in	mid- to late spr.	pretty bells of salmon-pink and spoon-shaped, evergreen leaves
Convallaria majalis	20/60cm 8/24in	mid- to late spr.	between strap leaves arching stems carry waxy, white bells with a ravishing scent
Doronicum 'Miss Mason'	45/30cm 18/12in	mid-spr. to early sum.	cheerful, yellow daisies complement bright green leaves
Epimedium x **warleyense**	25/25cm 10/10in	early to mid-spr.	sprays of short-spurred, orange flowers; attractive foliage although less dense than that of most epimediums
Helleborus niger Christmas rose	30/45cm 12/18in	mid-win. to early spr.	saucer-shaped flowers, sometimes tinged green or pink; leathery, evergreen leaves
Primula denticulata drumstick primula	30/50cm 12/20in	early to late spr.	packed, globular heads of pale mauve to rose-red flowers over rosettes of mealy leaves; needs moist soil
Pulmonaria angustifolia azurea	25/45cm 10/18in	mid-spr.	pink buds open to rich blue flowers as narrow, unspotted leaves develop
Pulmonaria rubra 'Redstart'	30/60cm 1/2ft	late win. to mid-spr.	evergreen with hanging clusters of deep pink flowers over a long period
MEDIUM TO TALL			
Brunnera macrophylla	45/45cm 18/18in	mid- to late spr.	sprays of small but vivid blue flowers, forget-me-not in style; large leaves
Euphorbia characias wulfenii	120/90cm 4/3ft	early to late spr.	huge heads of yellow-green flowers on an impressive plant with grey-green foliage through winter
Euphorbia polychroma	45/60cm 1½/2ft	mid- to late spr.	makes an arresting clump of yellow, tinged with green, for weeks
Helleborus orientalis Lenten rose	60/45cm 2/1½ft	late win. to early spr.	distinguished evergreen with saucer-shaped flowers ranging from white to deep plum, often beautifully speckled
Paeonia mlokosewitschii	45/75cm 1½/2½ft	late spr.	peerless when, for a brief time, lemon-yellow petals cradle darker stamens; good, grey-green foliage, red and flower-like when it emerges

BORDER PERENNIALS FOR LATE SPRING AND EARLY SUMMER

Name	height/spread	flowering season	description
BACK OF BORDER			
Cephalaria gigantea	1.8/1.2m 6/4ft	early to mid-sum.	scabious flowers of pale yellow wave high on wiry stems
Crambe cordifolia	1.8/1.5m 6/5ft	early sum.	the airy mass of small, white flowers camouflages the plant's coarseness; close to, the scent is pungent
MID-BORDER			
Achillea 'Moonshine'	60/45cm 2/1½ft	early to mid-sum.	wide heads of cool yellow flowers and feathery, silver foliage all year
Anchusa azurea 'Loddon Royalist'	120/45cm 4/1½ft	early to mid-sum.	coarse foliage but worth tolerating for the intense blue of the flowers
Aquilegia McKana hybrids columbine	90/45cm 3/1½ft	late spr. to early sum.	elegantly spurred flowers in a wide colour range
Baptisia australis	90/45cm 3/1½ft	early sum.	spikes of indigo-blue, pea flowers over blue-green leaves
Campanula lactiflora 'Prichard's Variety'	90/45cm 3/1½ft	early to mid-sum.	large heads of lavender-blue flowers on leafy stems
Campanula persicifolia	75/30cm 2½/1ft	early to late sum.	open bells of blue or white on wiry stems over evergreen rosettes; indispensable, self-seeding plants
Centaurea hypoleuca 'John Coutts'	60/45cm 2/1½ft	early to mid-sum.	knapweed flowers of purplish-pink over grey-green leaves
Euphorbia griffithii 'Fireglow'	75/60cm 2½/2ft	late spr. to early sum.	brick-red flower bracts fuel hot colour schemes
Geranium psilostemon	90/90cm 3/3ft	early to mid-sum.	eye-catching, black-centred, magenta flowers; handsome, divided leaves
Hemerocallis lilioasphodelus	75/45cm 2½/1½ft	late spr. to early sum.	refined trumpets of clear yellow; very sweetly scented
Iris 'Braithwaite' tall bearded iris	90/45cm 3/1½ft	early sum.	lavender standards and purple falls; one from a wide range
Iris sibirica 'Ego'	75/30cm 2½/1ft	early sum.	rich blue, small iris flowers topping grassy leaves
Lupinus 'The Chatelaine' lupin	90/45cm 3/1½ft	early sum.	one example of the many hybrid lupins; densely packed spires with pink and white flowers
Paeonia 'Bowl of Beauty' peony	90/60cm 3/2ft	early sum.	handsome foliage and sumptuous, deep pink, semi-double blooms with a large, cream boss; needs support
Paeonia 'Festiva Maxima' peony	90/60cm 3/2ft	early sum.	fragrant, double flowers of pure white with random red flecks
Papaver orientale 'Beauty of Livermere' oriental poppy	90/60cm 3/2ft	early sum.	although grandiose and untidy after flowering, the vivid red blooms are magnificent; needs support
Papaver orientale 'Black and White' oriental poppy	75/60cm 2½/2ft	early sum.	all oriental poppies have their merits; this has white flowers stamped in centre with bold, black blotches
Thalictrum aquilegifolium	90/45cm 3/1½ft	late spr. to early sum.	fluffy heads of small, purple flowers held above a lovely clump of blue-green foliage
FRONT OF BORDER			
Ajuga reptans 'Burgundy Glow'	20/30cm 8/12in	late spr. to early sum.	evergreen leaves, variegated rose and cream; spikes of blue flowers
Alchemilla mollis lady's mantle	45/60cm 1½/2ft	early sum.	versatile and companionable; rounded, velvety leaves and sprays of tiny, green flowers
Anthemis punctata cupaniana	35/45cm 14/18in	late spr. to early sum.	white, daisy flowers over sprawling, silvery foliage
Armeria maritima 'Düsseldorfer Stolz' thrift	15/20cm 6/8in	late spr. to early sum.	grassy hummock producing a long succession of wine-red flowers
Campanula lactiflora 'Pouffe'	25/25cm 10/10in	early to mid-sum.	mound of light blue bells
Dianthus 'Brympton Red' old-fashioned pink	30/30cm 12/12in	early to mid-sum.	crimson flowers with darker shading; like all old-fashioned pinks, deliciously fragrant
Dicentra 'Adrian Bloom'	38/30cm 15/12in	late spr. to mid-sum.	ferny, grey-green leaves and sprays of heart-shaped, carmine flowers
Geranium renardii	25/30cm 10/12in	late spr. to mid-sum.	purple-veined, near white flowers over pretty, sage-green leaves
Geranium sanguineum striatum	15/35cm 6/14in	early to late sum.	mats of pretty leaves well-covered with crimson-veined, pink flowers
Geum 'Borisii'	30/30cm 12/12in	late spr. into sum.	single flowers of vivid orange stand against the clump of hairy leaves
Incarvillea delavayi 'Bees' Pink'	25/30cm 10/12in	early to mid-sum.	large, dark pink, foxglove flowers over a clump of attractive leaves
Iris 'Blue Denim' dwarf bearded iris	25/20cm 10/8in	late spr. to early sum.	well-shaped, mid-blue flowers; one example from a wide range
Veronica gentianoides	30/25cm 12/10in	late spr. to early sum.	spires of pale blue flowers over a mat of dark green foliage
Viola cornuta Alba Group	25/45cm 10/18in	early to mid-sum.	masses of pure white, refined flowers

thriving in acid or alkaline soils, feature in appropriate sections (see pages 93, 99 and 103-5). Many of the ground-cover plants listed on pages 39-41 are also herbaceous perennials.

Placing perennials

The magnificent large-scale displays in herbaceous borders that had their heyday in the Edwardian era lasted only three to four months of the year and needed considerable amounts of time, labour and money to maintain them in a state of perfection. A border devoted to perennials measuring significantly less than 3m/10ft deep and 9m/30ft long looks mean if it is trying to cope with broad sweeps of colour and plants that are carefully graded according to height. It is not at all surprising that this kind of gardening is now so rare.

RIGHT The oriental poppies (*Papaver orientale*) are long-lived perennials that include some of the most sumptuous flowers of early summer. Their greatest fault is that they die down untidily in mid-summer so a foreground planting is needed to camouflage the wreckage. More sober than most is the heavily blotched 'Black and White'.

BELOW Although *Crambe cordifolia* is coarse in leaf, its small white flowers make a lovely airy mass in early summer. Here its cloud floats over *Geranium x magnificum*, a good border plant that is pretty in leaf and flower. The true geraniums (not the bedding plants that are correctly *Pelargonium* species and hybrids) include many excellent border plants.

HIGH-SEASON PERENNIALS FOR THE FRONT OF BORDERS

Name	height/spread	flowering season	description
Achillea x lewisii 'King Edward'	15/25cm 6/10in	mid- to late sum.	heads of pale yellow flowers spray out over grey-green foliage
Achillea ptarmica 'Nana Compacta'	30/30cm 12/12in	mid- to late sum.	plants covered by flat heads of daisy-like, white flowers
Astilbe x simplicifolia pumila	25/25cm 10/10in	mid- to late sum.	ferny growth, producing sprays of shell-pink flowers; best in a moist soil
Campanula carpatica 'Blaue Clips' ('Blue Clips')	20/20cm 8/8in	mid-sum. to early aut.	beautifully shaped blue bells smother a clump of toothed leaves
Campanula carpatica turbinata alba	25/25cm 10/10in	mid- to late sum.	lovely, saucer-shaped bells, white with a faint blue tinge
Dianthus 'Prudence' modern pink	30/25cm 12/10in	early to mid-sum.; sometimes aut. too	pale pink with a dark eye and lacing; modern pinks are longer flowering but old-fashioned pinks are usually fragrant
Diascia 'Ruby Field'	30/45cm 1/1½ft	mid- to late sum.	produces mats of small leaves and sprays of soft pink nemesia-like flowers over a long season; not reliably hardy
Diascia rigescens	45/60cm 1½/2ft	early to late sum.	dusty pink flowers on sprawling, stiff stems; may succumb in winter
Geranium 'Johnson's Blue'	40/40cm 16/16in	mid-sum.	blue flowers with dark veining produced in abundance over lovely, dense foliage
Geranium wallichianum 'Buxton's Variety'	30/75cm 1/2½ft	mid-sum. to early aut.	leafy plant producing a long succession of white-centred, blue flowers
Gypsophila 'Rosenschleier' ('Rosy Veil')	30/75cm 1/2½ft	mid- to late sum.	abundance of tiny flowers making an airy mound of pale pink
Prunella grandiflora 'Loveliness'	25/45cm 10/18in	mid-sum.	thick-set spikes of lilac-blue; may need checking
Salvia nemorosa 'Ostfriesland' ('East Friesland')	45/60cm 1½/2ft	mid- to late sum.	spikes of violet-blue flowers with purple bracts remain colourful for a long period
Sisyrinchium 'Quaint and Queer'	35/20cm 14/8in	mid-sum. to early aut.	cream-and-chocolate flowers on lax stems among grassy leaves
Stokesia laevis	35/45cm 14/18in	mid-sum. to early aut.	pale blue flowers with creamy centres over a long season
Veronica austriaca teucrium 'Crater Lake Blue'	45/45cm 18/18in	mid-sum.	exceptional for the vivid blue of the tiny flowers clustered on short spikes

HIGH-SEASON PERENNIALS FOR MID-BORDER

Name	height/spread	flowering season	description
WHITE FLOWERS			
Achillea ptarmica 'The Pearl'	60/45cm 2/1½ft	mid- to late sum.	small buttons of dazzling white, double flowers in branching heads
Astilbe x thunbergii 'Professor van der Wielen'	120/60cm 4/2ft	mid- to late sum.	lovely arching growth with airy sprays of tiny, creamy flowers
Campanula takesimana	60/45cm 2/1½ft	mid-sum.	arching stems dangle long, white bells with a purple flush and dark interior
Gypsophila paniculata 'Bristol Fairy'	90/90cm 3/3ft	mid-sum.	white cloud of tiny, double flowers masking plants past their best
Leucanthemum x superbum 'Beauté Nivelloise' shasta daisy	90/45cm 3/1½ft	early to late sum.	single, white daisies of unaffected charm; unlike many doubles, needs no staking
Scabiosa caucasica 'Miss Willmott' scabious	60/45cm 2/1½ft	early to late sum.	long-stemmed flowers with ruffled petals and pincushion centre in greenish-white
CREAM, YELLOW OR ORANGE FLOWERS			
Achillea 'Coronation Gold'	90/45cm 3/1½ft	mid- to late sum.	flat heads of yellow flowers over a long season; feathery foliage
Achillea 'Moonshine'	60/30cm 2/1ft	mid-sum.	dense, flat heads of pale yellow flowers over evergreen, feathery leaves of soft grey
Anthemis tinctoria 'E. C. Buxton'	90/90cm 3/3ft	early to mid-sum.	long and prodigal display of lemon-yellow daisies over ferny leaves
Hemerocallis 'Bonanza'	90/60cm 3/2ft	mid- to late sum.	light orange trumpets with maroon centres over strap-shaped leaves
Hemerocallis 'Stella de Oro' day lily	50/45cm 20/18in	mid-sum. to early aut.	compact and outstanding for the long succession of yellow flowers, orange at the throat
Kniphofia 'Sunningdale Yellow' red hot poker	45/30cm 1½/1ft	mid-sum.	slender plant with grassy foliage; cheerful yellow 'pokers'
Oenothera fruticosa glauca	45/30cm 1½/1ft	mid-sum.	bright yellow, silky cups open from reddish buds; the new leaves are prettily coloured
Phlomis russeliana	90/60cm 3/2ft	mid-sum.	stout stems, anchored in large, evergreen leaves, carry whorls of hooded, yellow flowers
Sisyrinchium striatum 'Aunt May'	45/30cm 1½/1ft	mid-sum.	grassy leaves with a creamy stripe, perfect with spires of soft yellow flowers
BLUE, MAUVE OR PURPLE FLOWERS			
Campanula 'Burghaltii'	60/30cm 2/1ft	early to mid-sum.	slender stems dangle dark buds that open to long, pale blue bells
Cynoglossum nervosum hound's tongue	60/60cm 2/2ft	early to mid-sum.	pretty sprays of intense blue, 'forget-me-not' flowers
Delphinium x belladonna 'Blue Bees'	120/60cm 4/2ft	mid-sum.	loose spikes of mid-blue flowers; a much freer plant than the tall hybrids
Eryngium alpinum	30/60cm 1/2ft	mid-sum.	several large, metallic-blue, cone-like flowers per stem, each magnificently dressed in a frilled ruff
Eryngium x tripartitum	75/60cm 2½/2ft	mid-sum.	steel-blue shower of small, cone-shaped flowers with spiny bracts
Geranium x magnificum	50/45cm 20/18in	mid- to late sum.	dense clumps of dark green leaves studded with violet-blue flowers deepened by dark veining
Geranium pratense 'Plenum Violaceum'	60/60cm 2/2ft	mid-sum.	clump of handsome leaves and exquisite double flowers of violet-blue
Linaria triornithophora snapdragon	90/60cm 3/2ft	early to late sum.	long flowering season with bird-like buds opening to purple and yellow
Scabiosa caucasica 'Clive Greaves'	60/45cm 2/1½ft	early to late sum.	long-stemmed flowers have ruffled, violet-blue petals surrounding a creamy pincushion
Thalictrum aquilegifolium	120/60cm 4/2ft	early to mid-sum.	fluffy heads of purple flowers over attractive ferny foliage
PINK FLOWERS			
Achillea 'Lachsschönheit' ('Salmon Beauty')	75/45cm 2½/1½ft	mid-sum.	feathery leaves and heads of small flowers fading from soft brick-red to pale peach; running roots
Astilbe x arendsii 'Federsee'	75/45cm 2½/1½ft	mid-sum.	in moist soils plumes of bright pink over ferny foliage
Astrantia maxima	60/30cm 2/1ft	mid- to late sum.	collared, rose-pink flowerheads are an intriguing cluster of tiny florets
Campanula lactiflora 'Loddon Anna'	120/60cm 4/2ft	mid-sum.	pink form of a superior bellflower
Echinacea purpurea 'Magnus'	90/45cm 3/1½ft	mid- to late sum.	deep pink petals ray out from a cone that glistens with a coppery sheen
Hemerocallis 'Pink Damask' day lily	75/60cm 2½/2ft	mid-sum.	a reputation to maintain as among the best of the pink day lilies
Lychnis coronaria	60/30cm 2/1ft	mid- to late sum.	although the white form is superior, the magenta flowers of this can electrify a dull border
Monarda 'Croftway Pink' bee balm, Oswego tea	90/45cm 3/1½ft	mid- to late sum.	aromatic foliage topped by tightly clustered heads of hooded flowers in strong pink
Sidalcea 'Rose Queen'	120/60cm 4/2ft	mid-sum.	graceful spikes of deep pink flowers of hollyhock shape
RED FLOWERS			
Astilbe x arendsii 'Fanal'	60/30cm 2/1ft	mid-sum.	in moist soils the attractive dark foliage is a good base to the deep red plumes
Cirsium rivulare atropurpureum	120/60cm 4/2ft	mid-sum.	unusual for the vibrant wine-red of its thistle flowers; prickly leaves and spreading roots
Cosmos atrosanguineus	75/45cm 2½/1½ft	mid- to late sum.	a curiosity with chocolate-coloured and chocolate-scented cupped flowers over dark foliage
Knautia macedonica	60/60cm 2/2ft	mid-sum.	branched stems carry deep crimson, pincushion flowers
Monarda 'Cambridge Scarlet' bee balm, Oswego tea	90/45cm 3/1½ft	mid- to late sum	aromatic foliage topped by tightly clustered heads of hooded, scarlet flowers

For the smaller garden, however, the mixed border is in so many ways a very much better solution. Shrubs give substance and interest throughout the year, bulbs provide a sequence of colourful detonations, marking the death of winter with a superb fireworks display, and perennials lighten what risks being a stodgy mixture with flowers and foliage.

Plants are listed here according to their most appropriate position in a border but ordering them too rigidly by height makes for a very unnatural effect and should be avoided.

Buying & planting perennials

Perennials are usually sold as container-grown specimens although some are available between autumn and spring as bare-root specimens. You can plant container-grown plants at any time, provided the ground is not frozen and you supply water during dry spells, but autumn and

The day lilies (*Hemerocallis*), as their common name suggests, have short-lived flowers but the succession continues over a long period. The clumps of strap-shaped leaves make dense ground cover but as they emerge in spring they have a wonderfully fresh beauty. The majority of the hybrid lilies flower in mid- to late summer.

spring planting give the best results. Look for plants that can be divided to make several plants. Bare-root specimens must be planted when dormant and as soon as they become available.

The ground of a newly created border must be prepared well in advance of planting. First, clear it of weeds and then dig it over systematically. Incorporate organic matter such as garden compost when digging and allow the border to settle for several weeks before you plant. When planting into established borders work organic matter into the soil over a larger area than the planting hole itself.

Some of its close relatives are bothersome weeds but the unusual colouring of its thistly tufts makes *Cirsium rivulare atropurpureum* highly ornamental. It is a prickly plant with spreading roots. Although the flower stems are tall, this plant does not need staking.

Staking perennials

There is a lot to be said for relying mainly on
perennials that require support only when they
are planted in exposed positions. Many are
naturally sturdy and nurserymen have tended to
concentrate on selections of compact growth. A
few that do need staking are well worth
growing, however, for the height they give to a
border, rarely achieved with such airy grace by
shrubs. Others needing support, such as the
heavy-headed but sumptuous peonies, have
flowers of exceptional quality.

The traditional method of stiffening the
middle ranks of herbaceous borders is to use pea
sticks – twiggy trimmings of trees such as hazel.
Two or three are pushed into the middle of
clumps and the tops bent over towards the
centre with the twigs interlaced. Purpose-made
supports are also available and include circles of
wire mesh on legs. Tall-growing delphiniums
and other giant perennials can be supported by
tying them to bamboo canes. Bear in mind that
supports that show conspicuously are more of
an eyesore than floppy plants. Always put
supports in early to avoid damaging plants.

Propagating perennials

Vegetative methods of propagation are
necessary to perpetuate selected cultivars.
Lifting and dividing perennials is the easiest
method and has the advantage of producing
plants quickly that are large enough for garden
use. Many perennials, including *Dianthus*, can be
propagated from tip cuttings, and some, such as
delphiniums, from basal cuttings. A few that
have thick roots, among them the oriental
poppies (*Papaver orientale*), are most easily
increased from root cuttings.

Seed of named cultivars collected in the open
garden will not come true. Where this is of little

consequence, collected seed is a cheap way of
raising a large number of plants. Packaged seed
bought from a reputable source can normally be
relied on to produce the plants described.

General care

Perennials that have been well chosen for the
available site require remarkably little attention
throughout the year. Excessive feeding is likely
to lead to lush and eventually floppy growth but
a moderate annual top-dressing of a balanced
slow-release fertilizer applied in early spring is
beneficial. An annually renewed mulch of
organic matter such as bark chippings, also
applied in spring, will conserve moisture and
discourage the growth of weeds. Watering
should only be necessary in extended periods of
drought. Deal promptly with any weeds that do

LEFT The large-flowered hybrid delphiniums, available in a wide colour range, make a stately show at the middle and back of borders that few other flowers can match. To achieve their full splendour they need to be grown in well-manured ground that is limy rather than acid, protected from slugs and snails and staked early in the season.

BELOW RIGHT The plume poppy (*Macleaya microcarpa* 'Kelway's Coral Plume'), although among the tallest perennials, rarely needs staking. If used at the back of a border, the foreground planting should not be so high that the beautiful lobed leaves are obscured for they are more ornamental than the flowerheads. The rather similar M. *microcarpa* runs very freely.

HIGH-SEASON PERENNIALS FOR THE BACK OF BORDERS

Name	height/spread	flowering season	description
Achillea filipendulina 'Gold Plate'	150/75cm 5/2½ft	mid- to late sum.	stiff stems present broad plates packed with tiny, golden flowers
Aruncus dioicus goat's beard	1.8/1.2m 6/4ft	mid-sum.	large clumps of ferny leaves topped by creamy plumes of tiny flowers
Campanula lactiflora	150/60cm 5/2ft	mid- to late sum.	large heads of powder-blue, bell flowers
Delphinium 'Black Knight'	150/90cm 5/3ft	early to mid-sum.	there are many of these classic perennials to choose from, their tall spires clustered with large flowers; this has deep blue florets with black centres
Delphinium 'Blue Jay'	150/90cm 5/3ft	mid-sum.	in the mid-blue range with a white eye
Delphinium 'Galahad'	150/90cm 5/3ft	mid-sum.	spires of pure white
Ferula communis 'Gigantea'	4/1.2m 13/4ft	mid-sum.	giant fennel, the yellow flowers carried high above finely cut foliage
Galega 'Lady Wilson'	150/90cm 5/3ft	mid-sum.	numerous spikes of small, pea flowers in mauve-pink
Macleaya cordata 'Flamingo'	180/60cm 6/2ft	mid- to late sum.	lobed, grey-green leaves and large plumes of pink and cream
Macleaya microcarpa 'Kelway's Coral Plume'	180/90cm 6/3ft	mid- to late sum.	similar to the above but tends to run
Rudbeckia laciniata 'Hortensia'	220/90cm 7/3ft	mid- to late sum.	bright yellow, double flowers on a wiry plant
Thalictrum flavum glaucum	150/60cm 5/2ft	mid-sum.	fluffy heads of tiny, pale yellow flowers over beautifully divided, blue-green foliage
Veratrum nigrum	180/60cm 6/2ft	mid-sum.	impressive clump of pleated leaves topped by a mahogany plume of tiny stars
Verbascum 'Cotswold Queen'	150/60cm 5/2ft	mid-sum.	hybrid mulleins make lovely spires but are not long-lived; this example has spires in a blend of cream, purple and orange

manage to grow for they will compete with perennials for water and nutrients.

Removing faded flowers will help to keep borders looking tidy and in the case of some perennials, among them delphiniums, may encourage plants to flower again. The main period for clearing up, however, is autumn, when dead leaves and stems should be removed. If, as with many grasses, the dead foliage and flowers remain attractive in winter, you can delay clearing until late winter or early spring.

A few perennials, among them peonies, are very long lived and are best left undisturbed. Many, however, tend to become woody or congested and less free-flowering with age, and are better lifted and divided every three to five years. In a herbaceous border this operation should form part of a regular cycle of rejuvenation. In mixed borders the operation is best carried out piecemeal, individual plants being lifted and divided as and when they need it. Do the work in mild weather between autumn and spring, when plants are dormant. Discard the woody centre of old plants but save healthy portions from the periphery that have roots and growth buds.

If grown in conditions that suit them, most perennials are largely trouble-free. However, the generalization that highly bred plants are more susceptible to pests and diseases holds true for some in this group of ornamentals. At one end of the scale are the large-flowered hybrid delphiniums but you may feel that their invaluable blues and splendid vertical accents make them well worth the trouble of keeping slugs at bay and fungal diseases under control.

BORDER PERENNIALS FOR LATE SUMMER AND AUTUMN

Name	height/spread	flowering season	description
FRONT OF BORDER			
Agapanthus 'Lilliput' African lily	50/30cm 20/12in	late sum.	refined dwarf hybrid, the heads of blue trumpets making a perfect accent at the front of a warm border
Aster amellus 'Sonia'	35/25cm 14/10in	late sum. to early aut.	clusters of large, mauve-pink flowers on short, stiff stems
Aster ericoides 'Esther'	60/30cm 2/1ft	early to late aut.	lovely for the late profusion of small, purple-pink flowers
Aster thomsonii 'Nanus'	35/25cm 14/10in	late sum. to mid-aut.	in moist soils masses of blue daisies on slender stems over a long season
Liatris spicata 'Kobold'	60/30cm 2/1ft	late sum.	erect bottle-brushes of intense lilac
Sedum 'Vera Jameson'	25/20cm 10/8in	late sum. to early aut.	dusty pink flowers terminate arching stems clothed in purple, fleshy leaves
Solidago 'Queenie' golden rod	20/15cm 8/6in	late sum.	dwarf version; makes a rounded mound with dense heads of bright yellow
MID-BORDER			
Agapanthus Headbourne hybrids blue African lily	90/60cm 3/2ft	late sum.	a hardy strain, long stems carrying heads of blue flowers over clumps of strap-shaped leaves
Anemone hupehensis japonica 'Bressingham Glow'	45/30cm 18/12in	late sum. to early aut.	neat plant with flowers of a deep, warm pink
Anemone x hybrida 'Honorine Jobert' Japanese anemone	120/60cm 4/2ft	late sum. to mid-aut.	dazzling white flowers with yellow stamens over shapely, dark green leaves; can be invasive
Aster x frikartii 'Mönch'	90/45cm 3/1½ft	late sum. to mid-aut.	long succession of lavender-blue, elegantly rayed flowers
Aster novae-angliae 'Andenken an Alma Pötschke'	90/30cm 3/1ft	early to mid-aut.	splash of bright red daisies, providing an unusual colour in autumn
Aster novi-belgii 'White Ladies' Michaelmas daisy	120/60cm 4/2ft	early to mid-aut.	vigorous, with yellow-centred, white daisies; many more to choose from, not all of good constitution
Codonopsis clematidea	60/60cm 2/2ft	late sum. to early aut.	lovely nodding bells of pale blue with surprising bold marks of purple and orange inside
Crocosmia x crocosmiflora 'Emily McKenzie'	60/30cm 2/1ft	mid- to late sum.	sprays of large flowers vivid with brown splashes on rich orange
Crocosmia 'Lucifer'	120/30cm 4/1ft	mid- to late sum.	stiff plants presenting flaming sprays
Dierama pulcherrimum wand flower, angel's fishing rod	150/60cm 5/2ft	late sum. to early aut.	paragon of gracefulness; wands arch over grassy, evergreen foliage; dangling, deep pink flowers wrapped in silver
Echinops ritro 'Veitch's Blue' globe thistle	90/45cm 3/1½ft	mid-sum. to early aut.	spherical heads of metallic blue top a base of grey-green leaves
Gaura lindheimeri	90-60cm 3/2ft	late sum. to mid-aut.	small butterfly flowers of pale pink fluttering over slender foliage
Gentiana asclepiadea willow gentian	60/45cm 2/1½ft	early aut.	narrow leaves and paired, blue trumpets along arching stems
Helenium 'Moerheim Beauty'	90/45cm 3/1½ft	mid- to late sum.	among a useful range with masses of daisy flowers from yellow to mahogany; bronze-red flowers
Knautia macedonica	60/30cm 2/1ft	late sum. to early aut.	airy show of crimson, scabious flowers
Kniphofia 'Percy's Pride' red hot poker	90/45cm 3/1½ft	late sum. to early aut.	cooler than many, with cream pokers tinged green
Penstemon 'Evelyn'	60/45cm 2/1½ft	mid-sum. to early aut.	fairly hardy, small-flowered example with spires of pink blooms over a long season
Penstemon 'Andenken an Friedrich Hahn' ('Garnet')	75/45cm 2½/1½ft	mid-sum. to early aut.	short spires of tubular, dark red flowers over a long season; not fully hardy
Phlox paniculata 'White Admiral'	75/90cm 2½/3ft	mid-sum. to early aut.	leggy plants but with heads of pure white flowers
Physostegia virginiana 'Summer Snow' obedient plant	90/60cm 3/2ft	late sum. to early aut.	splendid white alternative to pink and purple kinds
Platycodon grandiflorus balloon flower	45/35cm 18/14in	late sum.	amusing and lovely; balloon buds and saucer-shaped, blue flowers
Rudbeckia fulgida sullivantii 'Goldsturm'	90/45cm 3/1½ft	mid-sum. to early aut.	bushy plant, the daisy flowers having yellow petals raying from a dark brown cone
Sanguisorba canadensis	150/60cm 5/2ft	late sum. to early aut.	in moist soils elegant foliage topped by bottle-brush flowers of greenish-white
Schizostylis coccinea 'Sunrise' kaffir lily	75/25cm 30/10in	early to late aut.	grassy leaves and stems of star-shaped flowers, in this case salmon-pink
Sedum 'Herbstfreude' ('Autumn Joy')	75/60cm 2½/2ft	late sum. to early aut.	clumps of fleshy, grey-green leaves topped by flat heads of starry flowers, pink then coppery red
x **Solidaster luteus** 'Lemore'	75/30cm 2½/1ft	mid- to late sum.	loose heads of small, lemon-yellow flowers carried on wiry stems
BACK OF BORDER			
Aconitum carmichaelii 'Kelmscott'	150/60m 5/2ft	late sum. to early aut.	sinister and poisonous but beautiful; spires of hooded violet-blue flowers
Coreopsis tripteris	250/60cm 8/2ft	early to mid-aut.	small but effective yellow daisy flowers on slender stems
Helianthus salicifolius	220/60cm 7/2ft	early aut.	clump of deep green foliage during summer, then small yellow daisies
Kniphofia 'Prince Igor' red hot poker	220/90cm 7/3ft	late sum.	scarlet torches to light the back of a large border
Romneya coulteri tree poppy	180/90cm 6/3ft	mid-sum. to early aut.	magnificent poppies, white and finished with a golden boss; wandering tendencies
Rudbeckia 'Herbstonne' ('Autumn Sun')	180/60cm 6/2ft	late sum. to early aut.	a vigorous giant in moist soils with daisy flowers radiating lemon-yellow from a green knob
Salvia uliginosa	150/45cm 5/1½ft	early to mid-aut.	a graceful, open plant for a sheltered garden; airy sprays of blue flowers

BELOW The Japanese anemones (*Anemone x hybrida*), especially whites such as 'Honorine Jobert', add a lovely fresh note to the garden in late summer and autumn and provide relief from the dominant yellow. These wiry plants, which do not need staking, can spread rather too freely once established but in their first year they need to be coaxed along.

RIGHT The New Zealand flaxes (*Phormium*) make sword-like clumps of evergreen leaves that provide a useful contrast to more delicate plants. Breeders have concentrated on selecting purple-leaved and variegated forms. Here *Polemonium caeruleum album* has worked its way through the blades of *Phormium cookianum hookeri* 'Tricolor'.

BORDER PLANTS WITH ATTRACTIVE FOLIAGE

Name	height/spread	description
DECIDUOUS		
Acanthus mollis Latifolius Group bear's breeches	90/90cm 3/3ft	makes an impressive clump of glossy leaves with with wavy edges; spikes of purplish flowers in mid- to late summer
Acanthus spinosus	120/90cm 4/3ft	the leaves are spiny and more deeply cut than those of *A. mollis*
Alchemilla mollis lady's mantle	45/60cm 18/24in	even without the froth of lime-green flowers, worth a place for the velvety, rounded leaves
Artemisia ludoviciana latiloba	75/45cm 2½/1½ft	despite its running roots, a useful silvery plant with small, greyish flowers
Arundo donax	220/90cm 7/3ft	blue-grey leaves hang down from the stout clump of tall stems
Astrantia major 'Sunningdale Variegated'	60/45cm 2/1½ft	foliage prettily splashed with cream and yellow; greenish-white flowers in early to mid-summer
Crambe maritima seakale	60/60cm 2/2ft	large and waxy, blue-grey leaves, wavy at the edges; heads of white flowers in early summer
Cynara cardunculus cardoon	180/90cm 6/3ft	spectacular clump of arching, silver leaves of jagged outline; thistle flowers in summer
Foeniculum vulgare 'Purpureum'	150/30cm 5/3ft	a fennel with soft and hair-fine foliage in bronze and copper tones
Hakonechloa macra 'Alboaurea'	30/45cm 12/18in	in moist soils this grass makes bright clumps variegated in shades of cream, yellow and tan
Hosta fortunei 'Francee'	60/30cm 2/1ft	clumps of rich green leaves with a white edge; lavender flowers in summer
Hosta 'Halcyon'	30/20cm 12/8in	one of many short hostas; arrow-shaped leaves of silvery blue-grey; lilac flowers in mid-summer
Hosta 'Krossa Regal'	75/45cm 2½/1½ft	superb larger hosta; clump of large, arching, grey-green leaves; lilac flowers in mid-summer
Hosta 'Royal Standard'	75/45cm 2½/1½ft	impressive clump of heart-shaped, light green leaves; scented, white flowers in late summer
Iris pallida 'Argentea Variegata'	60/30cm 2/1ft	poor flowers but the blade-like leaves, striped blue-green and white, make a strong accent
Miscanthus sinensis 'Zebrinus'	150/45cm 5/1½ft	stems of narrow leaves with bold tiger banding; silky flower sprays in autumn
Rheum 'Ace of Hearts'	120/75cm 4/2½ft	large, heart-shaped leaves with crimson veins and reverse; pink flower plume in early summer
Stachys byzantina 'Silver Carpet' lamb's ears	15/45cm 6/18in	mats of silver, woolly ears; no flowers
EVERGREEN		
Ajuga reptans 'Atropurpurea'	20/20cm 8/8in	burnished purple-brown leaf rosettes and blue flowers in late spring; one of several forms
Bergenia 'Ballawley'	60/60cm 2/2ft	outstanding example; glossy leaves turn bronze in late autumn; dark pink flowers in spring
Festuca glauca 'Blaufuchs'	20/15cm 8/6in	bristly clumps of blue-grey for frontal positions; purple flower spikelets in mid-summer
Ophiopogon planiscapus 'Nigrescens'	25/20cm 10/8in	an appealing oddity with strap-like, arching leaves of green-tinged black; black berries
Phormium cookianum hookeri 'Tricolor'	120/30cm 4/1ft	blade-like leaves of dull green with red and cream margins

Shrubs for borders

So much emphasis is placed on the labour-saving merits of shrubs that it is easy to forget that they include some of the loveliest of garden plants. Some of the best-value ornamentals of all are shrubs that are memorable for more than one characteristic. Fothergillas, for example, have fragrant, catkin-like flowers in spring and leaves that colour magnificently in autumn. Even setting aside such high-performance plants, there are shrubs of outstanding ornamental value for every season of the year, some on account of their flowers but many, too, for their colourful foliage, their bright berries and even their vivid stems. Equally important but more difficult to classify is the character given to a plant by its branch structure and the size and density of its leaves. The contrast of these characters can go a long way to make a grouping of them a pleasure to the eye throughout the year.

Many shrubs, quite simply, deserve a place in borders without any consideration of their practical advantages but these, too, are considerable. Once established, most shrubs require very little further attention throughout what are often long lives. They provide the garden with a firmly structured component and are among the most effective informal screens.

The shrubs covered in this section thrive in open positions where the soil is reasonably fertile and well drained but with an adequate supply of moisture in the growing season. They are mainly of medium height, few of them growing taller than 2.5m/8ft. Taller shrubs that may be suitable for large borders are covered on pages 26-33 and some that are low-growing or prostrate feature among the ground-cover plants discussed on pages 38-41. Shrubs for specific conditions or uses are discussed elsewhere in the book.

BELOW LEFT The evergreen Mexican orange blossom (*Choisya ternata*) is worth a sheltered place in full sun or part shade simply for its glossy, aromatic leaves, each consisting of a fanned arrangement of three leaflets. In spring the luxuriant foliage shows off the fragrant, white flowers. The starry display they make is often repeated in autumn.

BELOW RIGHT The exquisite funnel-shaped flowers of the shrubby morning glory *Convolvulus cneorum*, white and yellow-centred but pink in bud, are carried over a long summer season. They rest among narrow, silver leaves of superfine silkiness. This delectable plant needs a sheltered position in full sun where the soil is well drained.

Shrub & mixed borders

Borders devoted exclusively to shrubs can make very successful features, especially when care is taken to build up a mixture in which deciduous and evergreen are balanced and where there is something of interest throughout the year.

Except for distant reaches of the garden, however, I would always prefer a mixed border. Shrubs, it is true, offer plenty of variety as well as anchoring a border. It is difficult, however, using shrubs alone to strike a balance between a slightly grim sobriety and an exaggerated bonhomie, with a heavy-handed reliance on some of the more extreme foliage colours. A border in which bays are planted among well-matched deciduous and evergreen shrubs, perennials and bulbs performs its structural role to perfection but is much lighter in effect.

Buying & planting shrubs

What I have said about buying and planting trees and large shrubs on pages 26-30 applies also to the purchase of smaller shrubs.

If you are creating a new border, you will need to prepare the ground thoroughly, as recommended for perennials (see page 49). If, on the other hand, you are incorporating shrubs into an existing border, prepare a generous planting hole each time, at least twice the diameter of the container the plant is in or, in the case of a bare-root plant, so that the roots can be spread out evenly. Fork over the base of the hole and add organic material such as well-rotted compost before positioning the shrub so that it is planted at its original depth – the soil level will show on the stem. Replace the soil, firm well and then water. In dry weather it is

VERSATILE SHRUBS FOR BORDERS

Name	height/spread	description
DECIDUOUS		
Berberis thunbergii 'Rose Glow'	1.5/1.8m 5/6ft	purple foliage with pink variegation even more vivid in autumn; pale yellow flowers followed by scarlet berries
Cornus alba 'Elegantissima'	1.5/1.5m 5/5ft	white-variegated foliage and in winter vivid red stems if hard pruned (necessary to limit size)
Daphne mezereum alba mezereon	1.5/1.2m 5/4ft	in late winter stems are wreathed in fragrant, white flowers; yellow berries in autumn
Fothergilla gardenii 'Blue Mist'	90/120cm 3/4ft	fragrant, white, catkin-like flowers in spring and grey-blue foliage that colours splendidly in autumn; for lime-free soils
Fuchsia magellanica 'Versicolor'	1.5/1.5m 5/5ft	graceful, with variegated leaves, pink-tinted and then grey-green, a perfect foil for troupes of slender dancing flowers in crimson and purple
Hydrangea quercifolia	1.8/1.5m 6/5ft	oak-like leaves that colour well in autumn; pyramidal, white flowerheads in summer age with a purple tinge
Spiraea thunbergii	1.8/2.2m 6/7ft	thick clusters of tiny, white flowers on dark twigs in early to mid-spring; foliage pretty when green and when it colours orange in autumn
Viburnum opulus 'Compactum'	2.2/2.2m 7/7ft	flat, white flowerheads in spring; good foliage colour in autumn and translucent scarlet berries
Weigela florida 'Foliis Purpureis'	1.5/1.5m 5/5ft	soft purple foliage which in early summer shows off flowers that open pink from red buds
EVERGREEN		
Brachyglottis 'Sunshine'	1.2/2.2m 4/7ft	grey-green leaves with felted, white reverse; in summer white buds open to yellow daisies
Choisya ternata Mexican orange blossom	1.8/1.8m 6/6ft	aromatic, glossy foliage all year and deliciously scented, white flowers in spring and often intermittently later; for a sheltered position
Convolvulus cneorum	75/60cm 2½/2ft	silver, silky foliage; a long succession of white, morning glory flowers open from pink buds
Erica x darleyensis 'Ghost Hills'	45/75cm 1½/2½ft	foliage in spring tipped cream; long season of pink flowers in winter and spring
Lotus hirsutus (Dorycnium hirsutum)	90/75cm 3/2½ft	silky, grey foliage; in summer white, pea flowers, tinged pink, are followed by red-brown seed pods
Mahonia japonica	2.5/2.2m 8/7ft	clustered tassels of fragrant, yellow flowers in in winter and handsome, jagged foliage all year
Rosmarinus officinalis 'Sissinghurst Blue'	120/90cm 4/3ft	refreshingly aromatic plant to brush against; blue flowers are borne freely in early summer
Yucca filamentosa Adam's needle	75/90cm 2½/3ft	clump of stiff, blade-like leaves with curling threads along the margins; spike, up to 1.8m/6ft tall, of fragrant, creamy bells in summer

BORDER SHRUBS WITH SPRING FLOWERS

Name	height/spread	flowering season	description
DECIDUOUS			
Chaenomeles x **superba** 'Rowallane'	1.2/1.8m 4/6ft	early to late spr.	small clusters of bright red flowers followed, usually, by quince-like fruit
Cytisus 'Lena' broom	90/75cm 3/2½ft	late spr. to early sum.	richly coloured example from the many free-flowering hybrids; smothering, pea flowers of red-brown and yellow
Cytisus x **praecox** 'Allgold'	1.2/1.5m 4/5ft	late spr.	stems arch with the mass of rich yellow flowers
Exochorda x **macrantha** 'The Bride'	1.5/1.8m 5/6ft	late spr.	loose-limbed beauty, dazzling with pure white flowers
Forsythia x **intermedia** 'Spectabilis'	2.2/2.2m 7/7ft	early to mid-spr.	stiff stems crowded with deep yellow flowers
Kerria japonica 'Golden Guinea' Jew's mallow	1.5/1.5m 5/5ft	mid- to late spr.	more graceful than the common double, with pretty flowers of deep yellow
Neillia thibetica	1.8/1.5m 6/5ft	late spr. to early sum.	neglected beauty; arching stems carry sprays of soft pink, tubular flowers
Paeonia suffruticosa 'Mrs William Kelway' tree peony	120/90cm 4/3ft	late spr.	example of the sumptuously beautiful but very expensive tree peonies; this is a ravishing semi-double of satiny white
Prunus glandulosa 'Alba Plena'	1.5/1.5m 5/5ft	late spr.	neat shrubby almond with double, white flowers
Prunus incisa 'Kojo-no-mai'	120/90cm 4/3ft	mid-spr.	intricately branched dwarf cherry, with gentle pink flowers fading to white; attractive foliage colours in autumn
Ribes sanguineum 'Pulborough Scarlet' flowering currant	2.2/2.2m 7/7ft	mid- to late spr.	reliably free-flowering; curiously scented, rich red blooms hang in dense clusters
Spiraea 'Arguta'	2.2/2.2m 7/7ft	mid- to late spr.	arching, wiry stems crammed with clusters of tiny, white flowers; dependable
Spiraea x **vanhouttei**	1.5/1.5m 5/5ft	late spr. to early sum.	dense clusters of small flowers create a snowy effect on arching stems
Viburnum carlesii 'Diana'	1.5/1.5m 5/5ft	mid- to late spr.	heads of richly scented, waxy flowers open to apple-blossom pink from red buds
Viburnum x **juddii**	1.8/2.5m 6/8ft	mid- to late spr.	small heads of pink buds open to very fragrant, white flowers
EVERGREEN			
Daphne x **burkwoodii** 'Somerset'	1.5/1.5m 5/5ft	late spr. to early sum.	semi-evergreen; clusters of very fragrant, starry pink flowers
Daphne retusa	90/60cm 3/2ft	late spr. to early sum.	rounded bush with leathery leaves bearing clusters of fragrant, pink flowers
Osmanthus delavayi	1.8/1.8m 6/6ft	mid-spr.	choice; white, tubular flowers, prettily set against dark green, exhale sweetness

BORDER SHRUBS WITH SUMMER OR AUTUMN FLOWERS

Name	height/spread	flowering season	description
DECIDUOUS			
Buddleja davidii 'Nanho Blue' butterfly bush	1.5/1.5m 5/5ft	mid-sum to early aut.	usefully compact; slender stems carry spikes of fragrant, violet-blue flowers
Ceanothus x **delileanus** 'Gloire de Versailles'	2.5/2.5m 8/8ft	early to late sum.	large shrub that can be pruned low in spring; profusion of powder-blue flowerheads
Deutzia x **elegantissima** 'Rosealind'	1.2/1.2m 4/4ft	early sum.	elegant, grey-green shrub with fragrant, deep pink flowers borne profusely in arching sprays
Deutzia ningpoensis (D. chunii)	1.2/1.2m 4/4ft	mid-sum.	arching stems carry long sprays of white flowers that are pink in bud
Hydrangea macrophylla 'Lanarth White' lacecap hydrangea	1.5/1.8m 5/6ft	mid- to late sum.	white flowerheads with starry, sterile flowers surrounding the dense centre
Hydrangea macrophylla 'Lilacina' lacecap hydrangea	1.8/2.2m 6/7ft	late sum.	showy, purplish-pink, sterile flowers ring the deeper toned, tiny, central flowers
Leycesteria formosa Himalayan honeysuckle	1.8/1.8m 6/6ft	late sum. to early aut.	arching growth; pendent clusters of white flowers clasped by claret bracts
Philadelphus 'Sybille' mock orange	120/90cm 4/3ft	early to mid-sum.	profusion of single, white flowers, mauve at the centre; rich scent
Spiraea japonica 'Walluf'	1.2/1.5m 4/5ft	mid- to late sum.	twiggy shrub with flat heads of crimson flowers
Spiraea nipponica 'Snowmound'	1.8/1.8m 6/6ft	early sum.	cascades of densely clustered small, white flowers on arching stems
Viburnum plicatum 'Pink Beauty'	1.8/2.5m 6/8ft	late spr. to early sum.	a charmer; dark green leaves and heads of creamy flowers that take on a pink tinge
EVERGREEN			
Cistus x **cyprius**	1.8/2.5m 6/8ft	early to mid-sum.	large, white flowers boldly blotched maroon on a spreading bush with sticky foliage
Cistus x **hybridus** (C. x **corbariensis**)	1.2/1.8m 4/6ft	late spr. to early sum.	masses of short-lived, white flowers opening from reddish buds
Cistus x **purpureus**	1.5/1.2m 5/4ft	late spr. to mid-sum.	grey-green foliage and many dark pink flowers blotched maroon
Deutzia x **hybrida** 'Mont Rose'	1.2/1.2m 4/4ft	early sum.	thickly clustered with starry, pink flowers and yellow anthers
Hebe 'Midsummer Beauty'	1.8/1.5m 6/5ft	mid-sum. to early aut.	long leaves with a purple reverse; many lax spikes of lilac flowers that fade to white; fairly hardy
Hypericum 'Hidcote'	1.2/1.2m 4/4ft	mid-sum. to early aut.	semi-evergreen with dark foliage; saucer-shaped, bright yellow flowers
Olearia x **haastii**	1.8/1.8m 6/6ft	mid- to late sum.	until decked by fragrant, white daisy flowers, a sombre, dense shrub
Yucca gloriosa	120/90cm 4/3ft	early to mid-aut.	from a base of strap-shaped leaves mature plants send up a stiff stem dangling creamy bells

The tree mallows are often short-lived, a case perhaps of exhausting themselves with months of non-stop flowering. The light pink with red eye of *Lavatera* 'Barnsley' is easier to combine with other flowers such as *Lythrum salicaria* than the rather hard pink of *L.* 'Rosea'. Cut back hard in spring and plants will flower on vigorous new growth from mid-summer.

LONG-FLOWERING BORDER SHRUBS

Name	height/spread	flowering season	description
DECIDUOUS			
Coronilla valentina 'Citrina'	120/90cm 4/3ft	mid-win. to late spr.	lax stems carry clusters of lemon-yellow, pea flowers
Hydrangea paniculata 'Kyushu'	120/90cm 4/3ft	mid-sum. to early aut.	compact form of a splendid shrub with pyramid heads of white florets
Hydrangea 'Preziosa'	1.2/1.2m 4/4ft	mid-sum. to mid-aut.	mop-head with pink flowers turning to red; foliage colours in autumn
Indigofera heterantha	1.8/1.8m 6/6ft	mid-sum. to mid-aut.	purple-pink flowers non-stop for 3 months; for a sheltered position
Potentilla fruticosa 'Katherine Dykes'	1.2/1.5m 2/5ft	late spr. to late sum.	primrose-coloured flowers in abundance
Potentilla fruticosa 'Tangerine'	60/120cm 2/4ft	late spr. to late sum.	scarlet buds open to orange flowers that fade to yellow
Syringa microphylla 'Superba'	1.5/1.5m 5/5ft	late spr. to early aut.	open, twiggy bush with sprays of fragrant, purplish flowers in flushes
Viburnum plicatum 'Nanum Semperflorens'	1.8/1.5m 6/5ft	late spr. to early aut.	compact form of a spreading plant with flat heads of white flowers
EVERGREEN			
Abelia x **grandiflora**	1.8/1.2m 6/4ft	mid-sum. to early aut.	semi-evergreen; masses of tubular flowers, white with a pink tinge
Erica carnea 'Eileen Porter' heath	45/60cm 1½/2ft	late aut. to early spr.	one of many heaths with a long flowering season in winter; flowers of carmine-red
Erica x **darleyensis** 'Arthur Johnson'	60/90cm 2/3ft	late aut. to early spr.	one of several with a long flowering season; sprays of deep pink flowers
Viburnum tinus 'Eve Price'	1.2/1.2m 4/4ft	late aut. to early spr.	marathon runner; clusters of pink buds open to white flowers

The snowball bush (*Viburnum opulus* 'Roseum', and more familiar as *V. opulus* 'Sterile') has round heads of sterile flowers, their shape repeated here in the foreground alliums. The flowers of the viburnum open green but change to white. The non-sterile cultivars of this species carry heavy crops of translucent red or yellow fruits in autumn.

essential to keep newly planted shrubs well watered. The smaller shrubs rarely need staking but in exposed positions screening is useful while they get established.

When setting out a new border, the temptation is to position plants too closely together with the result that when shrubs reach their mature size they are competing for the available space. It is worth considering at the outset how you intend to interplant so that bare earth is covered and the garden is ornamental. One option is to plant more closely than the ultimate scheme, preferably with fast-growing shrubs, the intention being to take some out as they mature and replant them elsewhere. Less expensive options to consider as fillers are perennials, biennials and annuals, with bulbs for additional colour in spring.

Pruning shrubs

Although some shrubs only achieve their full ornamental potential if pruned regularly, many perform perfectly satisfactorily with little or no pruning. The careful selection of shrubs to suit the space available will avoid the need to prune back unwanted growth. The harder a stem is cut back the more vigorous the subsequent growth will be, and ruthless pruning can initiate a cycle in which a badly placed shrub repeatedly demands more space.

Some formative pruning may help to establish a well-shaped plant yet this consists simply of removing weak growths and badly placed stems such as those that are crossing the main framework. If you are in any doubt at all about pruning, limit your action to this simple operation and to the removal of any dead,

The young leaves of *Spiraea japonica* 'Goldflame' are a rich orange-red, later turning to yellow and finally to pale lime-green. It is unquestionably a spectacular foliage plant, making a cheerfully sunny effect in early summer. Its beauty, however, is marred in mid- to late summer by bright pink flowers clashing with the yellow of its foliage.

BORDER SHRUBS WITH SILVER, GREY OR BLUE FOLIAGE

Many shrubs with grey-toned foliage do best in full sun where the soil is well drained. See also the flowering shrubs for hot, dry sites listed on page 95.

Name	height/spread	description
DECIDUOUS		
Lotus hirsutus (Dorycnium hirsutum)	90/75cm 3/2½ft	fine hairs give plant its silvered silkiness; white, pea flowers with a pink tinge in summer followed by red-brown seed pods
Potentilla fruticosa 'Vilmoriniana'	120/90cm 4/3ft	good silver to show off other plants and its own flowers of creamy white in summer
Salix lanata woolly willow	90/90cm 3/3ft	felting on the leaves creates a grey shrub; yellow catkins in early to mid-spring
EVERGREEN		
Artemisia arborescens 'Faith Raven'	120/90cm 4/3ft	upright silvery stand of aromatic, finely cut foliage; yellow flowers in summer
Artemisia 'Powis Castle'	90/120cm 3/4ft	rarely flowers but the mound of aromatic, silvery foliage is highly ornamental
Ballota pseudodictamnus	60/60cm 2/2ft	numerous stems with a dense cover of grey, woolly leaves; white flowers in mid-summer count for little
Brachyglottis 'Sunshine'	1.2/2.2m 4/7ft	grey-green leaves with a felted, white reverse; in summer masses of yellow daisies open from very pretty, white buds
Convolvulus cneorum	75/60cm 2½/2ft	narrow, silver leaves of soft silk; in summer white, morning glory flowers flare open from pink buds
Hebe pinguifolia 'Pagei'	20/75cm 8/30in	creeping, with a dense cover of blue-grey leaves; white flowers in late spring or early summer
Helichrysum italicum serotinum curry plant	30/60cm 1/2ft	sprawling, aromatic subshrub with narrow, silvery leaves; clusters of mustard-coloured flowers in summer
Helichrysum splendidum	75/75cm 2½/2½ft	dense, silver-grey mound with clusters of yellow flowers, which are often thought dispensable; not fully hardy
Ruta graveolens 'Jackman's Blue'	60/45cm 2/1½ft	aromatic and deeply divided foliage of an arresting blue-green; unimportant yellow flowers
Salvia officinalis sage	60/90cm 2/3ft	subdued grey-green foliage to calm excited neighbours; blue flowers in early to mid-summer
Salvia lavandulifolia	75/60cm 2½/2ft	aromatic, grey-green foliage with spikes of purple-blue flowers in mid-summer
Santolina chamaecyparissus cotton lavender	50/50cm 20/20in	silvery mound of finely dissected, aromatic leaves; yellow, button flowers in mid-summer

BORDER SHRUBS WITH GOLDEN FOLIAGE

Name	height/spread	description
DECIDUOUS		
Cornus alba 'Aurea'	1.8/2.5m 6/8ft	not so valuable for its stems but the soft yellow of the leaves is an asset
Corylus avellana 'Aurea' hazel	2.5/1.8m 8/6ft	large shrub that can be kept low; soft yellow leaves are a good contrast to dark foliage; long catkins in late winter
Ribes sanguineum 'Brocklebankii'	1.2/1.5m 4/5ft	lovely green-yellow leaves, best in shade; pink flowers in spring
Spiraea japonica 'Goldflame'	120/90cm 4/3ft	warm orange-brown foliage in spring turns to orange-yellow but, unhappily, the flowers in mid-summer are pink
Viburnum opulus 'Aureum'	1.8/1.5m 6/5ft	form of the guelder rose with the leaves flushed yellow; best with some shade
Weigela 'Looymansii Aurea'	1.5/1.8m 5/6ft	lime-green leaves, at their best with some shade; the flowers in early summer are awkwardly pink
EVERGREEN		
Choisya ternata 'Sundance'	90/90cm 3/3ft	compact and makes a striking yellow note; scented, white flowers in spring
Thuja occidentalis 'Rheingold'	90/60cm 3/2ft	dwarf conifer making a pyramid of golden foliage, most colourful in winter
Thuja orientalis 'Aurea Nana'	60/45cm 2/1½ft	dwarf, slow-growing conifer, dense and egg-shaped; the yellow is especially strong in spring

The proximity of *Allium christophii* flowerheads intensifies the rich tones of a purple-leaved smoke tree or Venetian sumach (*Cotinus coggygria*). There are several of these forms, including 'Royal Purple', which colours magnificently in autumn. Their flowerheads are also richly tinted.

BORDER SHRUBS WITH PURPLE, BRONZE OR RED FOLIAGE

Name	height/spread	description
DECIDUOUS		
Berberis x **ottawensis** 'Superba'	2.2/2.2m 7/7ft	remarkable for the reddish-purple of the foliage and red fruits in autumn
Berberis thunbergii atropurpurea	1.2/1.8m 4/6ft	deep bronze-purple version of a familiar shrub with showy berries in autumn
Corylus maxima 'Purpurea' filbert	3/3m 10/10ft	large shrub or small tree with rich purple leaves and dangling purple catkins in late winter; can be pruned low annually to enhance the foliage effect
Cotinus coggygria 'Royal Purple' smoke bush	3.7/3.7m 12/12ft	large shrub with rich red-purple foliage, brilliant in autumn, and smoky flowerheads in summer; can be pruned low annually with loss of flowers but enhanced foliage effect
Prunus x **cistena**	1.5/1.5m 5/5ft	foliage, red when young, deepens to purple; pale pink flowers in mid- to late spring, sometimes followed by purple fruit
Weigela florida 'Foliis Purpureis'	1.5/1.5m 5/5ft	soft purple foliage, which in early summer shows off flowers that open pink from red buds
EVERGREEN		
Mahonia x **wagneri** 'Moseri'	1.2/1.2m 4/4ft	young leaves are pale green but turn coral-red and most vivid in winter; yellow flowers in spring
Pieris formosa forrestii 'Wakehurst'	2.2/1.8m 7/6ft	pretty sprays of white flowers in spring are less eye-catching than the young leaves which are a glossy red; for acid soils
Pittosporum tenuifolium 'Tom Thumb'	1.2/1.2m 4/4ft	the green of young leaves contrasts with the red-brown of dense older foliage; for a sheltered position
Salvia officinalis 'Purpurascens'	60/90cm 2/3ft	soft purple, mat leaves mix readily with brighter foliage

damaged or diseased wood, making clean cuts at an outward-facing live bud or at a junction with a main stem.

Most of the spectacular deciduous shrubs of spring and early summer, among them forsythias, flower on wood produced the previous year. Removal of some of the old wood immediately after flowering will encourage the development of vigorous new stems; these will carry flowers in the following year. When cutting out old stems, aim to maintain a balanced shape.

Most of the shrubs that bloom in mid- or late summer produce their flowers on wood of the current season. They are best pruned in early spring. A few, including the butterfly bush (*Buddleja davidii*) and deciduous *Ceanothus*, will give their best floral display if cut back hard, with all or most of the growth made the previous year removed. Early to mid-spring is also the best time to prune shrubs grown for their colourful stems, such as *Cornus alba* 'Sibirica'. The young

BORDER SHRUBS WITH GOOD YEAR-ROUND GREEN FOLIAGE

Name	height/spread	description
Aucuba japonica 'Nana Rotundifolia'	90/75cm 3/2½ft	dense, compact form with small, glossy leaves; red berries in spring, provided there is a male plant nearby
Buxus sempervirens	2.2/1.5m 7/5ft	long valued for its glossy, dark green leaves; potentially larger but responds well to pruning
Camellia x **williamsii** 'Donation'	2.2/1.5m 7/5ft	camellias are large shrubs valuable on lime-free soils for glossy foliage and showy flowers in spring; this is compact with semi-double, pink flowers
Choisya ternata Mexican orange blossom	1.8/1.8m 6/6ft	outstanding for its aromatic, glossy foliage and fragrant, white flowers in spring; for a sheltered position
Myrtus communis tarentina	150/90cm 5/3ft	compact form with narrow, glossy leaves; in late summer produces white flowers freely
Osmanthus heterophyllus 'Gulftide'	2.2/2.7m 7/9ft	densely bushy with glossy, dark green, holly-like leaves; fragrant, white flowers in autumn
Quercus coccifera Kermes oak	2.2/1.5m 7/5ft	slow-growing, eventually up to 4.5m/15ft; small, dark green, holly-like leaves
Rhododendron yakushimanum	90/150cm 3/5ft	rhododendrons, which need moist, lime-free soil, are valuable for their foliage as well as their flowers; this example has deep green leaves, silvery at first and brown felted on the reverse; pink flowers in late spring
Viburnum davidii	75/120cm 2½/4ft	low mound of dark green leaves, prominently veined, followed by long-lasting blue berries provided both male and female plants present
Viburnum tinus 'Eve Price'	1.8/1.8m 6/6ft	compact with a good cover of dark green leaves on red stalks; white flowers in winter and spring

There are many variegated cultivars of the variable *Euonymus fortunei*. One of the brightest with cream or yellow variegation is the very popular 'Emerald 'n' Gold'. In winter the leaves take on a pink tinge. Here its yellow is complemented by the rich blue of *Veronica austriaca teucrium*, a summer-flowering perennial.

Border Shrubs with Variegated Foliage

Name	height/spread	description
DECIDUOUS		
Cornus alba 'Spaethii'	1.5/1.5m 5/5ft	yellow-variegated alternative to *C. alba* 'Elegantissima', also with red stems in winter
Fuchsia magellanica 'Sharpitor'	1.8/1.5m 6/5ft	elegant foliage with creamy white variegation; white and lavender dangling flowers in summer
Hydrangea 'Tricolor'	1.5/1.2m 5/4ft	blend of grey, green and yellow variegation; lacecap flowers of pink or white in summer
Potentilla fruticosa 'Abbotswood Silver'	1.2/1.5m 4/5ft	white edge to the leaves creates a silvered effect enhancing the whiteness of the flowers in summer
Ulmus parvifolia 'Frosty'	90/75cm 3/2½ft	neat shrubby elm; white teeth give a dainty edge to the leaves
Weigela 'Florida Variegata'	1.5/1.5m 5/5ft	leaves prettily highlighted by a yellow margin but, unhappily, the late spring flowers are pink
EVERGREEN		
Brachyglottis 'Moira Read'	1.2/1.8m 4/6ft	version of *B.* 'Sunshine' with the leaf centre pale green and cream; yellow daisies in summer
Buxus sempervirens 'Elegantissima'	1.8/1.2m 6/4ft	slow-growing dome of dark foliage with an irregular white leaf margin giving a cool effect
Buxus sempervirens 'Notata' ('Gold Tip')	2.2/1.5m 7/5ft	the gold tip to the leaves brightens the typically sombre box foliage
Euonymus fortunei 'Emerald Gaiety'	90/150cm 3/5ft	dense bush, the white edge to the leaves creating a crisp effect
Euonymus fortunei 'Emerald 'n' Gold'	90/90cm 3/3ft	bright yellow margin almost swallows the green centre of leaves on this dense bush
Hebe x **andersonii** 'Variegata'	90/75cm 3/2½ft	ivory edge makes the leaves showy; spikes of lavender flowers in late summer; not fully hardy
Salvia officinalis 'Icterina' sage	45/90cm 1½/3ft	aromatic leaves with a pale green and yellow edge and an irregular grey-green centre; rarely flowers
Salvia officinalis 'Tricolor'	45/75cm 1½/2½ft	less vigorous sage with variegation in purple, pink, grey and white
Vinca minor 'Argenteovariegata'	10/90cm 4/36in	useful white-variegated skirt to shrubs; blue flowers in late spring and early summer
Yucca flaccida 'Golden Sword'	90/75cm 3/2½ft	the low clump of yellow-variegated blades is valuable year-round; in late summer impressive spires carry cream flowers

stems are the most highly coloured. Cut out all old growth to just above ground level.

On the whole, evergreens require little pruning (see, however, pages 128-9 for topiary) but lavenders (*Lavandula*) and cotton lavender (*Santolina*) are exceptions. They need to be clipped back in spring to prevent them becoming straggly. Spring trimming will also help to keep heathers (*Erica*) neat.

Some variegated shrubs, themselves sports of green-leaved plants, have a tendency to produce stems that revert to the leaf colour of the parent plant. Stems showing reversion are usually more vigorous than those with variegated leaves. If left, they can take over and eventually you can be left with a shrub that shows little or no variegation. Cut out completely all reverted stems as soon as you spot them.

Propagating shrubs

The most common way to propagate shrubs is from cuttings, and hardwood cuttings are the least troublesome way to propagate many of the most popular. This and other vegetative methods such as layering and division ensure that the parent will be reproduced exactly. Many shrubs can be raised from seed but cultivars will not come true. Furthermore, the germination of shrub seed (and tree seed, too) can be slow and erratic and it may take a number of years before seed-raised plants are large enough to make their mark in the garden.

General care

Shrubs that have been planted in conditions that suit them require very little maintenance throughout the year. However, an annual feed of a slow-release fertilizer in early spring is beneficial and a mulch of bark chippings or similar material, renewed in spring after

Low Shrubs for the Front of Borders

Name	height/spread	description
DECIDUOUS		
Berberis thunbergii 'Bagatelle'	30/30cm 12/12in	dwarf form of a popular shrub making a neat ball of copper-red foliage
Cytisus x **beanii** broom	30/50cm 12/20in	gold, pea flowers make this semi-prostrate bush charming in late spring
Cytisus 'Dukaat' broom	50/45cm 20/18in	jaunty, upright bush with clear yellow flowers in mid-spring
Genista pilosa 'Lemon Spreader'	30/75cm 1/2½ft	cool profusion of lemon-yellow flowers over a tight mass of stems
Potentilla fruticosa mandshurica 'Manchu'	30/90cm 1/3ft	mat of silver-grey leaves spangled with white flowers
Spiraea japonica 'Little Princess'	60/75cm 2/2½ft	mound of dark green foliage, bronze early in the season, covered by heads of pink flowers in mid-to late summer
EVERGREEN		
Daphne cneorum 'Eximia' garland flower	10/50cm 4/20in	prostrate but rather loose shrub worth much for the wonderful fragrance of its tightly clustered, pink flowers in late spring and early summer
Erica x **darleyensis** 'Ghost Hills'	45/75cm 1½/2½ft	foliage in spring is tipped cream; long season of pink flowers in winter and spring
Halimium ocymoides 'Susan'	45/60cm 1½/2ft	in early to mid-summer masses of single, rose-like flowers, red in bud and then gold with a maroon blotch
Hebe 'Red Edge'	60/60cm 2/2ft	dome of grey-green, each leaf outlined in red; spikes of white flowers in summer
Helianthemum 'The Bride' rock rose	15/60cm 6/24in	one among many hybrids tailor-made for the front of borders, flowering profusely in early to mid-summer; white flowers over silver foliage
Helianthemum 'Wisley Pink' ('Rhodanthe Carneum')	15/60cm 6/24in	another fine rock rose, with pink flowers against soft grey
Lavandula angustifolia 'Hidcote' lavender	45/60cm 1½/2ft	aromatic lavenders are good at the front of borders; this compact form has deep purple flowers in mid- to late summer
Parahebe catarractae	30/30cm 12/12in	pretty in early summer with sprays of small, white flowers variably veined purplish-blue
Rosmarinus officinalis Prostratus Group rosemary	15/75cm 6/30in	aromatic with blue flowers in spring like other rosemaries; not fully hardy
Santolina pinnata neapolitana 'Sulphurea'	75/75cm 2½/2½ft	dome of grey-green foliage, feathery and aromatic, topped by primrose-yellow buttons in mid-summer

For a short period the garden may be more vividly colourful in autumn than at any other time in the year. *Euonymus alatus*, pictured here on the left, is outstanding for its fiery brilliance and there is room for it in many mixed borders. A smaller version, *E. alatus* 'Compactus', is also available. The sword-like leaves of *Phormium* 'Dazzler' retain their red tones all year.

fertilizing and when the soil is moist, will help conserve moisture and keep weeds down.

Some shrubs are grafted specimens and these may produce suckers from below the union of the scion (the cultivar) and the rootstock. If left, these suckers often develop at the expense of the cultivar. The best method of removal is to pull them away from the stem or root.

Although shrubs are potential victims for a wide range of pests and diseases, the problems that arise in gardens are usually the result of inappropriate selection and inadequate preparation of the ground before planting, poor drainage causing many failures that are often put down to other causes.

The most serious disease of woody plants is honey fungus, which forms fans of creamy fungus under the bark and dark strands on the roots, as well as the toadstool fruiting bodies. There is no effective treatment for this disease and all parts of affected plants should be removed and burned.

SHRUBS FOR AUTUMN FOLIAGE

For maples (*Acer*) see page 132.

Name	height/spread	description
Ceratostigma willmottianum	90/90cm 3/3ft	lovely blue flowers in late summer and autumn usually complemented by reddened foliage
Cornus alba 'Kesselringii'	1.8/1.8m 6/6ft	dark-green leaves turn red-purple in autumn; blackish-purple stems
Cotoneaster adpressus	45/150cm 1½/5ft	dull green leaves catch fire in autumn, when the bright red berries are also showy
Cotoneaster divaricatus	1.8/2.5m 6/8ft	dark green leaves turn brilliant red; pink flowers in early summer followed by purple berries
Euonymus alatus	2.2/2.2m 7/7ft	the crimson and scarlet foliage is among the most brilliant autumn displays; insignificant flowers but purple fruits with red seeds
Hamamelis vernalis 'Sandra'	1.8/1.2m 6/4ft	splendid orange and red in autumn but the yellow flowers in late winter are small
Nandina domestica 'Firepower' sacred bamboo	75/75cm 2½/2½ft	not a bamboo, in spite of its common name; this dwarf form has orange and red leaves in autumn and winter
Spiraea betulifolia aemiliana	75/60cm 2½/2ft	broad, oval leaves, which show off white flowers in summer, turn gold and bronze before falling
Vaccinium corymbosum 'Trovor' high-bush blueberry	1.8/1.5m 6/5ft	clusters of pink flowers on bare stems but the scarlet leaves in autumn are far more ornamental; edible, bloom-covered, black fruit; for moist, acid soil

BORDER SHRUBS WITH WINTER AND SPRING FLOWERS

Name	height/spread	flowering season	description
DECIDUOUS			
Chaenomeles speciosa 'Nivalis'	1.8/1.8m 6/6ft	mid-win. to mid-spr.	one of numerous cultivars at their peak in early spring but precocious in mild weather; clusters of pure white flowers
Daphne mezereum mezereon	150/90cm 5/3ft	late win. to early spr.	branches thickly clustered with fragrant, pink flowers; scarlet berries
Lonicera x purpusii 'Winter Beauty'	1.5/1.5m 5/5ft	mid-win. to early spr.	white, tubular flowers in small clusters are not showy but the scent is superb
Stachyurus praecox	2.2/2.7m 7/9ft	late win. to early spr.	small, greenish-yellow flowers hang catkin-like from purplish stems
Viburnum foetens	2.2/2.2m 7/7ft	mid-win. to early spr.	tight clusters of heavily scented white flowers show up against dark brown stems
EVERGREEN			
Daphne odora 'Aureomarginata'	1.2/1.2m 4/4ft	mid-win. to early spr.	nondescript bush with yellow-edged, glossy leaves valuable for richly scented, pink and white flowers in small clusters
Erica carnea 'Springwood White'	30/45cm 12/18in	mid-win. to early spr.	one of many named kinds with dense foliage and long-lasting flowers in white or pink; this is an outstanding white
Erica x darleyensis 'Arthur Johnson'	60/45cm 2/1½ft	late aut. to early spr.	one of several named cultivars that flower in winter; lilac-pink flowers
Erica lusitanica	1.8/1.2m 6/4ft	early win. to early spr.	bright green foliage and pink buds opening to white flowers; for acid soils and sheltered positions
Skimmia japonica 'Rubella'	1.5.1.5m 5/5ft	late aut. to early spr.	clusters of red buds are ornamental through winter until the flowers open white in spring

DECIDUOUS BORDER SHRUBS WITH ORNAMENTAL STEMS

Name	height/spread	description
Cornus alba 'Kesselringii'	2.2/3m 7/10ft	dense purple-black stems are useful as a contrast to reds
Cornus alba 'Sibirica'	1.8/2.5m 6/8ft	the most vivid red of winter stems and superb as a large clump
Cornus stolonifera 'Flaviramea'	1.8/2.5m 6/8ft	greenish-yellow stems; good for contrasting with red-stemmed *Cornus*
Corylus avellana 'Contorta'	2.5/2.5m 8/8ft	slow-growing puzzle of twisted twigs with dangling catkins in late winter
Leycesteria formosa	1.8/1.8m 6/6ft	pea-green stems; white flowers with wine-red bracts in late summer and autumn
Salix hastata 'Wehrhahnii'	1.8/1.5m 6/5ft	purplish-black winter stems show off silver catkins in early spring

Brightly coloured stems can be highly ornamental in the winter garden. Here the red of *Cornus alba* 'Sibirica' is set against the greenish-yellow of *C. stolonifera* 'Flaviramea'. Young stems are more strongly coloured than old wood so a regular pruning regime is necessary. One method is to cut to ground level some or all two-year-old stems in late winter.

BERRYING SHRUBS FOR BORDERS

Name	height/spread	description
DECIDUOUS		
Berberis wilsoniae	90/150cm 3/5ft	yellow flowers in late spring; coral-red berries and foliage colours well in autumn
Callicarpa bodinieri	1.8/2.2m 6/7ft	clusters of violet berries provide an unusual colour in autumn; the young foliage is bronze
Euonymus europaeus 'Red Cascade'	2.2/1.8m 7/6ft	large crops of crimson capsules open to show orange seeds; leaves colour in autumn
EVERGREEN		
Cotoneaster conspicuus 'Decorus'	1.8/1.8m 6/6ft	arching stems form a dense mound covered in white flowers in early summer and later massed with bird-proof, red berries
Cotoneaster franchetii	2.2/1.5m 7/5ft	arching growth and grey-green leaves; white-and-pink flowers; orange-red, oblong berries
Cotoneaster simonsii	2.2/1.5m 7/5ft	semi-evergreen; white flowers in early summer; long-lasting, bright scarlet berries
Gaultheria mucronata 'Mulberry Wine'	90/90cm 3/3ft	white flowers, followed by long-lasting, globular fruits in white, or shades of pink and red; rich red fruit; lime-free soil
Skimmia japonica reevesiana	75/90cm 2½/3ft	fragrant, white flowers in spring; long-lasting crimson berries remain attractive for weeks
Viburnum davidii	75/120cm 2½/4ft	dark green leaves, prominently veined; long-lasting, blue berries (male and female needed)

A role for roses

The rose has long held an unassailable position in the affection of gardeners and flower lovers. A core of species together with the accumulation of centuries of casual rose breeding and the prodigious output of the modern rose industry present the gardener with a staggering choice of roses, many of which are well suited to growing in beds and borders.

Two groups of roses, the hybrid teas and the floribundas, now reclassified respectively as large-flowered and cluster-flowered bush roses, have played a leading role in gardens this century and are the typical bedding roses.

Bush roses

Large-flowered and cluster-flowered bush roses have much in common, usually making compact bushes, flowering with astonishing freedom from early summer well into autumn and are available in a sweep of colour that takes in practically everything but true blue. They share, too, a disadvantage, that of being stiff-stemmed and charmless out of leaf.

The large-flowered types are remarkable for the refined, high-centred shape of their large blooms, while the cluster-flowered types produce smaller blooms but in large sprays. Patio roses are in effect compact forms of the cluster-flowered bush roses and can be used like them in beds and borders.

Shrub roses

The shrub roses are a very large group. They encompass wild roses and a number that are close to their wild parents, the various categories of old garden roses, such as the Albas and Damasks, and a number of shrub roses of more recent origin, including the English roses.

In this very heterogeneous grouping it is difficult to define common characteristics.

Almost all, however, are larger plants than the bush roses and are free from their angular gawkiness. A few are so lax that there is the option of training them as climbers and, conversely, some of the low-growing climbers can be grown as arching shrubs. The ground-cover roses (see the chart on page 38) are in effect low-growing modern shrub roses of dense habit and can also find a place in borders.

Placing roses

In a medium-sized to large garden there is much to be said for growing bush roses as permanent bedding plants. Roses grouped according to variety give a massed effect of colour over a long season and are a useful source of material for cutting. The vivid colours that have been bred into roses, often difficult to integrate in overall colour schemes, can seem appealingly cheerful in isolation. Variation in height can be achieved by using a combination of bush and standard forms.

There are, however, obvious and hidden disadvantages. Their ugliness in the dormant season is hard to disguise, even with generous interplanting. A bed of a single colour palls year after year and mixtures, unless carefully planned for height and colour, can create an agitating effect. Furthermore, herding roses together makes life easier for the pests and diseases that thrive on them. In the small to medium-sized garden the disadvantages of using bush roses as permanent bedding are generally so obvious that it is better from the outset to use them in combination with other plants, perhaps in small groups of three or so specimens.

Shrub roses have often been separated out in another way, reverentially cloistered in an area designated as a 'rose garden'. There is no denying the charm of a formal garden in which roses star, although supported by a cast of other plants, predominantly quietly spoken perennials. Most of our gardens, however, cannot accommodate such an extravagance, which can be dull over a long season. In general the shrub roses do well in more balanced borders, where perennials and other shrubs are given equal billing.

A contrasting option, best suited to formal schemes, is to isolate a single specimen in a bed of its own, perhaps with an underplanting. Most of the modern bush roses are frankly too ungainly to be used in this way. Much better, provided they are selected to be in scale with their setting, are some of the modern shrubs, such as 'Nevada', or weeping standards formed by budding ramblers on to a tall stem.

Planting roses

Roses are commonly sold as bare-root specimens, which become available in autumn, at the beginning of the dormant season. Bare-root roses need to be planted in mild weather between mid-autumn and late spring. When planting, ensure that the union of the rose and rootstock (most bought roses consist of a cultivar budded on a rootstock) is about 2.5cm/1in below the surface of the soil.

There is an increasing trend to sell roses as container-grown specimens. In theory roses grown in containers can be planted at any time of the year but planting in the dormant season gives the best results.

Although roses will tolerate light shade for a few hours during the day, they are best planted in full sun, in well-drained, humus-rich soil. If you are planting new beds of roses, dig the whole bed thoroughly well in advance and work in generous quantities of organic matter. Ground that has had roses growing in it should not be replanted with roses; the soil will be rose-sick and new roses will make stunted growth.

Pruning roses

On roses left to themselves, old stems that have borne flowers gradually die back to be replaced by new shoots low down. Pruning is a way of speeding up and tidying this natural process, taking out old wood when it is past its best to encourage vigorous new growth and keeping plants open so that the free circulation of air can minimize the risk of disease.

Pruning should be carried out after leaf fall but before leaf buds start to break in spring. The method of pruning varies according to the type of rose and to some extent on the way it is being used. First, always remove dead, damaged and diseased wood and weak growth. In shortening

BELOW LEFT Their blooms are the chief ornamental feature of most roses but in the case of *Rosa glauca* the small flowers and later the red hips are subordinate to the purple-tinged, grey-green foliage. Here the woolly-leaved *Stachys byzantina* and a single pink (*Dianthus*) are among the attractive, low-growing plants that contribute to a rich composite planting.

BELOW RIGHT *Rosa moyesii* and the slightly smaller *R. moyesii* 'Geranium' are heavily armoured and vigorous shrub roses that make large arching bushes. Their single flowers are followed by a magnificent display of bright red, flask-shaped hips. They are difficult to work around; geraniums and other low-maintenance ground cover make a suitable underplanting.

COMPANIONS FOR ROSES

Unless special conditions are mentioned, all of the plants listed will succeed in sunny positions where the soil is well drained and reasonably fertile.

Name	category	height/spread	description
Alchemilla mollis lady's mantle	perennial	45/60cm 1½/2ft	good for a soft edging of frothy, lime-green flowers in summer
Campanula persicifolia	perennial	75/30cm 2½/1ft	good-natured and self-seeds freely; spires of blue or white bells throughout summer
Dianthus 'Fair Folly'	perennial	25/25cm 10/10in	single flowers of dusty pink on white; one of many modern pinks with pretty single or double flowers in white, pinks and reds, often scented, in several flushes through summer
Dianthus 'Mrs Sinkins'	perennial	25/25cm 10/10in	wonderfully fragrant, white double in early summer
Digitalis purpurea foxglove	biennial	150/45cm 5/1½ft	tall spires of tubular flowers, purplish and spotted within, from early to mid-summer; lovely among old roses
Lavandula angustifolia 'Munstead'	evergreen shrub	60/60cm 2/2ft	aromatic lavenders and roses make a happy combination; this compact lavender has blue flowers mid- to late summer
Lilium candidum madonna lily	bulb	120/30cm 4/1ft	heads of pure white, fragrant trumpets in early to mid-summer; superb with old roses
Nepeta x **faassenii** catmint	perennial	45/45cm 18/18in	aromatic, grey-green foliage and sprays of lavender-blue flowers, especially in early summer, make a billowing edge
Santolina pinnata neapolitana	evergreen shrub	75/90cm 2½/3ft	feathery, grey-green foliage, good as a foreground; the yellow flowers produced in mid-summer can be sheared off
Stachys byzantina 'Silver Carpet'	perennial	15/45cm 6/18in	woolly-leaved, grey edging that goes well with all colours
Viola cornuta	perennial	25/45cm 10/18in	blue or white violet-like flowers make a refined skirting; best in the first half of summer
Viola 'Roggli Giants' pansy	annual	20/20cm 8/8in	also grown as a biennial; one of many desirable pansies; bushy with cheerful flowers in a good range of colours during summer and autumn

a stem, cut to just above an outward-facing leaf bud, with the cut sloping slightly back from the bud towards the base of the stem.

The most heavily pruned of all the roses are the large-flowered bush roses. These often develop crossing stems that should be cut out to keep bushes open. Cut out one or two old stems at the base and then shorten other stems to form a framework about 23cm/9in high, taller if the rose is particularly vigorous. Cluster-flowered bush roses are pruned in much the same way but not so severely, the framework left being about 35cm/14in high.

Generally, shrub roses do best when only lightly pruned and this is especially true of the species. After removing dead, damaged and diseased wood, cut out old stems that are flowering only sparsely. Shorten remaining stems by up to a third and cut back laterals that

Rosa 'Graham Thomas', named after one of the most influential plantsmen and gardening writers of this century, belongs to a group known as the English roses. These have been bred to combine the characteristic flower shape of the old roses with the vigour and repeat-flowering qualities of modern roses. Plant them in mixed borders.

have flowered to about 13cm/5in. The repeat-flowering roses, such as some of the bourbons and the English roses, do better with slightly heavier pruning and benefit from having twiggy growth thinned during the growing season.

Deadheading is, in effect, a form of pruning. Removing faded flowers of recurrent roses will encourage the production of more blooms. Spent flowers of large-flowered bush roses should be cut back to an outward-facing bud or shoot. Roses that produce sprays of flowers such as the cluster-flowered bush roses should have the whole truss cut back.

General care

Roses need generous feeding and they are worth treating with the fertilizers specially formulated for them. Apply fertilizer in the quantity specified by the manufacturer just as leaves begin to develop and repeat once or twice between then and just after mid-summer.

REPEAT-FLOWERING SHRUB ROSES

Most of the following roses start flowering in early summer.

Name	category	height/spread	description
WHITE			
R. 'Blanche Double de Coubert'	Rugosa	1.8/1.5m 6/5ft	dazzling white, loosely double flowers; sweetly scented
R. 'Nevada'	Modern shrub	2.2/2.2m 7/7ft	magnificent first flush of creamy white, semi-double flowers; fair scent
PINK			
R. 'Comte de Chambord'	Portland	120/90cm 4/3ft	stiff shrub with a long succession of very fragrant, bright pink flowers that are flat and quartered
R. 'Cornelia'	Hybrid musk	2.2/2.2m 7/7ft	dark foliage; clusters of small flowers in copper-toned pink; fair scent
R. 'Elmshorn'	Modern shrub	1.8/1.8m 6/6ft	two main flushes of cup-shaped, double flowers in strong carmine-pink
R. 'Erfurt'	Modern shrub	1.5/1.8m 5/6ft	copper-tinted young foliage; semi-double, pink flowers with white centres and conspicuous yellow stamens; fair scent
R. 'Frühlingsmorgen'	Modern shrub	1.8/1.5m 6/5ft	only a few flowers after the main flush but of rare beauty; single, pink with primrose centres and maroon stamens; fair scent
R. 'Lavender Lassie'	Modern shrub	1.2/1.5m 4/5ft	little scent but a good display of soft pink, pompon flowers
R. 'Louise Odier'	Bourbon	1.8/1.2m 6/4ft	exquisitely formed and well-scented, double flowers in lilac-tinged pink; good on support
R. 'Marguerite Hilling'	Modern shrub	2.2/2.2m 7/7ft	semi-double, pink flowers, the first flush prodigious; fair scent
R. 'Penelope'	Hybrid musk	1.8/1.5m 6/5ft	large clusters of semi-double flowers in a lovely creamy pink; fair scent
RED OR PURPLE			
R. 'Fountain'	Modern shrub	1.8/1.8m 6/6ft	dark green foliage; large, double, cupped, crimson flowers; fair scent
R. 'Madame Isaac Pereire'	Bourbon	2.2/1.8m 7/6ft	sumptuously double, purple-crimson blooms; ravishing scent; good on support
R. 'Reine des Violettes'	Hybrid perpetual	1.8/2.2m 6/7ft	grey-green foliage shows off double, quartered flowers of violet-purple; good scent
R. 'Roseraie de l'Haÿ'	Rugosa	2.5/1.8m 8/6ft	bright green foliage; loosely double, well-scented flowers of rich purple
R. 'The Prince'	English	75/90cm 2½/3ft	richly scented, deep purple rose in the old style
APRICOT OR YELLOW			
R. 'Buff Beauty'	Hybrid musk	1.8/2.2m 6/7ft	lax shrub; arching stems clustered with apricot or creamy flowers; good scent
R. 'Golden Wings'	Modern shrub	1.5/1.8m 5/6ft	large, single flowers of pale yellow borne prolifically; moderate scent
R. 'Graham Thomas'	English	1.2/1.5m 4/5ft	nicely scented double in the old style and of a splendidly rich yellow

In a good year the rose season opens in late spring with the single, yellow flowers of R. *xanthina* 'Canary Bird'. These are borne so profusely that they overlap along the arching stems. After the main flush there may even be a few odd flowers nestling in the attractive ferny foliage.

When choosing roses for small gardens it makes sense to give priority to those that repeat. There are, however, many superb shrub roses that flower only once in the summer. Of those with single flowers 'Complicata' is among the loveliest. Although usually categorized as a Gallica, it is highly individual in character and makes a large, spreading shrub.

SHRUB ROSES FLOWERING ONCE IN SUMMER

Unless other times are given, the following roses flower in early to mid-summer.

Name	category	height/spread	description
WHITE			
R. x **alba** 'Alba Maxima' Jacobite rose, great double white	Alba	2.5/2.5m 8/8ft	large shrub with grey-green foliage and double, fragrant, white flowers over a long period in mid-summer
R. 'Madame Hardy'	Damask	1.5/1.2m 5/4ft	few rivals among white roses; double, with a green eye; richly fragrant
PINK			
R. 'Céleste'	Alba	1.5/1.2m 5/4ft	double, soft pink and fragrant, beautifully displayed against grey-green foliage
R. 'Complicata'	Gallica	1.8/2.2m 6/7ft	fresh, single, pink flowers, pale at the centre; lightly fragrant
R. 'Fantin-Latour'	Centifolia	2.2/2.2m 7/7ft	blush-pink, double flowers, sometimes revealing a green eye; good scent
R. 'Fritz Nobis'	Modern shrub	1.8/1.8m 6/6ft	elegant, arching shrub with semi-double, salmon-pink, fragrant flowers with waved petals
R. 'Gloire des Mousseuses'	Moss	120/90cm 4/3ft	aromatic encrustation of light green moss; large, full-petalled flowers of bright pink
R. rubrifolia	Species	2.2/1.5m 7/5ft	the single, purplish flowers are less important than the grey-green foliage and good crop of hips
RED OR PURPLE			
R. moyesii 'Geranium'	Species	2.5/2.5m 8/8ft	small, bright red, single flowers in early summer followed by handsome, flask-shaped hips
R. 'Tuscany Superb'	Gallica	120/60cm 4/2ft	golden stamens and odd white streaks seem to intensify the rich purple of the double flowers; little scent
YELLOW			
R. 'Frühlingsgold'	Modern shrub	2.2/2.2m 7/7ft	large, semi-double, pale yellow flowers crowd the arching stems in early summer; rich fragrance
R. xanthina 'Canary Bird'	Species	2.2/2.2m 7/7ft	cascades of small, single, yellow flowers in late spring and early summer; very pretty foliage

BUSH ROSES

The following roses are described as cluster-flowered or large-flowered, terms now used instead of floribunda and hybrid tea.

Name	category	height/spread	description
WHITE OR CREAM			
R. 'Elina' ('Peaudouce')	large	90/75cm 3/2½ft	double, ivory flowers, lemon-centred, over dark foliage; fair scent
R. 'Iceberg'	cluster	75/60cm 2½/2ft	outstanding for flowering freely; creamy white with light scent
R. 'Margaret Merril'	cluster	75/60cm 2½/2ft	well-scented, blush-white flowers and dark foliage
R. 'Pascali'	large	75/45cm 2½/1½ft	gaunt bush with large, double flowers; little scent
R. 'Polar Star'	large	90/75cm 3/2½ft	shapely, double flowers with fair scent; dark foliage
PINK			
R. 'Anisley Dickson'	cluster	90/75cm 3/2½ft	double, salmon-pink flowers over thick, dark foliage; light scent
R. 'Beauty Queen'	cluster	75/60cm 2½/2ft	clusters of well-scented, mid-pink flowers; purplish foliage
R. 'Blessings'	large	90/75cm 3/2½ft	lightly scented, coral-pink flowers, produced with great freedom
R. 'City of Leeds'	cluster	75/60cm 2½/2ft	large clusters of semi-double, salmon-pink flowers; light scent
R. 'City of London'	cluster	75/75cm 2½/2½ft	well-scented, double flowers; taller on support
R. 'English Miss'	cluster	75/60cm 2½/2ft	shapely, double flowers of soft pink; good scent
R. 'Harry Edland'	cluster	90/60cm 3/2ft	fragrant, double flowers of lilac-pink
R. 'Many Happy Returns'	cluster	90/90cm 3/3ft	semi-double, blush-pink flowers on a lax shrub; fair scent
R. 'Prima Ballerina'	large	90/60cm 3/2ft	nicely scented large blooms of deep pink on an upright bush
R. 'Savoy Hotel'	large	90/60cm 3/2ft	large, double flowers, lightly scented, of pale pink
R. 'Silver Jubilee'	large	90/60cm 3/2ft	shapely, double flowers of silvery pink with apricot tints; light scent
APRICOT OR PEACH			
R. 'Apricot Silk'	large	90/60cm 3/2ft	moderately fragrant, double, apricot flowers over dark, glossy foliage
R. 'Clarissa'	cluster	90/45cm 3/1½ft	large clusters of soft apricot flowers; little scent
R. 'Elizabeth Harkness'	large	75/60cm 2½/2ft	large, double, well-scented flowers of buff with yellow tones
R. 'Grand-mère Jenny'	large	75/60cm 2½/2ft	double flowers of yellow flushed pink, produced freely; light scent
R. 'Southampton'	cluster	90/75cm 3/2½ft	large, double flowers are apricot with red flushes; good scent
RED OR PURPLE			
R. 'Alec's Red'	large	90/60cm 3/2ft	very large, cherry-red, double blooms of fine fragrance
R. 'Alexander'	large	150/75cm 5/2½ft	many large, double flowers in bright vermilion; light scent
R. 'Disco Dancer'	cluster	75/60cm 2½/2ft	double flowers of fiery red on a bushy plant with glossy foliage; light scent
R. 'Ena Harkness'	large	75/60cm 2½/2ft	weak neck but beautifully scented, double flowers of bright crimson
R. 'Escapade'	cluster	75/60cm 2½/2ft	single flowers of magenta-lilac; good scent
R. 'Fragrant Cloud'	large	75/60cm 2½/2ft	free-flowering with highly scented blooms of coral red
R. 'Josephine Bruce'	large	75/60cm 2½/2ft	double flowers of deep, velvety red and good scent but mildew-prone
R. 'Marlena'	cluster	45/45cm 18/18in	large clusters of double, bright crimson flowers; little scent
R. 'Melody Maker'	cluster	75/60cm 2½/2ft	clusters of large, double, light crimson blooms; light scent
R. 'Mister Lincoln'	large	90/60cm 3/2ft	well-scented, large flowers of deep velvety red
R. 'National Trust'	large	60/60cm 2/2ft	double, bright red blooms over good dark foliage; little scent
R. 'Royal William'	large	10/75cm 3½/2½ft	well-scented blooms of classic form and velvety, deep red over dark green foliage; good scent
R. 'Wendy Cussons'	large	90/60cm 3/2ft	well-scented blooms of pinky red on a bushy plant
ORANGE OR YELLOW			
R. 'Allgold'	cluster	60/45cm 2/1½ft	upright bush with medium-sized, bright yellow flowers
R. 'Amber Queen'	cluster	45/60cm 1½/2ft	large clusters of well-scented, double, amber-yellow flowers
R. 'Arthur Bell'	cluster	75/60cm 2½/2ft	double, golden flowers that fade as they age; good scent
R. 'Chinatown'	cluster	120/90cm 4/3ft	fragrant, double flowers, yellow with a pink flush over glossy foliage
R. 'Doris Tysterman'	large	90/75cm 3/2½ft	double, tangerine-orange flowers matched by bronzy foliage; light scent
R. 'Fellowship'	cluster	75/60cm 2½/2ft	double flowers of deep orange against glossy, dark green foliage; good scent
R. 'Just Joey'	large	75/60cm 2½/2ft	large, double flowers of coppery orange; good scent
R. 'King's Ransom'	large	90/60cm 3/2ft	free-flowering, double yellow; light scent
BI-COLOURED			
R. 'Champagne Cocktail'	cluster	90/75cm 3/2½ft	double flowers of yellow with pink flecks and reverse; fair scent
R. 'Oranges and Lemons'	cluster	75/60cm 2½/2ft	double flowers with startling combination of strong yellow and orange stripes; light scent
R. 'Piccadilly'	large	75/60cm 2½/2ft	yellow doubles with red reverse; light scent
R. 'Tequila Sunrise'	large	75/60cm 2½/2ft	double, yellow blooms edged with scarlet; light scent

Modern rose breeding has greatly extended the colour range available, especially among the cluster-flowered bush roses (still often referred to as floribundas). The dazzling orange-red of a rose such as 'Disco Dancer' is difficult to combine with other colours in a mixed planting and is probably most effectively used in a single-colour bedding scheme.

An organic mulch such as well-rotted stable manure will also add nutrients to the soil. Just as important is the fact that it will smother weeds and keep soil moist and at an even temperature. The mulch should be applied in early spring after planting and renewed annually after the first application of fertilizer.

Although roses like a well-drained soil, they require plenty of moisture in the growing season and irrigation may be necessary during periods of drought.

It is not surprising that a shadow lurks at the edge of the paradise garden filled with fragrant and beautiful roses. Although increasing efforts are being made to breed disease-resistant roses, many are not and even those that are sometimes show symptoms of disease if plants are under stress. Three fungal diseases are particularly troublesome. Of these the most common is mildew, which covers leaves and buds with a white powder. Black spot is another disfiguring and weakening disease, the black-spotted leaves yellowing and eventually falling. It is particularly prevalent in warm, wet summers. Rust is the least common of the major fungal infections but when orange patches show on the underside of leaves it can mean the beginning of the end. Good general cultivation and free air circulation reduce the risk of infection, but these diseases are difficult to contol without resorting to fungicides.

A quite different problem is presented by the fact that most commercially produced roses consist of a selected cultivar budded on to a rootstock. Some rootstocks have a tendency to produce suckers and if these are left they will develop at the expense of the cultivar. Cutting off suckers will only encourage more to develop. The best course is to trace the sucker back to the root and to pull it off.

The large-flowered bush roses, better known as hybrid teas, have small clusters or single blooms of good size. Like the cluster-flowered bush roses (floribundas), they are pruned hard and well fed to encourage a long flowering display. 'Just Joey', a richly toned and fragrant example, shows the characteristic fullness and high-centred shape.

Bulbs for beds & borders

One of the greatest satisfactions in gardening is seeing the explosions of colour from the flowers of bulbs, the almost effortless planting of which several months previously has virtually been forgotten. Spring is the great bulb season when no other category of plant can match them for sheer flower power. Bulbs, however, can be found for every season of the year and some that flower during summer, the lilies especially, are among the most elegant and sensationally beautiful of all garden plants.

The term 'bulb' has been used here in a broad sense to cover not only the true bulbs, such as tulips and daffodils, but a wide range of other plants that grow from swollen underground organs, for example cyclamen. These organs provide a source of food for the plant's growth at the end of a period of dormancy.

Bulbs can be grown in a variety of different ways. They are often naturalized (see page 36) or grown in raised beds and containers (see pages 144 and 147). Their versatility is such, however, that there is no garden where the beauty of beds and borders cannot be enhanced by the planting of a suitable selection.

Bulbs for bedding

One of the commonest ways of using bulbs is as spring bedding. The classics for this are tulips and hyacinths, plants that do not sulk under military discipline. Other plants can be used, for example grape hyacinths (*Muscari*) in spring and lilies in summer, but a more relaxed treatment may suit these better. Apart from municipal extravaganzas, large-scale bedding is largely a thing of the past but even on a small domestic scale, as many suburban gardens demonstrate, it can be a remarkably effective way of creating a bright effect, especially in spring.

Loosely grouped clumps of tulips make lovely splashes
of colour in borders just as the foliage of herbaceous
perennials is developing. Rather than leaving them in
the border, it is often more convenient to lift tulips
while still in leaf, immediately after flowering,
replanting in a nursery bed and allowing them to die
down before lifting the bulbs for storage.

Combining bulbs with other plants can
extend the interest of beds and enhance the
effect of the bulbs themselves. Among plants
that go happily with hyacinths are daisies,
polyanthus and winter-flowering pansies. The
formulae of tulips and wallflowers or tulips and
forget-me-nots have been heavily worked but
rarely fail to please. Sweet williams also make a
good combination with tulips, the sweet
william foliage backing the tulips and their
flowers following later.

Bulbs in borders

The principal disadvantage of the herbaceous
border is its long off-season. Bulbs are ideal for
extending the border's period of interest,
especially during the spring months. The
massed formality of bedding schemes would be
out of place but it is still best to plant in clumps
rather than scattering bulbs about. Clumps of
ten or a dozen daffodils or tulips make a greater
impact than the odd flower dotted about,
although one has to admit that cottage gardens
sometimes demonstrate how very pretty
random planting can be.

The strong practical reason for planting in
groups is that it simplifies the cultivation of the
border. If the position of bulbs is clearly
marked, they need not be disturbed when the
border is dug and it is an easier matter to devise
foreground planting that will mask the dying
foliage of the bulbs in early summer. Lifting
bulbs as soon as they have finished flowering
may be a better option but you need space in an
out-of-the-way corner of the garden where they
can be grown on until the leaves die down
naturally. Lifting bulbs is easier if they have
been planted in a basket made from wire netting
or a purpose-made container with base and
sides that are partially open.

RIGHT The Reticulata irises, including *Iris reticulata* itself and a number of hybrids, are very adaptable plants. They are at home among alpines and rock garden plants, good planted in containers, and lovely brightening the edges of borders in late winter. If left undisturbed – not easily achieved with any bulbs in borders – they will usually increase and flower freely.

Winter and Spring Bulbs

Unless special conditions are mentioned, all of the plants listed will succeed in sunny positions where the soil is well drained and reasonably fertile.

Name	height/spread	flowering season	description
DWARF BULBS			
Anemone blanda	10/10cm 4/4in	early spr.	flattish flowers, blue, pink or white, with numerous petals; suitable for shrub borders in sun or part-shade
Anemone coronaria poppy anemone	25/10cm 10/4in	late win. to mid-spr.	cheerful flowers in scarlet, blue, mauve or white; single (De Caen Group), double or semi-double (St Brigid Group)
Anemone x fulgens	30/15cm 12/6in	early to mid-spr.	single flowers of dazzling scarlet; short-lived
Chionodoxa forbesii glory of the snow	15/8cm 6/3in	late win. to early spr.	stems of starry, pale blue flowers with white centres; 'Pink Giant' is a pink form
Chionodoxa luciliae (C. gigantea) glory of the snow	20/10cm 8/4in	late win. to mid-spr.	lax spikes of starry blue flowers with white centres
Convallaria majalis 'Fortin's Giant' lily of the valley	20/60cm 8/24in	late spr.	when happy, a very vigorous spreader but suitable for a shrub border; this large-flowered selection has the waxy texture and scent of the familiar form
Crocus chrysanthus	8/5cm 3/2in	late win.	many exquisite and honey-scented cultivars, including 'Blue Pearl', soft blue with silvery lining; 'Cream Beauty', bright orange stigma in a creamy yellow cup; 'E. A. Bowles', rich yellow with purple feathering; 'Zwanenburg Bronze', bronzed exterior to rich gold blooms
Crocus sieberi 'Violet Queen'	10/5cm 4/2in	late win. to early spr.	yellow-centred, rounded flowers of violet-mauve
Crocus tommasinianus 'Ruby Giant'	10/8cm 4/3in	late win. to early spr.	rich purple form of one of the most obliging crocus species
Erythronium dens-canis dog's-tooth violet	20/10cm 8/4in	mid- to late spr.	purple flowers prettily poised over brown-blotched leaves; best in light shade among shrubs
Erythronium tuolumnense	30/15cm 12/6in	mid-spr.	prettily reflexed, yellow flowers up to 10 per stem; suitable for part-shade in shrub borders
Fritillaria meleagris snake's-head fritillary	38/10cm 15/4in	mid- to late spr.	beautifully chequered hanging bells in purple or greenish-white; for moist soil

Galanthus caucasicus snowdrop	15/8cm 6/3in	late win. to early spr.	broad, grey-green leaves and typical snowdrop flower with green markings at the tip of the inner petals only
Galanthus elwesii snowdrop	20/10cm 8/4in	late win. to early spr.	stocky plant with grey-green, strap-shaped leaves and green markings at the base and tips of inner petals
Galanthus 'S. Arnott' snowdrop	20/10cm 8/4in	late win. to early spr.	like a vigorous common snowdrop (*G. nivalis*) and scented
Hermodactylus tuberosus	30/10cm 12/4in	early to mid-spr.	iris-like flowers in an intriguing blend of green and velvety black
Hyacinthus orientalis Dutch hyacinth	25/15cm 10/6in	mid-spr.	densely clustered spikes of waxy flowers are graceless but blooms are powerfully fragrant; the range includes: 'City of Haarlem', pale yellow; 'Delft Blue', soft blue with darker tones; 'L'Innocence', ivory white; 'Pink Pearl', deep pink
Ipheion uniflorum 'Wisley Blue'	20/8cm 8/3in	mid- to late spr.	long season of star-shaped, blue flowers over grassy foliage that smells of onions
Iris histrioides 'Major'	10/10cm 4/4in	mid-win. to early spr.	violet-blue Reticulata iris with a gold crest; defiantly robust
Iris reticulata	10/10cm 4/4in	late win. to early spr.	violet-purple flowers with a gold crest; more slender than the former
Leucojum vernum	20/10cm 8/4in	late win. to early spr.	strap-shaped leaves and nodding, white flowers prettily tipped green; for moist soil
Muscari armeniacum 'Heavenly Blue' grape hyacinth	25/10cm 10/4in	mid- to late spr.	spikes densely clustered with little, scented bells, bright blue with a white rim; 'Cantab' is slightly dwarfer and a pale blue
Narcissus see page 75			
Scilla siberica Siberian squill	15/8cm 6/3in	early spr.	several flowers per stem, several stems per bulb; little can match the brilliance of the blue flowers
Tulipa see page 76			
LARGER BULBS			
Fritillaria imperialis crown imperial	90/30cm 3/1ft	mid-spr.	brick-red bells cluster beneath a green tuft on a tall stem rising out of glossy leaves
Fritillaria persica 'Adiyaman'	120/30cm 4/1ft	mid-spr.	spikes of about 20 pendulous flowers of deepest plum above grey-green foliage
Leucojum aestivum 'Gravetye Giant' summer snowflake	60/20cm 24/8in	mid- to late spr.	clusters of white bells, fringed with green tips, above dark green, strap-shaped leaves; for moist soils
Narcissus see page 75			
Tulipa see page 76			

DAFFODILS AND NARCISSI (*NARCISSUS*)

Most of the daffodils and narcissi listed here are scented to some degree.

Name	height	flowering season	description
N. 'Barrett Browning'	45cm/18in	mid-spr.	rounded face of white petals and orange cup
N. 'Cheerfulness'	50cm/20in	mid- to late spr.	several double flowers per stem; white with yellow centre and very fragrant
N. 'Dove Wings'	35cm/14in	mid-spr.	pale yellow trumpet and swept-back, ivory petals
N. 'February Silver'	25cm/10in	early spr.	milky petals and pale yellow trumpet
N. 'Geranium'	45cm/18in	mid- to late spr.	clustered heads of white flowers with showy orange cups
N. 'Hawera'	20cm/8in	mid- to late spr.	free-flowering charmer with several small-cupped, clear yellow flowers per stem
N. 'Jack Snipe'	20cm/8in	early to mid-spr.	jauntily swept-back, creamy petals and short primrose trumpet
N. 'Liberty Bells'	30cm/12in	mid-spr.	choice, with several drooping flowers of lemon-yellow per stem
N. 'Little Witch'	25cm/10in	early to mid-spr.	nicer than she sounds; bright yellow trumpet and reflexed petals
N. 'Merlin'	35cm/14in	mid- to late spr.	glistening white petals and green-eyed, gold cup with ruffled, orange rim
N. 'Petrel'	20cm/8in	mid- to late spr.	like a white version of 'Hawera'
N. 'Rippling Waters'	35cm/14in	mid-spr.	creamy, short-cupped flowers, 3 to a stem, nodding prettily
N. 'Rip van Winkle'	20cm/8in	mid-spr.	a curiosity, with petals and trumpet reduced to a cluster of yellow shreds
N. 'Salmon Trout'	40cm/16in	mid-spr.	white petals and a large cup turning from pale yellow to pink
N. 'Suzy'	50cm/20in	mid- to late spr.	fine scented jonquil, each stem with 3-4 flowers, yellow with an orange cup
N. 'Tête-à-Tête'	15cm/6in	early spr.	usually 2 yellow trumpets per stem
N. 'Thalia'	40cm/16in	mid- to late spr.	3-4 snowy flowers, with swept-back petals, per stem
N. 'Topolino'	20cm/8in	mid-spr.	elegantly twisted, creamy petals; pretty yellow trumpet with frilled edge
N. 'Trevithian'	50cm/20in	mid-spr.	very elegant and wonderfully scented, with 2-3 short-cupped, yellow flowers per stem

Narcissus cyclamineus, an early-flowering, dwarf species with swept-back petals, is a parent of many fine hybrid daffodils of short to medium height. One of the best of these for general use is the optimistically named 'February Gold'. In the northern hemisphere the nicely poised flowers rarely open before early March but are then long lasting.

The shrub border or a mixed border in which shrubs dominate is an even better location for many bulbs, which can be tucked into positions where there is little chance that they will be disturbed by digging. There is nothing like a succession of bulbs to lighten the sometimes heavy and constipated look of shrubs en masse. It has to be remembered that although many bulbs like an open position, those that are suitable for naturalizing in woodland can be established happily among deciduous shrubs where the positions will be lightly shaded in summer. Many of the shorter-growing daffodils and narcissi are particularly suitable for this kind of planting. The proportions of their refined flowers are more in scale with other plants than those of the really beefy large hybrids. Most lilies are better for having shade at the base, but almost all of them need to be able to lift their heads into sunlight.

Planting bulbs

Bulbs are usually sold in the dry state during their dormant period. As a general rule, they should be purchased as soon as they become available and planted without delay. This is partly because bulbs often deteriorate rapidly in the haphazard conditions in which they are stored at many of the outlets that sell them. Early planting also gives them a chance to

TULIPS (*TULIPA*)

All of the following tulips are best lifted once the foliage has died down and the bulbs stored for replanting in the autumn.

Name	height	flowering season	description
WHITE			
T. 'Diana'	35cm/14in	mid-spr.	before opening fully the flowers are egg-shaped on sturdy stems
T. 'Schoonoord'	30cm/12in	mid-spr.	short-growing double, packed with petals
T. 'White Triumphator'	60cm/2ft	late spr.	lily-flowered, with pointed petals
PINK OR APRICOT			
T. 'Angélique'	40cm/16in	late spr.	well-shaped double of soft pink
T. 'Apricot Beauty'	40cm/16in	mid-spr.	softest apricot, shading to cream
T. 'China Pink'	60cm/2ft	late spr.	lily-flowered, with gently recurved petals of strong pink
T. 'Peer Gynt'	45cm/18in	mid-spr.	soft pink on a paler base
RED			
T. 'Couleur Cardinal'	35cm/14in	mid-spr.	purplish bloom to cardinal-red flowers
T. 'Halcro'	50cm/20in	late spr.	very sturdy, with flowers of carmine-red
T. praestans 'Fusilier'	20cm/8in	mid-spr.	3-5 scarlet-orange flowers per stem
T. 'Red Emperor'	40cm/16in	early to mid-spr.	splendid in shape and in its bright scarlet colour
T. 'Red Riding Hood'	20cm/8in	late spr.	black-centred flowers of vivid red over purple-marked leaves
MAUVE, PURPLE OR BLACK			
T. 'Blue Parrot'	60cm/2ft	late spr.	large flowers of purplish-violet but with contorted petals
T. 'Greuze'	60cm/2ft	late spr.	hearty flowers of violet-purple
T. 'Queen of Night'	75cm/2½ft	late spr.	close to a true black; sturdy
CREAM, YELLOW OR ORANGE			
T. 'Bellona'	38cm/15in	mid-spr.	rounded head of pure gold; fragrant
T. 'Concerto'	20cm/8in	early to mid-spr.	cream shading to yellow around a black base
T. 'Generaal de Wet'	35cm/14in	mid-spr.	warm orange over yellow; fragrant
T. 'West Point'	50cm/20in	late spr.	lily-flowered, with elegantly recurved petals of clear yellow
MIXED COLOURS			
T. 'Carnaval de Nice'	40cm/16in	late spr.	globular, double, white flowers streaked raspberry-red; white variegated leaves
T. 'Estella Rijnveld'	60cm/2ft	late spr.	fringed, red petals streaked white
T. 'Golden Artist'	25cm/10in	late spr.	wavy, yellow petals with a green exterior stripe
T. 'Heart's Delight'	25cm/10in	early to mid-spr.	white flowers with a carmine-red reverse and yellow base; purple-streaked leaves ·
T. 'Johann Strauss'	25cm/10in	early to mid-spr.	red reverse to white flowers with a yellow base; purple-streaked foliage
T. 'Prinses Irene'	35cm/14in	mid-spr.	vivid orange seared by a purple flame
T. 'Spring Green'	45cm/18in	late spr.	white petals with green feathering

RIGHT The most familiar gladioli in gardens are the large-flowered hybrids of South African species. In many temperate areas they need to be lifted annually before frosts damage the corms. *Gladiolus communis byzantinus*, from southern Europe and North Africa, can be left to look after itself in sunny borders and normally multiplies freely.

LEFT The alliums, members of the onion family, carry the bulb season through from spring into summer. *Allium aflatunense* flowers here with the last of the tulips. The spherical heads, packed with small flowers, look best when they seem to float over other plants; the principal disadvantage of some alliums is that foliage dies untidily during flowering.

establish good root systems before they make top growth. Of the spring-flowering bulbs, tulips do not benefit particularly from early planting, mid- to late autumn generally being considered the best time.

Snowdrops that are planted as dry bulbs often fail to establish well but planted 'in the green', that is immediately after flowering, while still in leaf, they generally settle down quickly and flower the following season. Specialist nurseries usually sell snowdrops in this state. A number of other small bulbs, including crocuses, can be moved 'in the green'.

It is a fair generalization to say that most bulbs like sun, at least during their flowering period, and a soil that is well drained. The drainage on heavy soils can be improved by incorporating grit. In the wild, bulbs are often found at surprising depths but most are best planted with a depth of soil above them that is equivalent to two or three times the height of the bulb. In lighter soils they can be planted deeper. In borders, reduce the risk of bulbs

ABOVE Tulips come in a much wider colour range than any other spring bulbs, a reflection of the intensive breeding that has been carried out over the centuries. They are well suited to finely judged colour schemes in borders. Here 'China Pink', a lily-flowered hybrid, lightens the deep tones of the new leaves of *Rheum palmatum* 'Atrosanguineum'.

LATE SPRING AND SUMMER BULBS

Unless special conditions are mentioned, all of the plants listed will succeed in sunny positions where the soil is well drained and reasonably fertile. These bulbs are suitable for permanent planting unless annual lifting is suggested.

Name	height/spread	flowering season	description
Allium aflatunense 'Purple Sensation'	90/30cm 3/1ft	late spr. to early sum.	dense sphere packed with tiny flowers of deep purplish-violet
Allium caeruleum	60/15cm 24/6in	early to mid-sum.	deep blue flowerheads, 8cm/3in wide, on wiry stems
Allium christophii	45/20cm 18/8in	early sum.	open sphere, as much as 25cm/10in across, around which radiate silvery purple stars
Allium giganteum	120/30cm 4/1ft	early sum.	tight ball, 10cm/4in wide, composed of star-shaped, purple flowers
Allium karataviense	20/20cm 8/8in	late spr. to early sum.	large balls of pale lilac flowers over broad, strap-shaped leaves
Allium oreophilum	30/10cm 12/4in	early sum.	loose heads of rose-pink flowers over linear leaves
Cardiocrinum giganteum	250/90cm 8/3ft	mid- to late sum.	a giant lily relative with a massive stem drooping creamy trumpets; fragrant
Crinum x **powellii** 'Album'	75/45cm 2½/1½ft	late sum. to early aut.	the loveliest form of a fine hybrid; strong stems carry heads of funnel-shaped, sweetly scented, white flowers over strap-shaped leaves
Galtonia candicans summer hyacinth	120/30cm 4/1ft	late sum.	green-tinged, white bells hang from a stout stem; slightly fragrant
Gladiolus communis byzantinus	60/15cm 24/6in	early sum.	stems of vivid, wine-red flowers best cooled by grey foliage nearby
Gladiolus 'Nymph'	45/15cm 18/6in	early to mid-sum.	an example of the refined, small-flowered hybrids often listed under G. x colvillei or G. nanus; white with delicate rose markings
Gladiolus 'The Bride'	45/15cm 18/6in	early to mid-sum	from the same group as 'Nymph'; pure white flowers
Lilium see page 78			
Nectaroscordum siculum bulgaricum	120/30cm 4/1ft	late spr. to early sum.	a giant of the onion tribe with loose heads of hanging flowers in an unusual combination of green, cream and purple
Nomocharis pardanthina	90/30cm 3/1ft	mid- to late sum.	choice lily relative having down-turned, pink flowers, with a purple eye and blotching on the fringed petals; for moist soils
Tigridia pavonia tiger flower	50/20cm 20/8in	mid-sum. to early aut.	flowers are a succession of gaudy beauties that last a day; 3 large petals, usually red, yellow or white, and separated by small spotted petals, radiate from a spotted cup; lift before frosts
Triteleia laxa (**Brodiaea laxa**)	45/10cm 18/4in	early sum.	heads of upward-facing, blue flowers, the petals marked with a darker blue centre line
Tulipa see page 76			

LILIES (*LILIUM*) FOR SUMMER BORDERS

Unless special conditions are mentioned, all of these lilies will succeed in sun or part-shade where the soil is well drained and reasonably fertile. Individual plants have a spread of about 30cm/12in. Stem-rooting lilies should be planted at a depth of about 20cm/8in.

Name	height	flowering season	description
SHORT-STEMMED (under 90cm/3ft)			
L. 'Apollo'	60cm/2ft	late sum.	heads of upward-facing, star-shaped flowers of soft cream, tinged pink outside
L. 'Côte d'Azur'	35cm/14in	early to mid-sum.	creamy buds open to upward-facing, pink flowers
L. 'Elvin's Son'	30cm/12in	late sum.	upward-facing, yellow flowers on short stems
L. 'Mont Blanc'	75cm/2½ft	early to mid-sum.	each stem carries 5-6 star-shaped flowers of creamy yellow
L. 'Red Carpet'	40cm/16in	mid- to late sum.	upward-facing flowers of sheeny orange-red
LONG-STEMMED (over 90cm/3ft)			
L. 'African Queen'	1.2m/4ft	mid- to late sum.	trumpets of a lovely soft orange
L. 'Black Dragon'	1.5m/5ft	mid-sum.	magnificent, fragrant, waxy trumpets, 15cm/6in wide, pure white inside and red-purple outside; stem-rooting
L. 'Bright Star'	1.2m/4ft	mid- to late sum.	creamy flowers open flat to reveal an orange star; recurved petals; stem-rooting
L. candidum madonna lily	1.5m/5ft	mid- to late sum.	botrytis-prone but sublime; up to 20 fragrant trumpets per stem, the white petals, yellow at the base, are recurved at the tip; likes sun and lime
L. 'Connecticut King'	1.2m/4ft	early to mid-sum.	bright yellow, upward-facing flowers, with a green-tinged centre, opening flat
L. 'Corsage'	90cm/3ft	mid-sum.	outward-facing flowers with recurved petals of pale pink fading to a greenish-cream centre that has conspicuous maroon spots
L. 'Enchantment'	90cm/3ft	early sum.	the upward-facing flowers are orange-red with black spots in the throat
L. 'Fire King'	90cm/3ft	mid-sum.	outward-facing flowers of fierce orange-red with purple spotting
L. 'Golden Splendour'	1.5m/5ft	mid-sum.	tall stems carry numerous richly scented trumpets of soft yellow; stem-rooting
L. 'Journey's End'	90cm/3ft	late sum.	outward-facing giant stars, the petals, with their tips turned back, are dark pink, paler at the edge; stem-rooting
L. 'Marilyn Monroe'	1.2m/4ft	mid-sum.	heads of upward-facing, star-shaped flowers of strong yellow
L. martagon turk's-cap lily	1.2m/4ft	mid-sum.	up to 50 curiously scented, turk's-cap flowers per stem, purplish-pink and heavily spotted; stem-rooting
L. martagon album	1.2m/4ft	mid-sum.	as the above but the nodding flowers are creamy and unspotted
L. monadelphum (szovitsianum)	90cm/3ft	early to mid-sum.	splendid, yellow turk's-cap lily, the fragrant, nodding flowers usually spotted purple inside; stem-rooting
L. 'Pink Perfection'	1.2m/4ft	mid-sum.	trumpet lilies of regal descent, deep pink to purple; stem-rooting
L. regale regal lily	1.5m/5ft	mid-sum.	outstanding; up to 25 fragrant trumpets per stem, white stained purple outside, the base of the throat yellow; stem-rooting
L. speciosum rubrum	1.5m/5ft	late sum. to early aut.	nodding, fragrant flowers with recurved petals of rich pink, heavily spotted and with hairy protruberances at the centres; stem-rooting and intolerant of lime
L. 'Stargazer'	1.2m/4ft	mid- to late sum.	branched stems carry several upward-facing flowers, very elegant in bud; they are stained and flecked pink on the white; richly scented; stem-rooting
L. 'Sterling Star'	90cm/3ft	mid- to late sum.	upward-facing, white stars peppered with brown spots
L. x testaceum	1.2m/4ft	mid-sum.	a very old hybrid with pale apricot flowers, the petals curved back tightly from the orange anthers; fragrant

being damaged accidentally when digging by planting bulbs deeper than usual.

The stem-rooting lilies, those that form roots above the bulb, should be planted deeply. The madonna lily (*Lilium candidum*), however, is an exception to the general rule about planting depth and should be planted with the top of the bulb just below the surface of the soil.

Bulb care & propagation

Many bulbs can be left from year to year with little more than a light annual feed and a general fertilizer in early spring. Provided the foliage is allowed to die down naturally, colonies are likely to expand as a result of natural division. If colonies become congested, they can be lifted and divided in the dormant season. Splitting off natural divisions is by far the easiest and fastest way to increase bulb stocks. It is true that many bulbs are easy to raise from seed and some, such as the regal lily (*Lilium regale*), reach flowering size remarkably quickly. It is much more common, however, for bulbs to take four or more years to flower when raised from seed.

Bedding tulips deteriorate if left in the ground from one season to the next. They are best lifted after the foliage has died and stored dry before replanting in autumn. Bulbs that are not fully hardy, such as the large-flowered hybrid gladiolus, also need lifting. I have made no attempt to include representatives of the highly bred gladioli here, largely because the range of cultivars available changes so rapidly. The sweetly scented species *Gladiolus callianthus* 'Murieliae' requires the same sort of treatment.

Bulb problems

Provided you start with healthy bulbs, you may go for many years with very few problems. Many bulbs, it is true, make a neatly packaged and appetizing meal for rodents such as squirrels, voles and mice, and these pests are not

AUTUMN BULBS

Unless annual lifting is recommended, the following can be planted permanently. Colchicums thrive in sun or part-shade but other plants listed need full sun.

Name	height/spread	flowering season	description
Amaryllis bella-donna	75/30cm 2½/1ft	early to mid-aut.	before foliage emerges stems carry 3 or 4 large, pink, sweetly scented trumpets; best at the base of a warm wall
Colchicum 'Autumn Queen'	20/15cm 8/6in	early to mid-aut.	clusters of rich purple-pink flowers with subdued chequering and a white throat
Colchicum 'Lilac Wonder'	20/15cm 8/6in	early to mid-aut.	lightly chequered flowers of rosy violet teetering on slender stems
Colchicum speciosum	20/15cm 8/6in	early to mid-aut.	purplish-pink goblets, often with a white throat
Crocus kotschyanus kotschyanus (C. zonatus)	8/5cm 3/2in	early to mid-aut.	bright orange spots mark the inner base of lilac petals
Crocus speciosus	13/5cm 5/2in	mid-aut.	yellow anthers and scarlet stigmas brighten lilac-blue flowers, often darkly veined; all forms are worth growing
Cyclamen hederifolium	10/10cm 4/4cm	late sum. to late aut.	little shuttlecocks in shades of magenta or pink and even lovelier in white, poised over silvered leaves, themselves a feature to late spring
Gladiolus callianthus 'Murieliae' **(Acidanthera bicolor murieliae)**	90/20cm 36/8in	early to mid-aut.	white flowers, blotched maroon at the centre and exhaling a scent of refined sweetness, arch elegantly from stiff stems; lift before frosts
Leucojum autumnale autumn snowflake	25/10cm 10/4in	late sum. to early aut.	small, white flowers dangle from slender, wiry stems
Nerine bowdenii 'Mark Fenwick'	75/15cm 30/6in	early to late aut.	heads of long-lasting, glistening pink, spidery flowers appear just before strap-like leaves develop; best at the base of a warm wall
Sternbergia lutea	15/10cm 6/4in	early to mid-aut.	crocus-like, yellow flowers with a satiny sheen; best at the base of a warm wall

ABOVE There is a strong family resemblance among many of the colchicums. Like *Colchicum speciosum*, most grown in gardens flower in the autumn while still leafless and their colour range is limited to mauve, pink and purple (in these shades sometimes chequered) or white. The colchicums deserve to be more widely used as an inter-planting among shrubs.

Although easily grown, there is nothing common about the regal lily (*Lilium regale*). In mid-summer its magnificent, fragrant trumpets can transform a pedestrian plot into a border of distinction. In the usual form the exterior is flushed purple. No less beautiful are the white forms of the Album Group, with no exterior purple stain.

easily discouraged. Some gardeners report that bulbs are left alone if moth balls are planted among them. Making a barrier of wire netting just below the surface of a bed is worth considering if you are planting unusual bulbs.

Of other pests the most troublesome are slugs, some attacking the bulbs themselves (lilies on heavy soil are particularly prone to damage), others demolishing the buds of early bulbs such as crocuses and dwarf irises. Planting lilies in grit gives some protection as does a mulch of sharp gravel around dwarf bulbs and these measures may be more acceptable than chemical controls in the form of slug pellets.

Aphids are sap suckers which may in themselves cause considerable damage to plants, but this is compounded by their unpleasant way of passing on viral diseases, for which there is no effective treatment. Lilies are particularly prone to these diseases; plants stunted by them should be lifted and burned.

Of other diseases the most crippling is botrytis, species of fungus that show initially as spotting or mottling on foliage and stems. The beautiful madonna lily is regrettably one of its favourite victims. The disease can spread quickly but spraying early with a fungicide, such as one containing benomyl, will usually control it.

Quick changes

There are several categories of plants that lend themselves to short-term planting schemes, such as the sequence of bedding that is still sometimes featured on a grand scale in large public gardens. Although expensive in terms of plants and labour, it can be very impressive when carried out with style. Bold bedding schemes of this type can be adapted to smaller gardens although caution is needed. Uniform bedding plants with massive flowerheads of vibrant colour look fine as a distant regiment but are much less appealing close to. A freer grouping of short-lived plants that have been arranged by height and colour makes a lovely regular feature in a garden and can be an extremely successful way of filling beds and borders while waiting for other schemes to mature or in an interval before a permanent scheme is implemented.

The shortest lived of suitable plants are annuals, which complete their whole life-cycle in a single growing season. They are classified as hardy or half-hardy. In most cool temperate regions hardy annuals can be sown in spring, or even in the early autumn of the preceding season, directly where they are to flower. It is usually not safe to plant half-hardy annuals outdoors until late spring or early summer. Some plants grown as half-hardy annuals are actually half-hardy perennials that flower freely in their first season. Of the biennials, plants that take two growing seasons to complete their life-cycle, wallflowers are the best known. These plants are often used most successfully with bulbs such as tulips (see page 76), that are lifted after their flowering has finished.

Many of the plants that are listed later in the book as being suitable for patios and terraces (see especially pages 146-53) can be added to the suggestions given in this section.

The opium poppy (*Papaver somniferum*) self-seeds so freely that it can be a nuisance but few nuisances are dressed with such imperial splendour. The seedheads themselves are attractive and distinctive in shape, with the result that they are often left until after the copious seed has been spilt. In fact, unwanted plants are easily weeded out.

Easy Plants from Seed

These hardy annuals need a sunny position and will thrive in ordinary, even poor soils. The various cultivars available provide a range of heights. To extend their season, make a succession of sowings and deadhead regularly.

Name	height/spread	flowering season	description
Calendula officinalis pot marigold	60/35cm 24/14in	late spr. to early aut.	bushy plants covered with cheerful daisy flowers in yellow or orange
Centaurea cyanus cornflower	75/30cm 2½/1ft	early sum. to early aut.	the classic cornflower, fringed with flowers of intense blue, has versions in pink and white
Chrysanthemum carinatum	60/30cm 2/1ft	early sum. to early aut.	single flowers with a purple disc surrounded by petals that are strikingly banded; good colour range other than blue
Clarkia elegans	60/30cm 2/1ft	mid-sum. to early aut.	stems clustered with double flowers in shades of pink and purple or in white
Nigella damascena love-in-a-mist	60/20cm 24/8in	mid- to late sum.	beautiful for the blue or white flowers and balloon-like, purplish seed pods, all with thread-like mountings
Papaver rhoeas Shirley Series	60/30cm 2/1ft	early to late sum.	single and double flowers of nonchalant charm in shades of red and pink or in white
Papaver somniferum opium poppy	75/30cm 2½/1ft	early to mid-sum.	large, single or double flowers, pink, purple or white, over grey-green leaves
Salvia viridis (S. horminum)	45/20cm 18/8in	early sum. to early aut.	the pink or purple flowers count for less than the showy bracts in shades of blue and pink or in white
Silene coeli-rosa	45/15cm 18/6in	early to late sum.	an airy show of pretty 'viscaria' flowers with notched petals in pinks, blues and white
Tropaeolum majus Whirlybird Series nasturtium	30/45cm 12/18in	mid-sum. to early aut.	compact nasturtium with spurred flowers in a good range of colours, excluding blues, over nearly circular leaves

Buying plants

For a near-instant effect garden-ready summer bedding plants can be bought in spring. One great advantage of buying plants rather than sowing seed is that separate colours are available of some selections which as seed can only be bought mixed. For planting a large area, bedding strips provide a cheaper option than individually potted plants.

Half-hardy plants often become available long before all risk of frost is past. If you buy early, continue hardening off until it is appropriate to plant out. Always look for sturdy, compact growth and healthy foliage.

FOLIAGE FILLERS

The following, mainly fast-growing plants for short-term schemes include some that are half-hardy and tender. These need to be started into growth under glass and those to be kept for more than one season need protection from frost.

Name	height/spread	grown as	description
Beta vulgaris 'Rhubarb Beet' ruby chard	60/25cm 24/10in	biennial	very ornamental edible vegetable with vivid red stalks and reddish-green leaves
Brassica oleracea ornamental cabbage	40/45cm 16/18in	hardy annual	large, flower-like heads of thick and often crinkly, green leaves with dashing pink, red or white centres and markings
Canna 'Lucifer'	120/45cm 4/1½ft	tender perennial	hybrid cannas need heat to flower well but their broad leaves, purplish in this example, are highly ornamental; lift rhizomes before frosts
Coleus blumei Wizard Series	30/25cm 12/10in	tender annual	serrated and fringed leaves of variable shape and with vivid colour mixtures, including red, cream and bronze; flowers are best removed
Eucalyptus globulus gum	1.5/1.2m 5/4ft	half-hardy shrub	fast-growing tree with silver-blue young foliage; as a shrub it can be raised annually from seed
Helichrysum petiolare	45/150cm 1½/5ft	half-hardy annual	fast-growing, trailing stems insinuate felted, grey-green leaves among other plants
Kochia scoparia trichophylla burning bush	90/60cm 3/2ft	half-hardy annual	bushy plants with dense cover of narrow, pale green leaves turning deep red in autumn
Lunaria annua variegata	75/30cm 2½/1ft	biennial	coarsely toothed, heart-shaped leaves with lovely white variegation; heads of crimson honesty flowers in spring followed by seed discs
Melianthus major	150/90cm 5/3ft	half-hardy perennial	handsomely jagged, blue-grey leaves; worth lifting annually before frosts
Plecostachys serpyllifolia (Helichrysum microphyllum)	30/90cm 1/3ft	half-hardy perennial	fast growing with trailing stems densely clothed in small leaves, felted grey
Ricinus communis castor-oil plant	150/90cm 5/3ft	half-hardy annual	open shrub; fingered, mid-green leaves up to 30cm/12in across
Ricinus communis 'Impala'	120/90cm 4/3ft	half-hardy annual	in this form of the castor-oil plant the leaves are deep purple or bronze
Senecio maritima 'Silver Dust'	30/30cm 12/12in	half-hardy annual	silver, filigree foliage associating well with all colours
Silybum marianum	90/60cm 3/2ft	biennial	thistle grown for the spectacular white marbling of its spiny leaves
Smyrnium perfoliatum	75/60cm 2½/2ft	biennial	yellow-green leaves encircle the stems; tiny, matching flowers are borne in summer
Zea mays ornamental maize	150/60cm 5/2ft	half-hardy annual	a stout stem carries strap-shaped leaves, variegated pink, cream and white; silky flower tassels followed by cobs

The white pattern wandering over the bright green leaves of the milk thistle (*Silybum marianum*) makes it one of the most eye-catching of variegated plants. It is a biennial, seed of the previous year germinating in spring to produce plants that flower the following summer. Here it makes a cosy partnership with chives.

SHORT-TERM WINTER AND SPRING SCHEMES

All of these plants succeed in sun where the soil is well drained and reasonably fertile. Although mainly short-lived perennials, they are usually treated as biennials.

Name	height/spread	flowering season	description
Bellis perennis 'Pomponette' common daisy	10/15cm 4/6in	early spr. to early sum.	neat, button-like, double daisies in red, pink or white over a dense clump of leaves
Erysimum (Cheiranthus) cheiri 'Fire King' wallflower	45/30cm 18/12in	mid-spr. to early sum.	tall example with flowerheads of intense brick-red; fragrant
Erysimum (Cheiranthus) cheiri Tom Thumb Series	20/15cm 8/6in	mid-spr. to early sum.	dwarf strain of wallflowers with the colour range and fragrance of the taller kinds
Erysimum hieraciifolium 'Orange Bedder' Siberian wallflower	30/30cm 12/12in	mid-spr. to mid-sum.	masses of fragrant, warming orange flowers of typical wallflower simplicity
Myosotis 'Blue Ball' forget-me-not	20/20cm 8/8in	mid-spr. to early sum.	compact with sprays of deep blue flowers; full sun or part-shade
Primula Barnhaven Strain polyanthus	20/20cm 8/8in	late win. to late spr.	an outstanding range with flowers of moderate size; superb colour choice includes gold-laced
Primula Pacific Series polyanthus	23/20cm 9/8in	late win. to late spr.	large-flowered but unsophisticated colours
Viola x wittrockiana Universal Series winter-flowering pansy	20/20cm 8/8in	mid-win. to early sum.	remarkably resistant to bad weather; single pansy colours and combinations

Several salvias, members of the sage family, that are currently enjoying a vogue are tender perennials. Two robust plants that have long been in cultivation are valuable for the way the bracts surrounding their flowers extend their ornamental season. Clary (*Salvia viridis*) is a colourful annual, while the tall *S. sclarea turkestanica*, illustrated here, is biennial.

The more familiar bedding plants can also be bought as seedlings or plugs (rooted individually in compost with high levels of fertilizer), either mail order from seed suppliers or direct from garden centres. These are much less expensive than garden-ready plants but seedlings have to be pricked out and they and the plugs need to be kept frost-free and hardened off before planting out.

Raising plants from seed

Hardy annuals are the most confidence-boosting of all plants to grow from seed. Reasonably good results can be achieved with some plants using seed harvested in the garden but in general it is best to start with named seed from a reputable supplier. Many hardy annuals flower best when grown in rather spartan conditions; on a rich diet they tend to produce leaf at the expense of flowers.

To ensure even germination, it is important that the plot is raked over and worked so that the surface layer becomes a fine crumbly tilth. Seed can be scattered evenly and then lightly raked into the surface before this is firmed with the flat side of the rake. Alternatively, sow seed in shallow grooves or drills, not more than 1cm/½in deep, marked out with a hoe. This method can make weeding easier. Do not sow thickly and thin plants after germination.

Sow biennials in tidy rows in a well-prepared nursery bed during late spring or early summer. Thin as necessary and keep plants weeded during the summer months before carefully lifting and planting in early autumn in the position where they are to flower.

Half-hardy plants should be sown thinly in pots or trays of a proprietary seed compost in late winter or spring. Placing pots or trays in a heated propagator will keep them at a uniform temperature and humidity but you can create similar conditions by covering the pot or tray with a polythene bag and then placing the container in a warm part of the house. As soon as seedlings begin to break the surface, place the pot or tray in full light. Early transplanting (pricking out) into a potting compost with more generous spacing gives seedlings the best

Tall Summer-flowering Annuals and Biennials

Unless special conditions are mentioned, all of the plants listed will succeed in sunny positions where the soil is well drained and reasonably fertile. There can be considerable variation in height and flowering period, depending on the time seed is sown and growing conditions. The main season for the following plants is from mid-summer to early autumn.

Name	height/spread	category	description
Alcea rosea hollyhock	270/45cm 9/1½ft	biennial or annual	tall spires, clustered with single or congested double flowers in a wide range of colours, excluding blue, over coarse leaves
Amaranthus caudatus love-lies-bleeding	120/45cm 4/1½ft	half-hardy annual	bushy plants dangle numerous tassels, 45cm/18in long, of crimson flowers; in 'Viridis' the tassels are green
Cleome hassleriana (C. spinosa) spider plant	120/45cm 4/1½ft	half-hardy annual	curious heads of scented flowers with protruding stamens; mainly white and pink but also in darker shades
Dahlia 'Evening Mail'	120/90cm 4/3ft	tuber lifted annually	example of a yellow, semi-cactus-flowered dahlia with large, double blooms
Digitalis purpurea albiflora	120/30cm 4/1ft	biennial	very beautiful, white-flowered form of the common foxglove
Digitalis purpurea Excelsior Hybrids	150/30cm 5/1ft	biennial	unlike the common foxglove, the spires, which are cream, pink and purple, cluster all round the stems and stand out horizontally
Eryngium giganteum	120/60cm 4/2ft	biennial	attractively jagged, thistly plant with silver-blue flowerheads all summer
Helianthus annuus sunflower	30m/30cm 10/1ft	hardy annual	giants with flowers 30cm/12in or so across; yellow petals circle dark-coloured discs; different heights available
Nicotiana langsdorfii	120/30cm 4/1ft	half-hardy annual	tube-like flowers that open into a small bell are curious for their shape and green colour
Nicotiana sylvestris	120/45cm 4/1½ft	half-hardy annual	sturdy stems carry large leaves and spires of fragrant, white, trumpet flowers
Onopordum giganteum cotton or Scotch thistle	180/75cm 6/2½ft	biennial	superbly structured, silver-grey thistle which is beautiful all summer; purplish-pink flowers
Salvia sclarea turkestanica	120/30cm 4/1ft	biennial	clustered spires of white and mauve flowers with long-lasting purplish bracts stand stiffly above aromatic foliage

MEDIUM-HEIGHT ANNUALS AND BIENNIALS FOR SUMMER

The following plants flower over a long summer season, especially if deadheaded regularly. Unless otherwise stated, they thrive in sunny positions where the soil is well drained and reasonably fertile.

Name	height/spread	description
GROWN AS HARDY ANNUALS		
Coreopsis tinctoria 'Golden Crown'	60/25cm 24/10in	the daisy-like flowers, with notched petals, are rich yellow with a reddish-brown centre
Lavatera trimestris	60/45cm 2/1½ft	shallow trumpet flowers in veined pink ('Silver Cup') or dazzling white ('Mont Blanc')
Rudbeckia hirta 'Goldilocks' black-eyed susan	60/30cm 2/1ft	double or semi-double example, with orange-yellow petals surrounding a mahogany knob
GROWN AS HALF-HARDY ANNUALS		
Antirrhinum majus 'Trumpet Serenade' snapdragon	30/15cm 12/6in	from a wide range of sizes and flower shapes; compact with spikes of trumpet-shaped flowers, frilled at the mouth, in pastel shades
Callistephus chinensis Andrella Series China aster	60/30cm 2/1ft	single and double flowers in a range of heights; this is single, with many narrow petals around a yellow disc; colours include blue, purple, red, pink and white
Dahlia 'Redskin'	30/30cm 12/12in	moisture-loving; semi-double flowers in lilac or pink as well as warm colours over bronzy foliage
Eschscholzia californica Californian poppy	30/15cm 12/6in	bright, velvety flowers, mainly orange, yellow or cream, over ferny foliage
Malope trifida	90/30cm 3/1ft	flared, purplish-red flowers, prominently veined, in summer and early autumn
Nicotiana alata 'Lime Green'	75/30cm 2½/1ft	version of the tobacco plant (see next entry) with green flowers; grow in sun or light shade
Nicotiana alata Sensation Series tobacco plant	90/30cm 3/1ft	scented, tubular flowers, starry at the mouth, in red, pink, white or cream; grow in sun or light shade
Petunia Resisto Series	25/30cm 10/12in	rain-resistant petunias with single, flared trumpets in a wide range of colours
Salpiglossis sinuata 'Splash'	50/30cm 20/12in	trumpet flowers, conspicuously veined, in a good, multi-coloured range
Salvia farinacea 'Victoria'	45/30cm 18/12in	spikes of small, tubular flowers that are felted and violet-blue, like the stem
Salvia patens	60/30cm 2/1ft	lipped flowers of invaluable blueness; 'Royal Blue' is of gentian intensity, 'Cambridge Blue' paler
Tagetes 'Crackerjack' African marigold	60/30cm 2/1ft	mophead with double flowers in shades of yellow and orange over aromatic, dark green leaves
Tagetes patula 'Naughty Marietta' French marigold	30/25cm 12/10in	aromatic foliage and single, yellow flowers with a maroon, star-like marking; one of many, although most are more dwarf
Zinnia Ruffles Series	60/30cm 2/1ft	sturdy, upright example with packed double flowers in a colour range including pinks, reds and yellows
GROWN AS BIENNIALS		
Matthiola Brompton Series	45/30cm 18/12in	spikes of single or double, fragrant flowers in shades of pink, red, purple, yellow and in white
Papaver nudicaule Iceland poppy	60/30cm 2/1ft	various strains, some shorter, all with hairy stems; fragrant, tissue-paper flowers in pastel or bright colours, especially orange and yellow

chance of making strong, healthy plants. After pricking out keep pots or trays in a warm and well-lit position and water as necessary. Plants need to be acclimatized over several weeks to conditions outdoors. Harden them off in a cold frame or under a cloche, polytunnel or improvised plastic cover, gradually increasing the level of ventilation.

General care

Vigorous plants that have been given a good start require relatively little maintenance during their growing season. Keep weeds down but only water during prolonged periods of drought. Do not feed hardy annuals but give a light application of a general-purpose liquid fertilizer to bedding plants in mid-season and to biennials just as they are coming into flower.

Medium-sized to tall annuals can be knocked about by wind. Individual staking may be necessary for tall plants such as hollyhocks (*Alcea rosea*) but a better solution for most is to put in pea sticks (twiggy trimmings of trees such as hazel) while plants are young. The flowering season of many plants can be extended by deadheading but in a large-scale planting this may not be practicable. To fill gaps caused by failures in bedding schemes it is always worth having a few reserve plants in a spare corner.

As with all plants, the seedling stage can be critical, those raised under glass being particularly vulnerable to damping off, which causes plants to collapse and rot. Once the soil-borne diseases that are the cause have attacked, the situation is irretrievable, but good hygiene, the use of a sterilized compost and the occasional application of a fungicide will usually prevent the problem arising.

Birds can do a lot of damage to seedlings. A web of black thread criss-crossed between sticks just above ground level is still probably the best defence. You may feel that chemical measures are the only way of defeating the secretive thuggery of snails and slugs. In general, however, you need to take a relaxed view of the damage caused by pests and diseases to mature specimens of plants that have a short life.

The usefulness of annuals and biennials as fillers in mixed borders often goes unrecognized. They are particularly valuable in the early stages of a garden's development but can also be used as a regular feature in established borders. The veined flowers of *Malope trifida*, a hardy annual, are produced over a long season in summer and autumn.

LOW PLANTS FOR SUMMER BEDS AND BORDERS

Unless special conditions are mentioned, all of the plants listed will succeed in sunny positions where the soil is well drained and reasonably fertile. In general, they will flower over a long period, especially if regularly deadheaded.

Name	height/spread	description
GROWN AS HARDY ANNUALS		
Dianthus chinensis Baby Doll Series	15/25cm 6/10in	numerous fringed flowers, often boldly zoned, usually in shades of red or pink
Iberis umbellata Fairy Series candytuft	20/25cm 8/10in	bushy plants smothered by dense heads of tiny, red, pink, purple or white flowers
Limnanthes douglasii poached-egg flower	15/20cm 6/8in	masses of sweetly scented, white flowers with an orange-yellow centre; attractive to bees
Lobularia maritima 'Little Dorrit' sweet alyssum	15/30cm 6/12in	profusion of dense, rounded heads of sweetly scented, white flowers
GROWN AS HALF-HARDY ANNUALS		
Ageratum houstonianum 'Blue Danube'	15/15cm 6/6in	compact example with dense heads of whiskery, lavender-blue flowers on low hummocks
Dorotheanthus bellidiformis Livingstone daisy	15/25cm 6/10in	bright daisy flowers, in shades of pink, red, yellow or white, need sunshine to open
Impatiens Accent Series	15/20cm 6/8in	brims with flowers of vibrant colours; for moist soils and good in semi-shade
Lobelia erinus 'Crystal Palace'	15/20cm 6/8in	compact example with an unflagging show of small, dark blue flowers over bronze foliage
Mimulus Malibu Series	15/25cm 6/10in	prettily flared, tubular flowers, mainly in vivid yellow, orange or red; for moist soils
Nemesia strumosa Triumph Series	20/15cm 8/6in	bushy plants smothered with little funnel-shaped flowers in a range of bright colours
Phlox drummondii Twinkle Series	15/10cm 6/4in	compact with clusters of star-shaped flowers in brilliant colours, often with contrasting centres
Tagetes 'Lemon Gem'	15/15cm 6/6in	neat plant with aromatic, finely divided leaves and small, single flowers of pale yellow
Tagetes 'Paprika'	15/25cm 6/10in	aromatic hummocks of ferny leaves studded with yellow-centred, coppery, single flowers
Viola Clear Crystals Series pansy	20/20cm 8/8in	example of medium-sized pansies in a good range of clear colours; also grown as a biennial
Viola 'Prince Henry' viola	15/20cm 6/8in	velvety flowers of rich violet-purple with a gold eye and throat; less beefy than the pansy; also grown as a biennial
Viola 'Super Chalon Giants' pansy	20/20cm 8/8in	large, bicoloured flowers with ruffled petals; also grown as a biennial

Special Conditions

In the next world, perhaps, we will all be gardening in a sunny, open but sheltered site where the soil is a fertile, crumbly loam that is moisture-retentive but also well drained. Rebellious spirits among the most talented of gardeners will probably be impatient with the uniformity of this ideal, however, and petition for more extreme conditions. For, while it is true that these do impose limitations and problems, often quite severe, they also provide challenges which when taken up can produce gardens of superlative quality.

Almost all growing conditions can be modified to some extent to broaden the range of plants that can be grown, especially by generous applications of well-rotted organic material and the provision of shelter. Successful gardening, however, depends on recognizing the underlying nature of the growing conditions available and choosing plants that relish or at least tolerate them. There are so many plants to choose from that even unpromisingly dry or chalky soils, for example, can be planted in an interesting way.

Lavenders (*Lavandula*) are among the many shrubs from the Mediterranean region that do well in full sun where the soil is free draining. One of the most distinctive is *L. stoechas pendunculata*, with flower spikes topped by showy purple flags. Its flowering season coincides, as in this garden, with the orange-red *Tulipa sprengeri*, crimson *Gladiolus communis byzantinus* and purple-mauve alliums. In the background is the large, drought-tolerant perennial *Phlomis russeliana*, with whorls of hooded yellow flowers.

Shady gardens

Every garden has areas that are shaded for all or part of the day. Often, the shade is the hard-edged shadow cast by the house or by walls, fences and other architectural features, including pergolas and arches, or even that of planted features such as a formal hedge. The areas such shadows cover change through the day and also through the year as the sun moves. For instance, a border that might be barely touched by the shadow of a nearby wall or hedge in summer when the sun is high, may lie all winter in its sombre gloom.

The shade cast by trees or shrubs can be rather different. The amount of light that penetrates the canopy depends on the foliage and branching pattern of the tree. Some evergreens, such as yew (*Taxus*), cast very deep and more or less permanent shade. In full leaf, some deciduous trees cast only dappled shade or their growth is sufficiently narrow and upright for some light to get to the base of the tree but others, especially beech (*Fagus*), cast very deep shade. When deciduous trees are out of leaf, their branching system casts only light shade allowing plants that flower early in the season, many spring bulbs in particular, to flourish beneath them. Among the bulbs that are given in the charts on pages 36 and 135 there are many that can make a supremely beautiful underplanting beneath deciduous trees.

Creating borders in shade

Gardeners are sometimes heard lamenting the fact that so much of their garden is shady, the implication being that there is no way of planting it attractively. The simple truth, however, is that shade-loving and shade-tolerant plants are so numerous and include such a range of beauties that there is no difficulty in creating a superb garden for the

Areas of dry shade at the base of walls or in rooty ground under trees are notoriously difficult to plant. However, a few plants really thrive in these unpromising conditions. *Pachysandra terminalis* spreads freely and its notched leaves, which look sickly in full sun, are a good glossy green. The attractive cream-and-green P. *terminalis* 'Variegata' is much less vigorous.

PLANTS FOR DRY SHADE

All of these plants tolerate dry shade to some degree but perform better when humus is added to the soil.

Name	height/spread	flowering season	description
HERBACEOUS PERENNIALS, FERNS AND BULBS			
Bergenia 'Ballawley'	60/60cm 2/2ft	mid- to late spr.	large-leaved, evergreen perennial with vivid crimson flowers
Cyclamen hederifolium	10/15cm 4/6in	late sum. to late aut.	tough but choice tuber; shuttlecock flowers in white, pink or magenta; variegated leaves until late spring
Dryopteris filix-mas male fern	90/90cm 3/3ft	none	an obliging fern that will grow almost anywhere
Euphorbia amygdaloides robbiae	60/60cm 2/2ft	mid-spr. to mid-sum.	perennial with rosettes of evergreen leaves; yellow-green flowerheads
Geranium phaeum mourning widow	60/45cm 2/1½ft	late spr.	perennial with sombre, purple flowers; in 'Album' they are white
Helleborus foetidus stinking hellebore	60/60cm 2/2ft	mid-win. to early spr.	perennial; very dark, handsomely cut, evergreen leaves; clusters of green cups edged maroon
Iris foetidissima gladwyn, stinking iris	60/30cm 2/1ft	early sum.	evergreen perennial; insignificant flowers but brilliant orange seeds
Lamium galeobdolon 'Silberteppich'	25/180cm 10in/6ft	late spr. to early sum.	vigorous, spreading perennial; green-veined, silvery leaves; yellow flowers
Polygonatum x hybridum Solomon's seal	90/30cm 3/1ft	late spr.	rhizomatous perennial with graceful arching stems from which dangle clusters of greenish-white flowers
SHRUBS AND CLIMBERS			
Aucuba japonica spotted laurel	3/1.5m 10/5ft	early to mid-spr.	evergreen shrub; large- and plain-leaved forms include 'Crassifolia' (male) and 'Hillieri' (female), which has red berries
Hedera helix common ivy	300/90cm 10/3ft	mid-aut.	many cultivars (see page 21); plain-leaved forms are the most suitable for dry shade
Hypericum calycinum rose of Sharon	45/90cm 1½/3ft	early sum. to early aut.	evergreen shrub with an indefinite spread; golden flowers with a boss of stamens
Mahonia aquifolium Oregon grape	1.2/1.5m 4/5ft	early to mid-spr.	suckering shrub; glossy, spiny foliage; clotted heads of fragrant, yellow flowers; blue-black berries
Pachysandra terminalis	30/45cm 12/18in	mid-spr.	shrub for lime-free soils; fragrant, but insignificant flowers; evergreen foliage makes invaluable cover
Prunus lusitanica Portugal laurel	4.5/4.5m 15/15ft	early spr.	shrub; glossy, dark green leaves on red stems; scented, white flowers
Pyracantha 'Soleil d'Or'	2.5/2.2m 8/7ft	early sum.	thorny evergreen shrub with golden berries that persist through winter
Ruscus aculeatus butcher's broom	90/90cm 3/3ft	early to mid-spr.	shrub; clustered stems bear spiny, leaf-like growths; inconspicuous flowers; sealing-wax red berries
Sarcococca hookeriana humilis	75/75cm 2½/2½ft	late win.	hummocky evergreen shrub; dark leaves and tiny, fragrant flowers
Vinca minor periwinkle	10/90cm 4/36in	early spr. to early sum.	evergreen; blue or white flowers; several cultivars available

whole year even where little direct sunlight penetrates to the garden's floor.

True, some sites are more difficult than others. There is a general consensus that for areas of dry shade, for example a shadowed area where little rain penetrates and where the ground is thick with hungry and thirsty tree roots, the range of plants that will thrive is relatively small. But even for such an unpromising site, plants can be found, including some of considerable distinction, as the chart on page 89 shows.

The use of ground cover has already been suggested as one way of planting areas in shade (see page 41). Another approach, which involves the creation of a woodland effect, is outlined on pages 130-5.

Borders are perfectly feasible in shade. They can be established at the base of a wall by planting shade-tolerant climbers and shrubs such as those listed on page 14, perhaps with the addition of the climbing creamy white rose 'Madame Alfred Carrière', one of several roses that will perform well even when not in full

sun. A border can even be created on the shady side of a hedge, the dense dark green of yew (*Taxus*) showing off to superb effect white flowers such as the Japanese anemone, *Anemone x hybrida* 'Honorine Jobert'.

Some of the loveliest borders combine sunny and shaded areas. Very often such a border accommodates an existing small tree or large shrub. If you are starting from scratch and want a tree to feature in a border it might be worth considering one of those that cast light shade, as described on page 33.

WINTER- AND SPRING-FLOWERING SHRUBS FOR SHADE

All of these shrubs can be grown in partial shade, for example in dappled light under trees or where buildings create shadow for much of the day. Many also flourish in full sun. For rhododendrons, see page 132.

Name	height/spread	flowering season	description
DECIDUOUS			
Corylopsis pauciflora	1.8/3m 6/10ft	early spr.	twiggy bush with primrose-yellow flowers; for lime-free soil
Daphne genkwa	90/60cm 3/2ft	mid- to late spr.	slender bush; clusters of lavender-blue flowers with little scent
Kerria japonica 'Variegata'	90/90cm 3/3ft	mid- to late spr.	twiggy plant; white-edged, grey-green leaves; orange-yellow flowers
Lonicera x purpusii	1.8/1.8m 6/6ft	mid-win. to early spr.	the best winter-flowering shrubby honeysuckle; bewitchingly fragrant
Ribes odoratum	1.8/1.8m 6/6ft	mid- to late spr.	clusters of tubular, golden flowers, sweetly fragrant, followed by purple fruits; foliage colours well in autumn
Rubus 'Benenden'	2.5/3m 8/10ft	late spr. to early sum.	arching, thornless stems carry single, rose-like, white flowers
Weigela middendorffiana	1.2/1.2m 4/4ft	mid- to late spr.	clusters of pouch-shaped, yellow flowers, spotted orange in the throat
EVERGREEN			
Berberis x stenophylla 'Corallina Compacta'	30/30cm 12/12in	late spr.	spiny, neat shrub; many yellow flowers open from orange-red buds
Daphne pontica	90/150cm 3/5ft	mid- to late spr.	unshowy yellow-green flowers and glossy leaves; tantalizing scent
Osmanthus x burkwoodii	2.2/1.8m 7/6ft	mid- to late spr.	scented, white flowers; dark green, glossy leaves; useful as a hedge
Osmanthus delavayi	1.8/1.8m 6/6ft	mid-spr.	glossy leaves; clusters of tubular, fragrant, white flowers
Sarcococca hookeriana digyna	75/75cm 2½/2½ft	mid- to late win.	suckering shrub with dense, bright green foliage; tiny, inconspicuous but fragrant white flowers in winter
Viburnum tinus 'Gwenllian'	3/3m 10/10ft	late aut. to late spr.	free-fruiting so the light blue berries may be seen with the reddish buds and pink-tinged flowers
Vinca minor 'La Grave'	20/90cm 8/36in	early spr.	small-leaved form with numerous large, pale blue flowers

SUMMER- AND AUTUMN-FLOWERING SHRUBS FOR SHADE

All of the following shrubs can be grown in partial shade, for example in dappled light under trees or where buildings create shadow for much of the day. Many also flourish in full sun.

Name	height/spread	flowering season	description
DECIDUOUS			
Hydrangea arborescens 'Grandiflora'	1.5/1.5m 5/5ft	mid-sum. to early aut.	stems weighed down by heads of pure white, sterile flowers
Hydrangea aspera sargentiana	2.5/1.8m 8/6ft	late sum. to mid-aut.	large, bristly leaves; flat heads of small, mauve flowers ringed by large, white flowers that turn pink
Hydrangea aspera Villosa Group	2.5/3.7m 8/12ft	late sum.	velvety leaves and heads, up to 30cm/12in across, of blue fertile flowers surrounded by pale lilac florets
Hydrangea paniculata 'Brussels Lace'	2.5/1.8m 8/6ft	late sum. to early aut.	impressive pyramid heads of white flowers; best on lime-free soil
Hydrangea serrata 'Bluebird'	1.2/1.2m 4/4ft	mid- to late sum.	free-flowering lacecap; heads of violet-blue fertile flowers and pale pink or blue florets; will not produce a good blue on alkaline soil
Ligustrum japonicum 'Macrophyllum'	2.2/1.8m 7/6ft	late sum.	heads of small, white flowers show up well against handsome, evergreen foliage
Philadelphus 'Manteau d'Hermine' mock orange	90/150cm 3/5ft	early to mid-sum	compact example with long-lasting, fragrant, creamy white double flowers
Weigela 'Bristol Ruby'	2.5/1.8m 8/6ft	late spr. to early sum.	one of several good hybrids; upright growth and rich crimson flowers
EVERGREEN			
Desfontainia spinosa	1.8/1.8m 6/6ft	mid-sum. to mid-aut.	tubular, red flowers stand out against glossy, holly-like leaves
Rubus tricolor	60/180cm 2/6ft	mid-sum.	cup-shaped, white flowers on a plant covered with red bristles; edible red fruit

FOLIAGE SHRUBS FOR SHADE

All of the following shrubs, which are valued chiefly for their foliage, can be grown in partial shade, for example in dappled light under trees or where buildings create shadow for much of the day. Many also flourish in full sun. For rhododendrons and acers, see page 132.

Name	height/spread	description
EVERGREEN		
Buxus sempervirens 'Argenteovariegata' box	1.8/1.2m 6/4ft	one of several with brightening variegation; the dark, glossy leaves with a creamy edge show well in shade
Daphne laureola spurge laurel	90/120cm 3/4ft	attractively glossy, dark green foliage; green-yellow flowers in late winter
Fatsia japonica	3/2.5m 10/8ft	fingered, glossy leaves; clusters of cream flowers in autumn; black fruits
Hedera helix 'Erecta' ivy	90/120cm 3/4ft	non-climbing form of ivy with upright stems neatly clothed with dark leaves; 'Congesta' is similar but 45cm/18in tall
Ilex aquifolium 'Ferox Argentea' silver hedgehog holly	6/4m 20/13ft	male (non-fruiting) holly, which is very slow to reach its ultimate height; the cream-edged leaves are spiny over the whole surface
Ilex crenata 'Golden Gem'	75/60cm 2½/2ft	gold-suffused, small leaves with scalloped edge and no spines; female but flowers irregularly
Prunus laurocerasus 'Otto Luyken' cherry laurel	90/150cm 3/5ft	low, bushy laurel with glossy leaves; spikes of white flowers in late spring are followed by black fruit
Rhamnus alaternus 'Argenteovariegatus' Italian buckthorn	1.8/1.5m 6/5ft	beautiful variegation with grey marbling and irregular creamy margin; in cool regions the crops of black berries are uncertain; for a sheltered position
DECIDUOUS		
Sambucus racemosa 'Plumosa Aurea'	2.5/2.5m 8/8ft	the golden, finely cut leaves may scorch in full sun; lime-green in shade
Weigela 'Looymansii Aurea'	2.5/1.8m 8/6ft	the foliage is golden-green in sun, lime-green in shade; pink flowers in late spring and early summer

Good foliage plants are particularly valuable in the shady garden. The evergreen *Fatsia japonica*, sometimes known as the Japanese aralia, has hand-shaped leaves of glossy green. Clusters of white flowers in autumn are followed by dark fruits. Here its blue-toned companion is the handsome *Hosta sieboldiana elegans*, with large, quilted leaves.

Most hydrangeas do well in light shade where the soil is reasonably moist. The popularity of the numerous cultivars of *Hydrangea macrophylla* has led to the neglect of many good species and their cultivars, such as *H. arborescens* 'Annabelle'. A striking plant with a long flowering season in summer, its large heads of sterile flowers turn from lime-green to creamy white. 'Grandiflora' is another good cultivar.

Many of the plants listed in this book as being suitable for ground cover and for woodland gardens can easily join those discussed in this section. Taking into account the complete range of plants suitable for shady borders, foliage plants are very well represented, offering a wide range of shapes and textures as well as colours and in one genus alone, *Hosta*, there is an astonishing variety that goes a long way to justify the vogue that these plants enjoy. There is certainly no great problem in creating a superb shady garden in which flower colour hardly plays a part.

Particularly useful, provided they are used with moderation, are those foliage plants with variegated or yellow leaves. White or cream

BELOW The spires of drooping flowers that are typical of hostas have a quiet beauty but the species and numerous hybrids are grown mainly for their foliage. Their range of leaf colour, texture, shape and size is unmatched among perennials. The lushest clumps grow in moist shade. They are, however, an exquisite temptation to slugs and snails.

ABOVE The hearty clumps of metallic purple leaves have made *Heuchera micrantha diversifolia* 'Palace Purple' a popular foliage plant. It looks a much more elegant plant in early summer when loose sprays of tiny creamy flowers, showing a tint of pink, float above it. Here dense spires of a *Veronica longifolia* cultivar make an attractive contrast.

variegation can lighten a dark corner as effectively as pale-coloured or white flowers and Bowles' golden grass (*Milium effusum* 'Aureum') or *Symphytum* 'Goldsmith' can make sunny patches where no sun ever penetrates.

There are also plenty of good flowering plants suitable for shady areas, and many that last longer in flower when grown in shade than they do in full sun. Among the most spectacular to add are lilies (see page 78). Although many are happiest with their heads in sun for part of the day, most like their roots to be shaded.

Improving growing conditions

As well as creating shade, trees and shrubs take moisture and nutrients from the soil, often very greedily. Although the leaves they drop will form a mulch that eventually returns nutrients to the ground, the mulch is not thick enough and the process not fast enough for the artificially contrived conditions of a border. Mulching with well-rotted garden compost or stable manure and applying a general fertilizer in spring will help to conserve moisture and maintain fertility. Generous mulching will also benefit borders running along the base of walls and fences – these are often in rain shadow and only get a thorough soaking when rain is driven by wind or when they are watered.

Judicious pruning can often usefully reduce the density of shade, creating a more open effect and allowing a wider range of plants to be grown. For example, removing the lower branches of a tree, best done when it is young, allows morning and afternoon sunlight to get under the canopy and makes it possible to plant up to the base. Thinning out small branches on a tree with a lot of cluttered growth may benefit the tree as well as the plants growing beneath its canopy; such a job may need to be carried out by a qualified arboriculturalist.

Regular heavy pruning of many shrubs is generally undesirable as this may encourage even more vigorous growth, but for very overgrown shrubs there are other options. Some shrubs, including lilacs (*Syringa*), will generally respond well to periodic drastic reduction. A few shrubs, holly (*Ilex*) among them, can often be transformed from loose, informal specimens to formal topiary shapes that cast relatively little shade. For some shrubs the best course may be to take them out completely.

Small, enclosed gardens often have large areas in shade for much of the day. Painting walls or fences white makes the space seem bigger while many plants will benefit from the reflected light. Green foliage looks attractive against a white background, whether walls or a flooring material of light-coloured stone or gravel.

Perennials with Ornamental Foliage for Shade

All of the following plants can be grown in partial shade, for example in dappled light under trees or where buildings create shadow for much of the day, most performing best in a rich, moist soil. Many also flourish in full sun.

Name	height/spread	description
Ajuga reptans 'Atropurpurea'	20/30cm 8/12in	one of several good forms; glossy, purple foliage shows off blue flower spikes in spring
Arum italicum pictum	45/30cm 18/12in	spear-shaped, dark green leaves with white veins develop through winter; red berries in autumn
Astilboides tabularis (Rodgersia tabularis)	90/90cm 3/3ft	very large, circular leaves attached to the stem at their centre; creamy white flowers in late summer
Bergenia 'Wintermärchen'	30/30cm 12/12in	small, polished leaves with a carmine reverse; deep pink flowers in spring; foliage will colour better in sun
Brunnera macrophylla 'Hadspen Cream'	45/60cm 1½/2ft	an irregular cream border gives the large leaves distinction; sprays of blue, 'forget-me-not' flowers in spring
Epimedium x warleyense	30/30cm 12/12in	heart-shaped, light green leaves with a red-purple tinge; orange flowers in spring; most epimediums are superb foliage plants for shade
Filipendula ulmaria 'Aurea'	90/30cm 3/1ft	a meadow sweet with outstanding gold foliage in spring
Heuchera micrantha diversifolia 'Palace Purple'	45/45cm 18/18in	deep purple, heart-shaped leaves with an irregular edge and magenta reverse; in summer sprays of small, white flowers
Hosta fortunei 'Gold Standard'	75/90cm 2½/3ft	pale green, heart-shaped leaves turn gold in mid-summer except for a narrow, dark green edge; violet flowers in mid-summer
Hosta sieboldiana 'Frances Williams'	75/90cm 2½/3ft	large, blue waxy leaves with an irregular, wide, yellow margin; pale mauve flowers early summer
Hosta undulata albomarginata (H. 'Thomas Hogg')	75/90cm 2½/3ft	a narrow white edge highlights the mid-green leaves; violet, trumpet flowers in mid-summer
Lamium maculatum 'Pink Pewter'	20/60cm 8/24in	pure silver leaves edged green; pink flowers in spring
Lysimachia nummularia 'Aurea' creeping jenny	10/45cm 4/18in	creeping stems work gold leaves among other plants; cup-shaped, yellow flowers in summer
Milium effusum 'Aureum'	60/30cm 2/1ft	Bowles' golden grass has clumps of soft yellow leaves, especially beautiful in spring
Pulmonaria saccharata Argentea Group	30/60cm 1/2ft	evergreen and one of several pulmonarias with beautifully silvered leaves; pink buds open to blue flowers in spring
Rodgersia podophylla	90/90cm 3/3ft	each leaf consists of 5 large, roughly triangular leaflets, bronze when unfolding and coppery at maturity; creamy but unshowy flowers in summer
Symphytum 'Goldsmith'	25/45cm 10/18in	rather coarse foliage made beautiful by cream and yellow suffusions; flowers are best removed
Tellima grandiflora Rubra Group	60/45cm 2/1½ft	scalloped leaves, green with a purple reverse, turn bronze in winter; spikes of greenish flowers with a pink rim in early summer
Tolmiea menziesii 'Taff's Gold' pick-a-back plant	45/30cm 18/12in	semi-evergreen leaves randomly speckled green and gold; spikes of green and brown, bell flowers in spring
Viola riviniana (V. labradorica) Purpurea Group	15/45cm 6/18in	can be rampant but the purple foliage and mauve violets in spring are charming

Flowering Perennials for Shade

All of the following plants can be grown in partial shade, for example in dappled light under trees or where buildings create shadow for much of the day. Many also flourish in full sun.

Name	height/spread	flowering season	description
Alchemilla mollis lady's mantle	45/40cm 18/16in	early to late sum.	froth of tiny, yellow-green flowers over velvety, rounded leaves
Anaphalis triplinervis	30/30cm 12/12in	late sum.	woolly, silver-grey leaves and small heads of snowy flowers
Anemone hupehensis 'September Charm'	90/30cm 3/1ft	late sum. to mid-aut.	elegant, single, pink flowers, the outer petals tinted purple
Anemone x hybrida 'Honorine Jobert'	120/60cm 4/2ft	late sum. to mid-aut.	branching stems carry white flowers with yellow stamens; good foliage
Bergenia 'Bressingham White'	30/30cm 12/12in	mid- to late spr.	sprays of white flowers arch over large leaves; most bergenias are good in shade
Convallaria majalis lily-of-the-valley	20/60cm 8/24in	mid- to late spr.	sprays of waxy, bell-shaped and beautifully fragrant flowers; rampant
Corydalis cheilanthifolia	30/25cm 12/10in	late spr. to early sum.	spikes of spurred, green-yellow flowers over ferny foliage
Digitalis grandiflora	60/30cm 2/1ft	mid- to late sum.	spikes of soft yellow foxgloves with brown veining
Doronicum 'Miss Mason'	45/60cm 1½/2ft	mid- to late spr.	bright yellow daisies over a clump of heart-shaped leaves
Gentiana asclepiadea willow gentian	60/45cm 2/1½ft	early aut.	paired blue flowers strung along slender, arching stems
Geranium maculatum	60/45cm 2/1½ft	mid- to late spr.	lilac flowers borne over a clump of attractive, mid-green leaves
Geranium sylvaticum 'Album'	60/45cm 2/1½ft	late spr. to early sum.	beautifully fresh effect of pure white flowers against silver-green leaves
Geranium wallichianum 'Buxton's Variety'	30/75cm 1/2½ft	mid-sum. to early aut.	lax stems insinuate white-centred, blue flowers among other plants
Helleborus argutifolius (H. corsicus)	60/60cm 2/2ft	early to mid-spr.	evergreen outstanding for its 3-lobed, spiny-edged leaves and long-lasting clusters of green flowers
Helleborus orientalis Lenten rose	60/45cm 2/1½ft	late win. to early spr.	evergreen; nodding, saucer-shaped flowers in white, pink, crimson or deep plum, often speckled
Meconopsis x sheldonii	150/60cm 5/2ft	early sum.	spectacular clusters of large, cup-shaped, blue poppies over clumps of hairy leaves; for lime-free soil
Paeonia emodi	90/90cm 3/3ft	early to mid-sum.	luxuriant foliage; single, white, fragrant flowers with gold stamens
Polygonatum biflorum (P. commutatum) great Solomon's seal	180/90cm 6/3ft	late spr.	like a well-proportioned giant of the familiar Solomon's seal, with large clusters of dangling, white flowers
Pulmonaria 'Mawson's Blue'	25/25cm 10/10in	early to mid-spr.	plain-leaved pulmonaria with heads of funnel-shaped, blue flowers
Smilacina racemosa false spikenard	90/45cm 3/1½ft	late spr.	arching foliage and fluffy heads of fragrant, creamy flowers
Tricyrtis formosana	90/45cm 3/1½ft	early aut.	intriguing lily-like flowers, mauve with purple-brown spots
Viola cornuta	25/45cm 10/18in	early to mid-sum.	profusion of elegant, blue or white flowers, often repeating later

Hot, dry sites

Light soils, usually sandy or gravelly, are very free draining and have several advantages. They are usually easy to work and they normally warm up quickly in spring and early summer, encouraging precocious growth. Their inability to retain water, however, means that many plants cannot survive in them during long spells of desiccating wind or when, during torrid summers, there are extended periods with little or no rain. Where the annual rainfall is generally low, even a normal year can present serious problems. Furthermore, these soils are often low in fertility, nutrients usually being leached out of them quickly with free-draining water.

Choosing plants

If you are gardening on light soil, one approach is to plant on regardless, making no attempt to select plants according to their tolerance of drought. This works if you are prepared to ensure the survival of your plants through testing periods by regular watering. It is, however, a perilous course to follow, especially where there is the chance of a ban on the use of hose pipes or you want to go away on holiday. Pampered plants, unable to find sufficient reserves of moisture to maintain their lush life style, will rapidly collapse.

A far better solution is to choose plants that show a tolerance of drought and to confine watering to a relatively brief initial period when plants are getting established. There are, as it happens, large numbers of plants from many parts of the world that are well equipped to survive dry conditions, even during periods of protracted drought. Very often these are plants that are native to dry mountainsides, shoreline shingle or the impoverished hillsides of the Mediterranean. They are survivors of drought,

The rock roses (*Cistus*), mainly Mediterranean and North African in origin, bask happily in scorching sun and are best kept on short rations. Too rich a diet leads to lush growth that is vulnerable in cold winters. The tissue-paper flowers of *C. x pulverulentus*, as of all the rock roses, are individually short-lived but the buds continue to open over a long summer season.

FLOWERING SHRUBS FOR HOT, DRY SITES

Name	height/spread	flowering season	description
SPRING–FLOWERING			
EVERGREEN			
Rosmarinus officinalis 'Benenden Blue' rosemary	1.8/1.8m 6/6ft	early to mid-spr.	rich blue flowers; typical of these deliciously aromatic shrubs, demanding sun and good drainage
DECIDUOUS			
Caragana arborescens 'Pendula'	1.8/1.8m 6/6ft	late spr.	prostrate but often grown as a grafted standard; clusters of yellow, pea flowers
Cytisus x **kewensis**	45/120cm 1½/4ft	late spr. to early sum.	lax broom that makes a lovely cascade of creamy flowers
Cytisus 'Windlesham Ruby'	1.8/1.8m 6/6ft	late spr. to early sum.	one of many good hybrid brooms; masses of rich red, pea flowers
SUMMER–FLOWERING			
EVERGREEN			
Brachyglottis compacta	1.2/1.8m 4/6ft	early to mid-sum.	sprawling shrub; masses of yellow daisies; very beautiful white buds
Cistus x **cyprius**	1.8/2.5m 6/8ft	early to mid-sum.	dazzling, white flowers, blotched with purple; dark green foliage
Cistus x **pulverulentus**	90/120cm 3/4ft	early to mid-sum.	crumpled flowers of vivid crimson over grey-green foliage
Convolvulus cneorum	75/75cm 2½/2½ft	late spr. to late sum.	silky and silvery leaves; white flowers open from pink buds
x **Halimiocistus wintonensis** 'Merrist Wood Cream'	90/120cm 3/4ft	early to mid-sum.	grey-green foliage and numerous creamy flowers, their yellow centres ringed by dark crimson
Halimium ocymoides	75/90cm 2½/3ft	early sum.	grey-green foliage with chocolate-centred, yellow flowers
Helianthemum 'Jubilee'	20/25cm 8/10in	late spr. to late sum.	one of many floriferous rock roses; double, yellow flowers
Lavandula stoechas pendunculata	75/45cm 2½/1½ft	late sum.	grey shrub with purple 'ears' topping the flower spikes; like all lavenders needs good drainage
Lupinus arboreus tree lupin	1.2/1.2m 4/4ft	early to late sum.	spires of fragrant, usually yellow flowers; short-lived but fast-growing
Teucrium fruticans shrubby germander	1.5/1.2m 5/4ft	early to late sum.	aromatic, grey-green shrub for a sheltered position
DECIDUOUS			
Buddleja davidii 'Black Knight' butterfly bush	3/3m 10/10ft	mid-sum. to early aut.	dense heads of dark purple, fragrant flowers on arching stems; a feast for butterflies
Buddleja 'Lochinch'	3/3m 10/10ft	late sum. to early aut.	grey-green foliage and heads of fragrant, lilac-blue flowers
Caryopteris x **clandonensis** 'Heavenly Blue'	90/90cm 3/3ft	late sum. to early aut.	clusters of small, tubular flowers; aromatic, grey-green foliage
Colutea arborescens bladder senna	2.5/2.5m 8/8ft	early to late sum.	open shrub with ferny foliage and yellow, pea flowers followed by inflated, copper-red seed pods
Spartium junceum Spanish broom	3/2.5m 10/8ft	early to late sum.	green stems with fragrant, golden, pea flowers in profusion

GOOD FOLIAGE SHRUBS FOR HOT, DRY SITES

Name	height/spread	description
EVERGREEN		
Artemisia arborescens 'Faith Raven'	120/90cm 4/3ft	finely cut, aromatic, silvery foliage; bright yellow flowerheads in late summer and early autumn
Artemisia 'Powis Castle'	90/120cm 3/4ft	beautifully lacy, aromatic, silver-grey foliage; insignificant, dull yellow flowers in summer
Ballota pseudodictamnus	60/60cm 2/2ft	upright stems with woolly, grey-green leaves; tiny white flowers in summer
Lavandula lanata	75/75cm 2½/2½ft	woolly and very white lavender, easily lost in cold winters; dark purple flowers in summer
Melianthus major	1.8/1.8m 6/6ft	magnificently jagged, blue-green leaves; red-brown flower spikes in summer; somewhat tender
Phlomis fruticosa Jerusalem sage	120/60cm 4/2ft	woolly, grey-green leaves on stiff stems; whorls of yellow flowers and ornamental seedheads
Quercus coccifera Kermes oak	4/4m 13/13ft	dense, slow-growing shrub with small, spiny, holly-like leaves; tiny acorns
Ruta graveolens 'Jackman's Blue'	60/40cm 24/16in	aromatic subshrub with densely divided, blue-grey leaves; small, yellow flowerheads in summer
Salvia officinalis 'Icterina'	45/90cm 1½/3ft	pale green and yellow variegation on grey-green, aromatic leaves; seldom flowers; one of several good colour forms
Santolina chamaecyparissus cotton lavender	50/50cm 20/20in	soft, aromatic hummock of silver-grey, lacy foliage; lemon-yellow, button flowers in mid-summer
Santolina rosmarinifolia	60/90cm 2/3ft	finely cut foliage makes a dense bush of dark green; bright yellow flowers in mid-summer
DECIDUOUS		
Artemisia abrotanum southernwood, lad's love	90/90cm 3/3ft	sometimes semi-evergreen; downy, grey-green leaves are strongly aromatic; dull, yellow flowers in late summer

burning heat and in many cases of turbulent and desiccating winds, and they have special features that allow them to succeed where numerous other plants would fail.

In many cases the foliage of these plants gives a clue to their character. Some, such as most sedums, have fleshy leaves in which water is stored. Others have leathery or felted leaves, or leaves covered with silky hairs, all devices that help to slow water loss. Many have astonishingly deep root systems which allow them to tap reserves of moisture far below the surface of the soil. A considerable number of them are bulbous, their swollen underground organs allowing them to survive from one relatively brief flowering season, often coinciding with a short rainy season, to another.

Described in an anatomical way, the plants that thrive in hot, dry conditions sound unpromising as ornamentals but among them are many garden favourites, some, such as the lavenders and a number of herbs, which are loved as much for their foliage as for their flowers. When successfully grown they are no less appealing than plants that are only at home in much kinder conditions.

Creating borders in hot, dry sites

Mixed borders can be a highly effective way of planting hot, dry sites. For many gardeners the ideal is a Mediterranean medley in which compact shrubs, often aromatic, set off a mixture of summer-flowering perennials.

It is important to strike a balance between foliage and flowering plants. A high proportion of shrubs that thrive in these conditions have

ABOVE Full sun and free-draining soils suit most plants with grey or silver foliage and a meagre diet intensifies their colour. Cotton lavender (*Santolina chamaecyparissus*) is an aromatic evergreen that makes neat mounds if clipped in mid- to late spring to remove most of the previous season's growth. Plants that are not pruned carry yellow, button flowers in summer.

OPPOSITE The Mount Etna broom (*Genista aetnensis*) needs sun and is best on rather poor, freely draining soils. Unlike its smaller relatives, it is usually trained on a single stem to form a small, weeping tree with a sparse canopy that casts only light shade. The showers of yellow, pea flowers in late summer transform it into a fragrant plant of great beauty.

SHORT-LIVED PLANTS FOR SUN AND FREE-DRAINING SOILS

The following plants are summer-flowering and, in most cases, their season will be extended if they are regularly deadheaded.

Name	height/spread	description
GROWN AS HARDY ANNUALS		
Agrostemma githago 'Milas' corn cockle	75/25cm 30/10in	slender, swaying stems with lilac-pink flowers; the seeds are poisonous
Calendula officinalis 'Art Shades' marigold	60/60cm 2/2ft	an example of these very easy-going plants with double, daisy flowers in soft, warm colours
Echium platagineum 'Blue Bedder'	30/25cm 12/10in	bushy plants covered with deep blue, tubular flowers
Eschscholzia californica Ballerina Series Californian poppy	25/20cm 10/8in	an example of these gorgeously coloured plants with frilled, satiny petals
Gilia capitata	45/20cm 18/8in	pincushion, lavender-blue flowers over feathery foliage
Helipterum (Acroclinium) roseum	40/15cm 16/6in	daisy flowers with straw-textured, red, pink or white petals radiating from a yellow centre
Iberis amara Hyacinth-flowered Series	30/15cm 12/6in	flattish clusters of scented flowers in white and shades of pink or purple
Layia platyglossa (L. elegans) tidy tips	45/30cm 18/12in	yellow daisies, the notched petals tipped white
Lobularia maritima 'Rosie O'Day'	10/25cm 4/10in	rounded heads of sweetly scented, rose-pink flowers
Malope trifida	90/30cm 3/1ft	showy, mallow-like flowers of rosy purple
Tanacetum (Chrysanthemum) parthenium	30/25cm 12/10in	the herb feverfew is a bushy, aromatic plant with white, daisy flowers
Tropaeolum majus Jewel Series nasturtium	30/30cm 12/12in	compact example with spurred flowers in many colours, and which are more numerous when the soil is not rich
GROWN AS HALF-HARDY ANNUALS		
Cosmos 'Sea Shells'	90/45cm 3/1½ft	unusual single flowers with fluted petals in red, pink or white; dry conditions suit all cosmos
Dimorphotheca aurantiaca star of the Veldt	30/25cm 12/10in	elegant, orange, yellow or cream daisies on graceful stems; needs sunshine to open
Dorotheanthus 'Lunette'	10/15cm 4/6in	masses of flowers with glistening, yellow petals radiating from a brick-red centre
Gaillardia pulchella	45/30cm 18/12in	mostly found as double mixtures, the flowers, yellow, pink or red, with a crimson zone
Helichrysum bracteatum Monstrosum Series	90/30cm 3/1ft	an 'everlasting' with papery, double flowers in a wide colour range; good for drying
Xeranthemum annuum immortelle	60/45cm 2/1½ft	single or double papery flowers in pink, purple or white over silvery leaves; good for drying
GROWN AS BIENNIALS		
Glaucium flavum horned poppy	45/45cm 18/18in	biennial, yellow poppies over handsome, grey-green foliage
Verbascum olympicum	180/90cm 6/3ft	from a base of grey, felted leaves rises a giant candelabrum of yellow flowers

TREES FOR HOT, DRY SITES

Unless described otherwise, the following plants are deciduous.

Name	height/spread	description
Cercis siliquastrum Judas tree	6/4.5m 20/15ft	clusters of purplish-pink, pea flowers in late spring; seed pods redden in late summer
Elaeagnus 'Quicksilver'	3.7/3.7m 12/12ft	outstanding, silver-foliaged, small tree or shrub bearing tiny, fragrant flowers in late spring
Eucalyptus pauciflora niphophila	6/4.5m 20/15ft	elegant evergreen with blue-white bloom to bark; grey-green foliage; white flowers early summer
Genista aetnensis Mount Etna broom	6/5m 20/16ft	almost leafless, open shrub or weeping small tree with small, yellow flowers making a fragrant cloud in mid- to late summer
Hippophae rhamnoides sea buckthorn	6/4.5m 20/15ft	small tree or large shrub with narrow, silvery leaves; tiny, yellow flowers in spring are followed by long-lasting, orange berries, provided plants of both sexes are present
Juniperus chinensis 'Obelisk'	450/90cm 15/3ft	loosely columnar, evergreen conifer with aromatic, needle-like leaves
Tamarix tetrandra	3.7/3.7m 12/12ft	lightly foliaged and open with long sprays of pink flowers in late spring to early summer

silver or grey foliage (those listed on page 58 will almost all do well on a free-draining, sunny site). On a dull winter's day it may be difficult to appreciate their qualities but these plants come into their own in sizzling summer heat, cooling what might otherwise be colours of unsettling intensity.

Many of the shrubs – the brooms (*Cytisus*) are a case in point – flower with astonishing profusion and others, including the exquisite *Convolvulus cneorum*, remain in flower over a very long season. Not all of them are long-lived but most are fairly readily propagated and quick to reach flowering maturity. With many it is a wise precaution to root cuttings on a regular basis in order that old and tired plants can be replaced by younger stock.

It is no kindness to grow most of the shrubs and perennials listed here in rich, well-watered conditions. High living transforms them completely. Instead of being tough and compact, they become soft and lax, vulnerable to disease, especially rots, and to attack from pests. They are also much less likely to survive spells of cold weather, grey-leaved plants succumbing particularly readily when sodden ground becomes frozen.

To the shrubs and perennials described here should be added a generous selection of bulbs. The lilies on the whole do not do well where the soil gets baked but many other bulbs listed on pages 74-9 and on page 144 relish these conditions. The alliums, in particular, make superb additions in early summer to mixed borders on dry sites and the seedheads can remain attractive over a long period.

Many trees that are not natives of hot, dry areas can be established on sunny, free-draining sites provided they are given some help while they are getting their roots down. Generous

mulching helps; pieces of old carpet around the base of a young tree can be extremely effective in reducing water loss.

When planting a tree that must endure hot and droughty conditions, for example as a background to or component of a dry border, it is preferable, however, to use one that is really comfortable in free-draining conditions, such as those given in the short list on page 97. They are quicker to get established and make a natural-looking association with plants that require similar growing conditions.

A consolation for those who are beginning to make a garden on rather poor soils but in an open sunny position is that a number of the most cheerful annuals flower more freely in these conditions than on rich soils. The short-lived plants listed on page 97 can make a beautiful temporary bed in an established

ABOVE Tall perennials are commonly associated with moist growing conditions. But the cardoon (*Cynara cardunculus*), with handsome jagged leaves, and the globe thistle (*Echinops ritro*), with round steel-blue flowerheads, are large plants that do well with lavenders (*Lavandula*) and other plants that thrive in dry, sunny gardens.

RIGHT Several achilleas have flat heads packed with tiny, yellow flowers in summer. The strong horizontals made by the disks of *A. filipendulina* 'Gold Plate', held high on stiff stems, make a strong contrast to other flower shapes. In schemes based on the complementary colours of yellow and violet it coincides with lavenders (*Lavandula*) and Russian sage (*Perovskia*).

BELOW Although a rather short-lived, lightweight perennial, *Linum narbonense* in its best forms has flowers of such a deep blue that it is worth perpetuating. Here the flowers work their way through the daisies of *Anthemis punctata cupaniana*, an evergreen with silvered filigree foliage that flowers in early summer.

PERENNIALS FOR HOT, DRY SITES

Name	height/spread	description
Acanthus mollis bear's breeches	90/90cm 3/3ft	clumps of boldly lobed, glossy foliage topped by purple-and-white flower spikes mid- to late summer
Achillea filipendulina 'Gold Plate'	150/60cm 5/2ft	stiff-stemmed perennial with flat heads packed with tiny flowers of rich yellow
Anthemis tinctoria 'E. C. Buxton'	75/75cm 2½/2½ft	in summer masses of cream daisies over ferny, green foliage
Artemisia ludoviciana latiloba	75/60cm 2½/2ft	clustered stems of grey-white foliage and small, grey flowers in mid- to late summer
Centranthus ruber red valerian	90/45cm 3/1½ft	a weed but lovely for rough slopes and crumbling walls with red flowers in mid-summer; *C. ruber albus* has white flowers
Cynara cardunculus cardoon	180/90cm 6/3ft	sensational foliage plant with silvery, divided leaves and purple thistle heads in summer
Dianthus 'Musgrave's Pink'	15/10cm 6/4in	deliciously scented, white flowers in mid-summer; one of many suitable pinks
Echinops ritro globe thistle	120/60cm 4/2ft	steel-blue buds open to blue flowers in late summer over jagged, grey-green leaves
Eryngium maritimum sea holly	30/30cm 12/12in	jagged, blue-grey foliage and blue flowers in summer surrounded by spiny collars
Euphorbia characias wulfenii	120/90cm 4/3ft	clumps of evergreen, blue-grey foliage; long-lasting, lime-green flowerheads in spring
Euphorbia myrsinites	15/45cm 6/18in	sprawler with blue-green leaves and in early to mid-spring heads of lime-green flowers
Foeniculum vulgare 'Purpureum' bronze fennel	150/60cm 5/2ft	large clumps of hair-like, bronze foliage and heads of small, yellow flowers in summer
Gaura lindheimeri	90/60cm 3/2ft	airy display from late summer to early autumn of small, pale pink flowers
Glaucium flavum fulvum (**G. flavum aurantiacum**) horn poppy	60/75cm 2/2½ft	short-lived but lovely, orange poppies over blue-grey foliage from late summer to early autumn
Iris unguicularis 'Walter Butt'	30/40cm 12/16in	untidy leaves; scented, pale lilac flowers from autumn to spring; one of several good forms
Linum narbonense	60/45cm 2/1½ft	slender plants with single flowers of intense blue in early to mid-summer
Lychnis coronaria dusty miller	75/45cm 2½/1½ft	in mid-summer masses of deep magenta or white flowers on woolly, grey plants
Oenothera macrocarpa (**O. missouriensis**) evening primrose	25/60cm 10/24in	lax plant with long succession of lemon-yellow flowers, reddish at the base, from mid- to late summer
Salvia nemorosa 'Ostfriesland' ('East Friesland')	45/60cm 1½/2ft	spikes of violet-purple flowers with long-lasting, crimson-tinged bracts in summer
Sedum 'Herbstfreude' ('Autumn Joy')	60/60cm 2/2ft	fleshy, grey-green leaves form a base for large, flat flowerheads that darken from pink to bronze in late summer and early autumn
Stachys byzantina 'Silver Carpet' lamb's ears	15/45cm 6/8in	non-flowering and, in effect, makes an indefinitely spreading, dense carpet of woolly, grey leaves
Stipa gigantea	180/90cm 6/3ft	oat-like grass with arching growth; flowers turn burnished gold in mid- to late summer
Verbascum 'Helen Johnson'	75/30cm 2½/1ft	choice mullein with flowers of dusty pinkish-brown in mid- to late summer

Drought-tolerant Plants for Gravel

Unless described otherwise, the following are herbaceous perennials. All are remarkably tolerant of dry conditions and look attractive planted in open, sunny sites in a mulch of coarse gravel.

Name	height/spread	description
Acanthus spinosus Spinosissimus Group	75/45cm 2½/1½ft	although not free-flowering, redeemed by its silvery foliage of skeletal spininess
Allium giganteum	120/30cm 4/1ft	early summer-flowering bulb, producing a tight ball, 10cm/4in wide, of star-shaped, purple flowers
Asphodeline lutea asphodel	90/30cm 3/1ft	in late spring spires of starry, yellow flowers emerge from a base of grassy, grey-blue leaves
Asphodelus albus	90/30cm 3/1ft	clump of grassy leaves and in early summer a spire of white flowers tinted warmly by brown veining
Ballota acetabulosa	75/60cm 2½/2ft	evergreen shrubby plant; grey-green, felted leaves whitening in drought; small, pink flowers in summer
Centranthus ruber atrococcineus red valerian	75/60cm 2½/2ft	strong red version of a wayside plant that flowers throughout summer
Crambe maritima seakale	60/60cm 2/2ft	superb foliage, the waxy, blue-green leaves having a wavy edge; heads of creamy flowers in early summer
Eryngium maritimum sea holly	30/30cm 12/12in	spiny, blue-grey foliage topped in summer by thistly, blue flowers
Erysimum (Cheiranthus) 'Bowles' Mauve'	90/90cm 3/3ft	unscented wallflower but reasonably perennial and invaluable for its lilac-purple flowers throughout summer
Euphorbia characias wulfenii	120/90cm 4/3ft	stiff stems form large clumps of evergreen, blue-grey foliage; large heads of lime-green flowers, dark brown at the centre, are impressive throughout spring
Euphorbia myrsinites	15/60cm 6/24in	evergreen; prostrate stems of blue-green bear terminal heads of yellow-green flowers in spring
Ferula communis 'Gigantea'	3.7/1.2m 12/4ft	a truly giant fennel with a sturdy stem rising from dark green foliage to bear heads of yellow flowers in mid-summer
Gaura lindheimeri	90/60cm 3/2ft	understated charm in late summer and early autumn with pink-tinted white flowers airily displayed
Glaucium flavum fulvum horned poppy	60/60cm 2/2ft	usually biennial; orange poppies in late summer and autumn as an alternative to the more common yellow, over divided, grey-blue foliage
Lavandula angustifolia 'Folgate' lavender	50/50cm 20/20in	evergreen shrub; a compact lavender, the greyness of the foliage enhanced by dry conditions; lavender-blue flowers in mid-summer
Romneya coulteri Californian tree poppy	180/30cm 6/1ft	can be an irritating wanderer but in mid-summer the crumpled white poppies with yellow bosses are superb
Santolina chamaecyparissus nana	15/15cm 6/6in	evergreen shrublet with feathery foliage bleached to near white; yellow, button flowers in mid-summer
Sedum spectabile 'Septemberglut' ('September Glow')	45/45cm 18/18in	attractive clump of fleshy, grey-green leaves from spring to late summer, when they are topped by flat flowerheads that age from green, through pink to red
Stipa gigantea	180/90cm 6/3ft	arching stems carry golden, oat-like flowers over a dense clump of narrow leaves
Verbascum bombyciferum	150/60cm 5/2ft	biennial; a rosette of silver leaves throws up a branching stem with spikes of sulphur-yellow flowers

garden and are ideal as fillers for a garden that is in the process of being developed.

Although the biennials are often overlooked, tall-growing kinds, such as many of the verbascums and the magnificent scotch thistle (*Onopordum acanthium*), which should be deadheaded to prevent it from self-seeding too liberally, are especially valuable for giving height and bulk to young borders.

Improving growing conditions

It is quite unrealistic to expect that free-draining sandy or gravelly soils can be transformed into a moist loam. Nonetheless, incorporating moisture-retentive material in what would otherwise be very free-draining soils will do much to extend the range of plants that you can grow. Mix plenty of humus in the form of well-rotted garden compost, stable manure or the like into the soil before planting.

Bulbs for Baking

The following are all ardent sun-lovers. Although they need moisture in the growing season, these bulbs are best suited to sheltered positions where they get a good baking during summer; at the base of a sunny wall is ideal.

Name	height/spread	description
SPRING-FLOWERING		
Fritillaria imperialis crown imperial	90/30cm 3/1ft	tall stem topped by leafy tuft beneath which hang a clustered ring of orange, red or yellow bells
Hermodactylus tuberosus	25/8cm 10/3in	iris-like with flowers in an unusual combination of green and near black
Iris orchioides (I. bucharica)	45/15cm 18/6in	1-4 scented, cream-and-yellow flowers, with an orange crest on the falls
Tulipa saxatilis	45/20cm 18/8in	1-3 purplish flowers with yellow centres in late spring; spreads by stolons
SUMMER-FLOWERING		
Allium aflatunense 'Purple Sensation'	90/30cm 3/1ft	in late spring or early summer tall stems bear round heads of deep purple flowers
Allium giganteum	120/30cm 4/1ft	one of the tallest-growing *Allium* with densely packed, spherical heads of lilac-purple flowers
Tigridia pavonia tiger flower	50/20cm 20/8in	vivid flowers with 3 large petals, mainly red, yellow or white, and spotted centres in summer to early autumn
AUTUMN-FLOWERING		
Amaryllis belladonna	75/30cm 2½/1ft	3-4 pink or white, sweetly scented, trumpet flowers per stem; the leaves develop after the flowers
Nerine bowdenii 'Mark Fenwick'	60/15cm 24/6in	glistening and elegant beauty with 6-8 bright pink flowers per stem before the leaves develop
Sternbergia lutea	15/10cm 6/4in	superficially crocus-like with shining yellow flowers opening as the leaves develop

RIGHT A mulch of gravel helps conserve moisture, discourages weeds and gives plants a cool root-run. Plants also look attractive growing through a material that gives the garden a unified texture. Many plants other than those listed on the left can be grown in gravel. Shrubs such as the grey-leaved *Brachyglottis* 'Sunshine' are combined here with the woolly lamb's ears (*Stachys byzantina*) and the lime-green lady's mantle (*Alchemilla mollis*).

Mulching borders in spring before the soil dries out will help conserve moisture. Moderate feeding with a balanced fertilizer, also in spring, will maintain the level of nutrients in the soil. Avoid excessive feeding as this will encourage soft growth untypical of the plants that bask happily on a spartan living in free-draining soil.

Special bulbs
Some bulbs only flower freely when they are given a good baking during the summer months. Nerines and bulbs of a similar disposition (see the chart on page 100) do best

with a little special treatment; an ideal position is a bed at the foot of a warm wall. Raising the bed above ground level will make it drain even more sharply, especially if a compost containing a good proportion of coarse, gritty sand is used. Walls for such a bed rarely need to be more than about 30cm/12in high and can be constructed from a wide range of materials, including bricks and old railway sleepers.

Planting in gravel
An alternative to planting in conventional borders is to grow drought-tolerant plants in

loose groupings in a mulch of gravel with paths of the same material meandering between them. The plants given in the chart on page 100 are particularly suitable for this method of cultivation but almost all the plants covered in this section (see pages 94-101) can be grown in such a way. The ground should be well-prepared in advance, all perennial weeds being removed. The mulch can be applied to a depth of about 8cm/3in after planting. As well as ensuring free drainage round the neck of plants, the gravel also helps to conserve moisture and inhibits the growth of weeds.

Problem soils

To describe as problem soils those covered in this section indicates, perhaps, a slanted view of them. As many superb gardens demonstrate, the limitations posed by the soil are not so serious that one has to garden in a perpetual state of regret.

Heavy soils

Although they are often highly fertile, heavy clay soils are difficult to work. Water does not drain from them freely and in winter they are often soggy; when walked on in this state they can become seriously compacted. In summer they can bake to a concrete-like hardness.

Ground that is seriously waterlogged almost certainly requires the installation of a drainage system that will carry off excess water to a drainage ditch or soakaway. All heavy soils can be improved by the addition of organic matter, such as straw or garden compost. Digging in coarse grit will also help to create a more open texture. There are, however, a number of fine ornamentals (see page 103) that perform well even in cold and apparently inhospitable clay.

Alkaline soils

Although many ornamentals thrive in a wide range of conditions, the acidity or alkalinity of a soil is an important factor to take into account when choosing plants for a garden. This chemical balance of a soil is measured on a pH scale from 1 to 14, soils with a pH of 7 being neutral, those above being alkaline. You can use a simple soil-testing kit to give an approximate reading of the pH level of your soil. You simply mix a sample of soil with a chemical solution and match the result against a chart for colour.

Major modification of the chemical balance of a highly alkaline soil, such as the thin soils usually found over chalk, is hardly practicable

Goat's beard (*Aruncus dioicus*) is one of the most impressive perennials for heavy soils but will tolerate a wide range of conditions. In mid-summer creamy plumes top the clumps of fern-like leaves. Female plants, which have attractive seedheads (and generous self-seeding tendencies), cannot match male plants for extravagant plumage.

CLASSIC PLANTS FOR HEAVY SOILS

The following plants will succeed in slow-draining, typically clayey, soils but most are tolerant of a wide range of conditions.

Name	height/spread	description
EVERGREEN TREES AND SHRUBS		
Aucuba japonica 'Gold Dust'	2.5/2.5m 8/8ft	one of many forms, all tolerating a wide range of conditions; the showy leaves are speckled gold; red berries are produced provided a male plant is nearby
Berberis x **stenophylla** 'Corallina Compacta'	25/25cm 10/10in	a spiny dwarf from a genus tolerant of a wide range of conditions; bright orange flowers in late spring
Cotoneaster conspicuus 'Decorus'	30/250cm 1/8ft	white flowers in late spring are followed by long-lasting, orange-red berries; most species of cotoneaster are suitable
Pyracantha 'Mohave' firethorn	3.7/4.5m 12/15ft	a suitable genus with many good berrying shrubs; white flowers in early summer are followed by orange-red fruits
Skimmia japonica 'Fructu Albo'	75/75cm 2½/2½ft	low-growing female plant with fragrant, white flowers in spring followed by long-lasting, white berries if there is a male nearby; all skimmias are suitable
DECIDUOUS TREES AND SHRUBS		
Aralia elata 'Aureovariegata'	4.5/6m 15/20ft	large leaves, the many paired leaflets with a broad cream margin; fluffy heads of white flowers in late summer and early autumn; all forms suitable
Crataegus persimilis 'Prunifolia'	4.5/6m 15/20ft	from a genus providing many suitable small trees; white blossom in early summer followed by long-lasting red haws; good autumn foliage
Deutzia x **hybrida** 'Mont Rose'	1.5/1.5m 5/5ft	this genus provides many suitable shrubs; soft pink, starry flowers in early summer
Forsythia x **intermedia** 'Lynwood'	2.5/2.5m 8/8ft	forsythias are generally suitable and this good choice bristles with large, yellow flowers in spring
Malus x **schiedeckeri** 'Red Jade'	4.5/6m 15/20ft	most crab apples are suitable; this is a weeping example, with pink-and-white blossom followed by long-lasting, red fruit
Philadelphus 'Burfordensis'	3/3.7m 10/12ft	one of the most vigorous among a fragrant choice; single, white flowers in early summer
Prunus 'Hokusai' Japanese cherry	6/6m 20/20ft	one of many suitable flowering cherries; semi-double, pale pink flowers in mid-spring; the foliage, bronze when young, colours well in autumn
Ribes sanguineum 'King Edward VII'	1.8/1.8m 6/6ft	cascading sprays of rich pink flowers in mid- to late spring; all the flowering currants are suitable
Spiraea japonica 'Shirobana'	1.2/1.2m 4/4ft	small, flat flowerheads, some pink and some white on the same bush, in late summer; all the species and hybrids are suitable
Viburnum opulus 'Roseum' ('Sterile') snowball bush	4.5/3.7m 15/12ft	a valuable genus for these conditions; round heads of flowers, greenish at first and then white, in late and early summer; the foliage colours well in autumn
Weigela 'Candida'	2.5/2.5m 8/8ft	in late spring pale green buds open to pure white flowers; all species and hybrids suitable
PERENNIALS		
Aruncus dioicus goat's beard	1.8/1.2m 6/4ft	handsome clump of ferny leaves and in mid-summer creamy plumes of starry flowers
Astilbe x **arendsii** 'Fanal'	60/30cm 2/1ft	plumes of deep crimson flowers over dark, fern-like leaves in summer; one of many suitable hybrids
Hemerocallis 'Stafford'	75/60cm 2½/2ft	mahogany-red trumpets over strap-shaped leaves in summer; many good hybrids to choose from
Lobelia 'Dark Crusader'	90/25cm 36/10in	one of several hybrids which in mid-summer produce tall spires of deep red flowers over dark foliage
Lythrum salicaria 'Feuerkerze'	120/45cm 4/1½ft	sometimes known as 'Firecandle', this purple loosestrife has slender spires of vivid rose-red flowers in mid-to late summer
Rheum palmatum 'Atrosanguineum'	1.8/1.8m 6/6ft	handsome, deeply cut, large leaves, red at first but the upper surface turning green; plumes of red flowers in early summer
Trollius x **cultorum** 'Orange Princess'	75/45cm 2½/1½ft	all globe flowers suitable; in late spring and early summer this hybrid has globular flowers of intense orange-yellow

CLASSIC PERENNIALS FOR ALKALINE SOILS

In most cases the following plants do not require but tolerate very alkaline conditions.

Name	height/spread	description
Acanthus mollis Latifolius Group	90/90cm 3/3ft	impressive clump of large, shiny leaves topped in late summer with spikes of purple and white, hooded flowers
Achillea filipendulina 'Gold Plate'	150/60cm 5/2ft	stiff stems carry flat heads of yellow flowers in summer
Aconitum carmichaelii 'Arendsii'	120/30cm 4/1ft	spikes of hooded, dark blue flowers make a striking feature in early autumn
Aubrieta 'Doctor Mules'	8/30cm 3/12in	rich purple-blue flowers in spring; one of the many cultivars of a useful evergreen perennial
Bergenia 'Morgenröte' ('Morning Red')	45/45cm 18/18in	bright pink flowers in spring and summer over rounded, evergreen leaves
Brunnera macrophylla 'Langtrees'	45/60cm 1½/2ft	sprays of blue, forget-me-not flowers in spring; heart-shaped leaves prettily spotted with silver
Campanula lactiflora	150/60cm 5/2ft	superb in summer when topped by heads of powder-blue, bell flowers; all forms are good
Catananche caerulea 'Major'	75/45cm 2½/1½ft	lavender-blue daisies in summer over a clump of grassy foliage
Centranthus ruber albus	75/30cm 2½/1ft	lovely white valerian, flowering in summer, and tolerant of a wide range of conditions
Doronicum 'Miss Mason'	45/30cm 18/12in	bright yellow daisies in early to mid-summer
Erysimum (Cheiranthus) cheiri 'Harpur Crewe'	30/30cm 12/12in	alkaline conditions suit all wallflowers; this has fragrant, double, yellow flowers from late spring to mid-summer
Geranium pratense 'Plenum Violaceum'	60/60cm 2/2ft	exquisite, summer-flowering geranium with rich violet-blue, double flowers
Gypsophila 'Rosenschleier' ('Rosy Veil')	30/75cm 1/2½ft	in mid- to late summer tiny, pale pink, double flowers create a hazy mound
Helenium 'Sonnenwunder'	120/45cm 4/1½ft	clear yellow, daisy flowers in autumn; one of several invaluable hybrids
Linum narbonense	60/45cm 2/1½ft	in summer slender stems carry a long succession of silky, rich blue flowers
Lychnis chalcedonica Maltese cross	90/30cm 3/1ft	heads of vivid scarlet flowers in summer; the flower shape gives the plant its common name
Paeonia 'Festiva Maxima'	90/60cm 3/2ft	one of many choice perennial peonies; in early summer this has large, fragrant, double flowers, the white petals marked with crimson flashes
Salvia x **superba**	60/60cm 2/2ft	bushy plant producing many spikes of violet-blue flowers, their summer season extended by persistent red-purple bracts
Scabiosa caucasica 'Clive Greaves'.	60/60cm 2/2ft	long summer display of lavender-blue, pincushion flowers
Sidalcea 'Sussex Beauty'	120/45cm 4/1½ft	one of several cultivars with spikes of hollyhock-like, silky flowers in summer; this is deep pink
Stachys byzantina 'Silver Carpet' lamb's ears	15/45cm 6/18in	invaluable, evergreen carpeter with woolly, silver-grey foliage; non-flowering
Verbascum 'Cotswold Cream'	120/60cm 4/2ft	stems of apricot-buff flowers make telling vertical accents in summer; unfortunately short-lived
Veronica spicata 'Heidekind'	30/40cm 12/16in	one from a useful range of edging plants; spikes of pink flowers in mid-summer

CLASSIC TREES AND SHRUBS FOR ALKALINE SOILS

Name	height/spread	description
EVERGREEN		
Aucuba japonica 'Picturata'	3/2.5m 10/8ft	all forms tolerate a wide range of conditions; this male has large leaves with a central yellow splash
Berberis x **lologensis** 'Apricot Queen'	3/2.5m 10/8ft	*B. darwinii*, one parent of this hybrid, does not like lime, unlike most berberis; rich apricot flowers in spring are followed by purple berries
Buxus sempervirens	2.2/1.5m 7/5ft	boxes are versatile evergreens, outstanding for their dense, dark green foliage
Ceanothus impressus	3/3m 10/10ft	many *Ceanothus* are lime-tolerant; this is good as a wall-shrub, with deep blue flowers in spring
Cotoneaster salicifolius 'Rothschildianus'	4.5/4.5m 15/15ft	from a genus that is generally lime-tolerant; white flowers in summer are followed by rich yellow fruits
Potentilla fruticosa 'Tangerine'	1.2/1.5m 4/5ft	genus of plants adaptable to many conditions; yellow flowers are tinted orange-red throughout summer
Prunus lusitanica Portugal laurel	4.5/4.5m 15/15ft	fine alternative to *P. laurocerasus* which does not do well on thin soils over chalk; chiefly remarkable for its dark green leaves on red stalks; takes clipping
Rosmarinus officinalis	1.5/1.5m 5/5ft	all rosemaries are suitable; aromatic, narrow leaves and blue flowers in late spring
Taxus baccata 'Elegantissima'	6/4.5m 20/15ft	dense and upright yew with yellow foliage; very adaptable conifer with many named forms
DECIDUOUS		
Buddleja davidii 'Royal Red' butterfly bush	4/4m 13/13ft	most shrubs in this genus are lime-tolerant; arching stems carry plumes of fragrant, reddish-purple flowers from mid- to late summer
Cercis siliquastrum Judas tree	6/4.5m 20/15ft	purple-pink, pea flowers cluster on naked stems in late spring; seed pods redden in late summer
Crataegus x **lavallei** 'Carrierei'	6/7.5m 20/25ft	one from a genus tolerant of lime; clusters of white flowers in late spring are followed by long-lasting, orange-red fruits; leaves turn red in autumn
Deutzia setchuenensis corymbiflora	1.8/1.2m 6/4ft	from an obliging genus; graceful shrub with heads of star-shaped, white flowers in summer
Euonymus alatus 'Compactus'	90/250cm 3/8ft	low form of a shrub with exceptionally vivid autumn colouring; from a genus that is generally lime-tolerant
Forsythia giraldiana	3.7/3m 12/10ft	tolerant of chalk, like the hybrids; its less extravagant display of yellow flowers starts late winter
Malus x **zumi** 'Golden Hornet' crab apple	6/4.5m 20/15ft	in an important group of lime-tolerant ornamentals; outstanding for long-lasting, yellow fruits that follow the white blossom in spring
Philadelphus 'Avalanche' mock orange	1.5/1.8m 5/6ft	like most of the hybrids very tolerant of chalky soil; arching branches bear single, white, fragrant flowers in early summer
Prunus triloba 'Multiplex'	3.7/3.7m 12/12ft	twiggy example that thrives in alkaline soil; double, pink flowers mid- to late spring
Sorbus aria 'Lutescens'	6/4.5m 20/15ft	creamy white leaves are arresting in spring before turning grey-green; the white flowers in late spring or early summer are followed by scarlet berries
Syringa vulgaris 'Maud Notcutt' common lilac	3.7/3m 12/10ft	vigorous, white-flowered example of the many cultivars, with large heads of fragrant flowers in late spring

CLASSIC PLANTS FOR ACID SOILS

In most cases the following plants require, and if not prefer, acid conditions. This applies also to most rhododendrons (see page 132).

Name	height/spread	description
TREES AND SHRUBS		
Arbutus x **andrachnoides**	3/2.5m 10/8ft	evergreen with leathery leaves; peeling, reddish-brown bark; white spring flowers, sometimes followed by strawberry-like fruit
Calluna vulgaris 'H. E. Beale' Scotch heather, ling	50/50cm 20/20in	typical of the many forms of this shrubby evergreen; spikes of pale pink, double flowers
Camellia x **williamsii** 'Donation'	2.5/1.8m 8/6ft	first-rate example of a large group of lime-hating evergreens; glossy foliage and showy, semi-double, pink flowers in spring
Cornus nuttallii	6/3m 20/10ft	deciduous; in spring showy white bracts, which develop a pink tinge, surround inconspicuous flowers; strawberry-like fruits
Corylopsis pauciflora	1.8/3m 6/10ft	deciduous; drooping clusters of pale yellow flowers in early spring
Enkianthus campanulatus	2.5/1.5m 8/5ft	drooping clusters of creamy bells with red veins; brilliant red foliage in autumn
Erica cinerea 'C. D. Eason'	30/45cm 12/18in	all bell heathers are summer-flowering and evergreen; this example has red flowers
Eucryphia glutinosa	3/2.5m 10/8ft	deciduous tree or shrub smothered with white flowers in late summer; good autumn colour
Fothergilla major	2.5/1.8m 8/6ft	bottle-brush flower spikes, white and fragrant, appear before the leaves in late spring; foliage colours magnificently in autumn
Gaultheria (Pernettya) mucronata 'Cherry Ripe'	1.2/1.2m 4/4ft	one of several cultivars of this evergreen, grown for the long-lasting berries borne by female plants; this has large, bright red berries
Hamamelis x **intermedia** 'Arnold Promise' witch hazel	3.7/3m 12/10ft	deciduous, with spidery, fragrant flowers in winter; the foliage is red in autumn; one of several fine hybrids
Kalmia latifolia 'Ostbo Red' calico bush	3/2.5m 10/8ft	all forms of this evergreen are delectable; red, clustered buds open in early summer to dark-centred, saucer-shaped flowers
Lithodora diffusa 'Heavenly Blue'	10/60cm 4/24in	evergreen with dazzling blue flowers studding trailing stems in summer
Magnolia liliiflora 'Nigra'	2.2/1.8m 7/6ft	in early summer, and sometimes later, purple-red flowers with a much paler inside; among several magnolias disliking lime
Pieris formosa forrestii	3.7/4.5m 12/15ft	evergreen with brilliant scarlet young foliage and profusion of white flowers in spring
Stewartia pseudocamellia	5/3.7m 16/12ft	deciduous; attractive for its flaking bark, autumn foliage and white flowers in summer
PERENNIALS		
Cornus canadensis	15/60cm 6/24in	creeping ground cover; crowded foliage studded in summer with white flowers; red berries
Gentiana sino-ornata	15/30cm 6/12in	autumn-flowering evergreen sheeting the ground with trumpets of a breath-taking, intense blue
Sanguinaria canadensis 'Plena'	15/30cm 6/12in	double flowers of scrupulous whiteness among pretty leaves in spring
Smilacina racemosa false spikenard	90/45cm 3/1½ft	leafy perennial with fluffy heads of cream flowers in spring and early summer; fragrant

but its fertility and ability to retain moisture can be improved by the copious addition of organic matter, such as garden compost. There are, fortunately, many garden plants that are at their best on alkaline soils, of which those listed on page 104 are only a sample.

Acid soils

Acid soils, that is those giving a reading below 7 on the pH scale, can be made more alkaline by liming or the addition of a lime-rich material such as mushroom compost. This can be beneficial if you plan to grow vegetables but is rarely justified in the ornamental garden. It is far better to choose from the wide range of plants that thrive in acid soils such as those listed on this page. In addition to these there are many woodland plants that are happy only in acid conditions. These include a number of the trees and shrubs listed on pages 131-5, the most important group among them being the rhododendrons and azaleas.

Camellias are in the top rank of flowering evergreens that are intolerant of lime. In a moist, acid soil *Camellia x williamsii* 'Donation' shows the genus at its ornamental best. Some camellias hold their flowers when they are brown and faded; an advantage of the Williamsii hybrids is that the flowers drop when they are over.

Ponds & damp conditions

Mirroring sky and surroundings when calm, lively with sound and broken light when moving, water is in itself a potentially beautiful feature to add to the garden. The existence of a water feature also provides opportunities for introducing a number of fine plants that require a watery environment or only attain their full beauty when they are grown in moist ground.

Making & siting pools

Fortunate indeed is the gardener who has a natural water feature, but happily for those who have not there are now many materials available from which pools can be made. Using concrete or puddled clay calls for some experience and is relatively laborious but flexible liners and rigid pre-formed shapes make the creation of water features a fairly simple operation. The most durable liners are made from butyl rubber but reinforced PVC, which is cheaper, is a satisfactory alternative. Pre-formed pools, which are available in geometric and irregular shapes, are usually made of fibreglass or PVC.

It is best to site a pool in an open position but where it is integrated in the overall garden scheme. Try to avoid overhanging trees as these create shade, depriving most ornamental aquatics of the sun they need to thrive, and any leaves that fall may cause a build-up of chemicals in the water that are toxic to fish.

In a formal garden, a pool of simple geometric shape can be a major focal point; raising it and furnishing it with a fountain operated by a recirculating pump will give it greater emphasis. A formal pool's architectural quality and the visual and sound effects of water generally count for more than the planting.

For an informal pool to be convincing it is not enough for it simply to have an irregular

Tall-growing perennials make a lovely edging to a large pool. Great clumps of triangular leaves with roughly serrated edges anchor *Ligularia* 'The Rocket' to the pond side. In summer dark stems, crackling with golden sparks, shoot away from these handsome mounds of foliage. All the plants in this genus need soggy soil conditions to make lush growth.

PERENNIALS WITH ORNAMENTAL FLOWERS FOR BOGGY GROUND

Although all of the following plants relish boggy conditions, some grow well in borders on moist soils.

Name	height/spread	flowering season	description
Astilbe x **arendsii** 'Amethyst'	90/60cm 3/2ft	early to mid-sum.	feathery spikes of lilac-pink flowers over ferny foliage; one of many *Astilbe* relishing moist soil
Astilbe x **simplicifolia** 'Bronce Elegans'	30/25cm 12/10in	mid- to late sum.	charming example of dwarf *Astilbe*; bronze-toned foliage and sprays of tiny flowers blending cream and salmon-pink
Cardamine pratensis 'Flore Pleno'	25/15cm 10/6in	mid- to late spr.	the double cuckoo flower or lady's smock has spires of double, pale lilac flowers over deeply cut leaves
Darmera peltata	90/60cm 3/2ft	early to mid-spr.	umbrella-like leaves preceded by flat heads of pink flowers
Eupatorum purpureum	220/90cm 7/3ft	early to mid-sum.	imposing, with stout stems bearing frothy, purplish-pink flowerheads
Filipendula purpurea	120/90cm 4/3ft	mid-sum.	clumps of fingered leaves topped by flat heads of tiny, reddish-purple flowers
Gunnera manicata	2.5/3m 8/10ft	mid-spr. to early sum.	a giant with prickly stems bearing boldly cut leaves, 1.8m/6ft or more across; large cone of insignificant green flowers
Inula magnifica	180/90cm 6/3ft	late sum.	good bristly foliage; stout, branching stems bear large, yellow daisies
Iris ensata (kaempferi) 'Alba'	60/30cm 2/1ft	early to mid-sum.	pure white form among many of a beautiful iris revered in Japan
Ligularia dentata 'Desdemona'	120/60cm 4/2ft	mid- to late sum.	large, heart-shaped leaves, bronze with reddish underside; orange-yellow daisies
Ligularia 'The Rocket'	150/90cm 5/3ft	late sum.	from a mound of elegant, rounded leaves, serrated at the edge, black stems carry spires of small, yellow flowers
Lobelia 'Queen Victoria'	75/30cm 2½/1ft	late sum.	spire of scarlet flowers over beetroot leaves; one of many hybrids for moist soil
Lysichiton americanus	1.2/1.8m 4/6ft	early spr.	yellow, arum flowers, 30cm/12in high, are impressive though rankly scented, and followed by large, handsome leaves
Lysichiton camtschatcensis	90/90cm 3/3ft	early spr.	a plant to match its close relative, with white, fragrant flowers
Lythrum salicaria 'Feuerkerze'	90/45cm 3/1½ft	mid- to late sum.	also known as 'Firecandle', this purple loosestrife sends up several slender spires of vivid, deep pink flowers
Primula florindae giant cowslip	60/60cm 2/2ft	early to mid-sum.	heads of drooping, yellow bells powdered with white meal; fragrant
Primula japonica 'Postford White'	60/30cm 2/1ft	late spr. to mid-sum.	vigorous example of this candelabra primula; yellow-centred, white flowers
Primula pulverulenta	60/30cm 2/1ft	early to mid-sum.	candelabra of wine-red flowers on mealy white stems over pale green leaves
Rodgersia pinnata 'Superba'	120/75cm 4/2½ft	mid-sum.	handsome, divided leaves with bronze tints, and a plume of tiny, rosy flowers
Trollius x **cultorum** 'Canary Bird'	90/45cm 3/1½ft	late spr. to early sum.	one of several lovely hybrids; attractive, cut foliage and double, cupped flowers of lemon-yellow
Zantedeschia aethiopica 'Crowborough'	90/60cm 3/2ft	mid-spr. to early sum.	arum lily with arrow-shaped leaves and elegant flowers consisting of a funnel-like white spathe surrounding a yellow spike

DECIDUOUS TREES AND SHRUBS FOR WATERSIDE PLANTING

Name	height/spread	description
Alnus glutinosa 'Imperialis' black or common alder	10/4m 33/13ft	slow-growing form of a classic waterside tree; finely divided leaves and catkins in early spring
Amelanchier lamarckii	4.5/7.5m 15/25ft	profusion of white flowers in spring; the leaves, bronze in spring, colour brilliantly in autumn
Betula pendula 'Tristis' silver birch	7.5/3m 25/10ft	symmetrical weeping tree with silvery bark and light foliage; silver birches are highly adaptable trees
Cornus alba 'Aurea'	1.8/1.8m 6/6ft	less vigorous than most of the *Cornus* with coloured stems; grown mainly for its soft yellow foliage
Cornus alba 'Sibirica'	1.8/2.5m 6/8ft	outstanding for the vivid red of its stems in winter; needs to be coppiced regularly to ensure a succession of young wood
Cornus stolonifera 'Flaviramea'	1.8/2.5m 6/8ft	good as a contrast with the preceding *Cornus*; bright yellow-green stems in winter if coppiced
Mespilus germanica medlar	6/6m 20/20ft	small tree with white blossom in late spring followed by edible, brown fruit, like large rose hips
Salix alba sericea silver willow	12/6m 40/20ft	fast-growing but can be coppiced to maintain it as a shrub; superb, silver-grey foliage but insignificant catkins
Salix hastata 'Wehrhahnii'	1.8/1.5m 6/5ft	dark, purplish stems spangled with silver catkins appear in spring before the leaves develop
Salix irrorata	3/4.5m 10/15ft	in winter the purple twigs are covered with a white bloom; male catkins in spring are silvery pink with brick-red anthers; best coppiced regularly
Spiraea × vanhouttei	1.5/1.5m 5/5ft	prodigious quantities of white flowers in small, dense clusters along arching stems in late spring and early summer
Spiraea veitchii	3/3m 10/10ft	arching red branches bear heads of white flowers from early to mid-summer

PLANTS FOR THE WATER MARGIN

The following plants are happiest when growing in shallow water at the margins of pools, but may also thrive in boggy conditions.

Name	height/spread	description
Acorus calamus 'Variegatus' sweet flag	90/30cm 3/1ft	sword-like leaves with bold cream-and-green variegation; insignificant flowers but the crushed leaves are pleasantly scented
Butomus umbellatus flowering rush	90/45cm 3/1½ft	narrow foliage and in late summer stout stems bear heads of pink flowers
Calla palustris bog arum	30/30cm 12/12in	glossy, heart-shaped leaves grow from creeping rhizomes; small, white flowers in late spring followed by red berries
Caltha palustris marsh marigold	45/30cm 18/12in	shiny, deep green leaves and waxy, cup-shaped, spring flowers of rich gold
Glyceria maxima variegata	120/45cm 4/1½ft	grass with cream-and-green variegation that is tinged pink when it emerges in spring
Houttuynia cordata 'Flore Pleno'	30/30cm 12/12in	heart-shaped, aromatic leaves of bluish-green and in summer white, double flowers
Iris laevigata Japanese iris	60/30cm 2/1ft	green, sword-like foliage and in summer lavender-blue flowers; there are also named forms, some double, in various colours
Iris pseudacorus yellow flag	120/60cm 4/2ft	very vigorous; blue-green leaves; in late spring to early summer stems carry 5 or more yellow flowers
Iris versicolor 'Kermesina'	60/30cm 2/1ft	narrow, grey-green leaves; in early summer flowers of deep plum with white markings
Myosotis scorpioides 'Mermaid' water forget-me-not	15/30cm 6/12in	sprawling perennial with blue flowers like those of the common forget-me-not in early summer and later
Sagittaria sagittifolia arrowhead	60/60cm 2/2ft	arrow-shaped leaves and in summer spikes of white flowers with a dark centre
Schoenoplectus lacustris tabernaemontani 'Zebrinus' zebra rush	90/45cm 3/1½ft	a striking effect is created by the stems which are banded alternately green and white

outline. Pre-formed pools often sit conspicuously in gardens with their predictable, mass-produced irregularity blatantly exposed. The edge of such a pond should be disguised with marginal and waterside plants and the pool needs to be set in the ground in a position where it might occur naturally. Avoid siting ponds in frost pockets where they are very likely to freeze over for long periods.

Making bog gardens

Natural water features are often bordered by a transitional zone where the soil is permanently moist. As a surprisingly large number of impressive ornamental plants thrive in these conditions, creating boggy conditions at the edge of an informal pool can greatly enhance its overall effect. Although a pool made with a liner or a pre-formed shape has no natural seepage to keep the surrounding ground moist, you can make a boggy area artificially. The simplest method is to excavate an area adjacent to the pool, line it with PVC or polythene sheeting and then fill with soil. Periodic irrigation will keep the area boggy.

Below the surface

Balanced planting and stocking is necessary to maintain a well-oxygenated pool (essential for fish) in which the growth of algae is kept in check. Submerged plants produce oxygen and also use up the nutrients on which algae feed.

Common submerged plants, including Canadian pondweed (*Elodea canadensis*) and spiked milfoil (*Myriophyllum aquaticum*), are usually sold as bunches of weighted cuttings. Two or three containers planted up with bunches and sunk at a maximum depth of 90cm/3ft will help to keep the water reasonably clear.

Shading the water with the floating foliage of water lilies and other aquatics will also discourage the growth of algae. Having about one-third of the surface covered gives fairly effective control while still leaving a clear surface to reflect light. Moving water will also help to boost oxygen levels but many aquatics, including water lilies, do not thrive where there is movement or spray from fountains.

RIGHT There are many good flowering plants that give colour to the waterside. In the overall scheme, however, contrasts of foliage shape, size and texture count for more than the relatively fleeting display of flowers. Many plants that thrive at the water margin spread vigorously and the most aggressive will need cutting back periodically.

BELOW RIGHT The arum lily (*Zantedeschia aethiopica*) has spear-shaped leaves of glossy dark green, making it a foliage plant of distinction. For its full magnificence, however, this plant needs to be seen in summer, when its white, funnel-shaped spathes unfurl. It can be planted in boggy ground (see page 107) or just below water level in deep mud.

Waterside planting

Trees and large shrubs, so beautiful when reflected in natural bodies of water, present problems for the gardener who has a small or even moderately large artificial pool. As well as creating shade, they drop leaves and their roots may cause damage when they are in close proximity to a pool. The trees listed on page 108 are suitable only for planting as background to fairly large bodies of water and even the shrubs (also listed on page 108) may be out of scale with a small pond.

Getting the scale right when selecting perennials that like boggy conditions is also extremely important. Real giants, such as the magnificent *Gunnera manicata*, are superb where there is room for their astonishing annual growth but they are much too large for the average suburban garden. In addition to the plants described on page 107, it is worth considering ferns and grassy plants, of which a small selection is given on page 111. These are foliage plants of tremendous beauty, giving a richly textured edge to ponds and remaining attractive over a long season. Bamboos, such as *Fargesia murieliae* and *F. nitida* are also valuable for their elegant evergreen foliage.

Many of the plants that can be grown in boggy conditions will also do well in reasonably moist ground and make good border plants. This is true of some of the primulas and also of the astilbes, plants with highly ornamental foliage, which is frequently bronzed, as well as showy flower plumes.

WATER LILIES AND OTHER DEEP-WATER AQUATICS

Except where stated, the following perennials flower in summer. The dimensions given are for the maximum depth of water allowed for planting, followed by the approximate surface spread. A selection of water lilies (*Nymphaea*) for shallow water is included in the chart Aquatics for small ponds (see page 111).

Name	depth/spread	description
Aponogeton distachyos water hawthorn	90/120cm 3/4ft	white, fragrant flowers, forked and curiously toothed, over a long season
Nuphar lutea brandy bottle, yellow pond lily	1.8/2.5m 6/8ft	small, yellow flowers nestle among leathery, circular leaves; for a large pool
Nymphaea 'Amabalis'	75/120cm 2½/4ft	star-shaped, salmon-pink flowers with yellow stamens that turn orange
Nymphaea 'Comanche'	60/90cm 2/3ft	rounded flowers turn from deep orange to bronze
Nymphaea 'Escarboucle'	1.8/2.5m 6/8ft	fragrant and crimson, cupping bright yellow stamens; for large ponds
Nymphaea 'Froebelii'	75/120cm 2½/4ft	deep red flowers with orange stamens; purplish leaves
Nymphaea 'Gladstoneana'	2.5/3m 8/10ft	handsome, dark green, circular leaves and large, white, cupped flowers with yellow stamens; for large bodies of water
Nymphaea 'Marliacea Albida'	75/120cm 2½/4ft	beautiful, white cups, the outside of the flowers often tinged pink, are held just above the water
Nymphaea 'Marliacea Carnea'	1.5/2.2m 5/7ft	scented, pink cups filled with yellow stamens; the young leaves are purplish; for large ponds
Nymphaea 'Marliacea Chromatella'	75/120cm 2½/4ft	fine, yellow cups with pink tones; the leaves show dark blotching
Nymphaea 'Rose Arey'	75/120cm 2½/4ft	pink, star-shaped, fragrant flowers with yellow stamens; young, red foliage greens as it ages
Orontium aquaticum golden club	45/60cm 1½/2ft	pencil-like, gold and white flower spikes rise above narrow, glaucous leaves; suitable for moving water

Marginals

Plants that are happy with their feet in water are particularly useful for disguising the edge of informal pools. They can be planted in shallow water, up to about 15cm/6in deep. Although they will root readily in the soil of natural pools, in artificial pools they are best planted in baskets. This will help to check their often vigorous growth and make them easier to control. Some marginals that are beautiful in a wild setting spread so aggressively that they should be avoided completely. These include the reedmaces *Typha angustifolia* and *T. latifolia* and also the reed *Phragmites australis*. Even the marginals described on page 108 will be too vigorous for small pools, for which more suitable plants are suggested on page 111.

It is impossible to incorporate marginals naturally in a formal pool. However, the Japanese iris (*Iris laevigata*) has many highly bred forms of sumptuous beauty and these do not seem at all out of place when carefully grouped in a formal setting.

Water lilies and deep-water aquatics

The flowers of many water lilies, borne over a long summer season, are exceptionally beautiful and a pool without them looks curiously undressed. As it happens, the floating pads perform an important role in starving algae of the light that allows them to multiply prodigiously. Cultivars need to be selected according to the depth of water at which they are to be planted. The most vigorous, such as

Nymphaea 'Gladstoneana', are happy in water 2.5m/8ft or more deep and can spread over an area with a diameter of more than 3m/10ft. At the other end of the scale are some real pygmies (see page 111) suitable even for tubs and other containers planted as water gardens.

The glamour of water lilies tends to eclipse the quieter beauty of other deep-water aquatics but these are on the whole more tolerant of moving water. All of these plants are best

RIGHT Pools of geometric shape do not provide a comfortable setting for marginals but water lilies never seem out of place, the shape created by their whimsical coverage of the surface making a nice contrast with a formal outline. Choose water lilies that will suit the depth at which they are to be grown and plant in containers.

The grassy, evergreen tufts of the great drooping sedge (*Carex pendula*) are transformed in summer when the greenish-brown flower spikes dangle from arching stems. At the waterside this sedge, with its lax elegance, makes a very beautiful contrast to plants with substantial leaves or those that make stiffly upright growth.

AQUATICS FOR SMALL PONDS

The dimensions given here for water lilies (*Nymphaea*), all of which flower in summer, are for the maximum depth of water allowed for planting, followed by the approximate surface spread.

Name	height/spread	description
MARGINALS		
Acorus gramineus 'Variegatus'	25/15cm 10/6in	grassy semi-evergreen, the stiff leaves variegated cream on dark green
Caltha palustris 'Flore Pleno' marsh marigold	30/30cm 12/12in	compact form with appealing double flowers in spring that are golden with green tints at the centre
Iris laevigata 'Variegata'	45/30cm 18/12in	bold variegation with foliage striped ivory-white and green; lavender-blue flowers in summer
Juncus effusus 'Spiralis' corkscrew rush	60/30cm 2/1ft	a curiosity, with stems spiralling in corkscrew fashion
Typha minima	45/30cm 18/12in	grassy, dwarf bulrush with cylindrical seedheads following the late summer flowers
WATER LILIES		
Nymphaea 'Aurora'	45/75cm 1½/2½ft	cup-shaped flowers change from yellow to orange then red; purple-mottled foliage
Nymphaea x **helvola**	30/45cm 12/18in	star-shaped, yellow flowers; heavy purple mottling to the leaves
Nymphaea 'Laydekeri Rosea'	60/90cm 2/3ft	dwarf water lily with pink flowers that darken as they age; reddish underside to the leaves

planted in baskets that are sunk to the appropriate depth. Garden soil can be used for the compost but, to prevent it from discolouring the water, the basket should be lined with hessian and the surface of the compost covered with pea gravel after planting.

Water and wildlife

The plants listed in this section are all suitable for pools that are essentially ornamental in character. However, more and more gardeners are drawn to the idea of making pools where the chief aim is to provide a habitat for or to attract wildlife. The plants for these pools should be predominantly natives for these will provide the food and shelter that insects, birds, amphibians and small mammals need. Some that are indigenous to northern Europe – flowering rush (*Butomus umbellatus*), marsh marigold (*Caltha palustris*) and yellow flag (*Iris pseudacorus*) among them – are in fact listed here because of their ornamental value.

FERNS AND GRASSY PLANTS FOR WATERSIDE PLANTING

Name	height/spread	description
Carex elata 'Aurea' **(C. stricta** 'Bowles' Golden')	60/45cm 2/1½ft	in late spring and early summer a grassy clump of bright gold, which turns green; this sedge has brown flower spikes in summer
Carex pendula great drooping sedge	120/90cm 4/3ft	a broad-leaved, lax sedge useful to contrast with stiffer plants
Matteuccia struthiopteris ostrich plume fern	90/60cm 3/2ft	for a sheltered position; the lacy shuttlecocks of pale green warrant superlatives
Miscanthus sacchariflorus Amur silver grass	270/90cm 9/3ft	bamboo-like, non-invasive grass for large-scale plantings; arching, ribbon-like leaves
Miscanthus sinensis 'Zebrinus'	150/60cm 5/2ft	graceful tiger grass with leaves banded green and yellow; also good in borders
Onoclea sensibilis sensitive fern	45/90cm 1½/3ft	invasive but its light green fronds, renewed all summer, are lovely
Osmunda regalis royal fern	1.5/1.2m 5/4ft	superb in spring when copper-brown fronds unfold; also lovely in its summer green and autumn tan

Special Effects

There is a risk in presenting planting suggestions in charts focused on special requirements and particular conditons that the versatility of many plants may go unrecognized. This is especially so when making plant recommendations to suit particular styles of gardening. There are, for example, many plants of relatively recent introduction that can be grown very effectively in a cottage garden style. Those with a sentimental attachment to the cottage garden tradition, however, will only be satisfied with a core of authentic plants long cherished in simple country gardens.

Some of the charts in this chapter are intended, therefore, to point gardeners in the direction of reliable old favourites, including useful herbs and vegetables, essential components of the traditional cottage garden. There are suggestions, too, for plants particularly suited to formal and woodland gardens. In addition, there is a section on fragrant and aromatic plants. What is puzzling to those who have learned to appreciate the role scent can play in the garden is the extent to which it is so often neglected. Scented plants, whether fragrant or aromatic, hardly belong to a specific style of gardening but they do warrant special consideration.

Frost and snow can work miraculous transformations in a garden, highlighting some features while hiding or camouflaging others. In this magnificent formal garden, enclosed by the ruled line of a superb evergreen hedge, frost has picked out the bushy heads of unusual trained standards. These are specimens of the early Dutch honeysuckle (*Lonicera periclymenum* 'Belgica'), with flowers in early summer that are particularly fragrant in the evening.

Cottage garden mixtures

The idea of the cottage garden, with its jostling mix of familiar flowers, herbs and vegetables, continues to be a powerful influence on gardening today. The reality of the gardens cultivated by the rural poor in the past may have been far removed from the idealized versions created in the nineteenth century, which are in general the models that excite sentimental attachment. There is, however, a recognizable tradition of small country gardens in which useful plants – vegetables, fruit, culinary and medicinal herbs – are economically grown cheek by jowl with ornamentals. It has had an enormous influence on grander gardening. This is partly because the cottage garden provided a sanctuary for good hardy plants when, in the nineteenth century, bedding schemes were the rage. It is also because when the qualities of hardy perennials were once again recognized, the association of plants so casually effective in the cottage garden inspired, as Gertrude Jekyll freely acknowledged, the more sophisticated groupings of the herbaceous border.

Designing a cottage garden

The design of cottage gardens recorded and sometimes idealized by Victorian and Edwardian artists such as Helen Allingham follow simple patterns. A common formula shows a cottage front draped with roses, honeysuckle and other climbers, approached by a straight, narrow path bordered by familiar flowers, behind which grow vegetables, fruit and herbs. Just as common is a tiny front garden packed with flowers, with useful plants grown at the side or back of the cottage. All have in common a matter-of-fact economy in the use of space, the area available being devoted to planting or access, the arrangement not

ABOVE The astrantias (*Astrantia*) have a quaint beauty that has secured a place for them in many old gardens. Branching stems carry several flowerheads, each consisting of a central pincushion surrounded by a collar of bracts. They are happy in sun or light shade. Here the flowerheads of *A. major* are set against the bronzy foliage of an astilbe.

LEFT The idea of the cottage garden remains an inspiration to modern gardeners. The density and apparent casualness of this planting backed by a simple wooden fence captures its spirit. The garden is seen here in early summer, when it is dominated by clumps of sumptuous oriental poppies (*Papaver orientale*) and the spires of delphiniums.

allowing for leisure areas, such as lawns or patios, or elaborate design schemes.

The modern cottage gardener might want to make some adaptations to a scheme dictated by a frugal life style and the degree of adaptation will depend on personal taste. However, if your intention is to create a cottage garden that is authentic in mood, any hint of pretension – an architectural fountain or artfully positioned statuary – will strike a false note.

Labour-saving planting, such as the use of extensive ground cover, is also at odds with the spirit of the cottage garden. You do not have to garden with the skills of the old florists,

AUTHENTIC PERENNIALS AND BULBS FOR COTTAGE GARDENS

Name	height/spread	description
PERENNIALS		
Aquilegia vulgaris columbine, granny's bonnet	75/30cm 2½/1ft	pretty, grey-green leaves and in late spring and early summer short-spurred flowers in blue, purple, pink or white; self-seeds freely
Astrantia major masterwort	60/40cm 24/16in	curiously beautiful plants, the pincushion flowers white, tinged pink
Campanula persicifolia 'Boule de Neige'	45/25cm 18/10in	one of several double forms, this with white flowers in summer
Convallaria majalis rosea lily-of-the-valley	15/60cm 6/24in	treasured pink variation of a favourite among fragrant, spring flowers
Dianthus 'Brympton Red' old-fashioned pink	30/15cm 12/6in	single crimson flowers with white markings; one of many fragrant, old-fashioned pinks that flower in early summer
Geranium sanguineum striatum	10/30cm 4/12in	dwarf form of the bloody crane's-bill with pale pink flowers, darkly veined, in summer
Lychnis chalcedonica Maltese cross	75/30cm 2½/1ft	heads of brilliant scarlet flowers for early summer
Lychnis coronaria dusty miller	60/30cm 2/1ft	in mid-summer masses of startling deep magenta or white flowers on self-seeding, woolly plants
Paeonia officinalis 'Rubra Plena'	60/75cm 2/2½ft	peony with heavy, double, red flowers of a rich tone in late spring or early summer
Papaver orientale 'Mrs Perry'	75/60cm 2½/2ft	single, pink cultivar from early this century; all cultivars look at home in cottage gardens
Polemoneum caeruleum Jacob's ladder	60/30cm 2/1ft	spikes of blue and, more rarely, white flowers over ferny foliage in early to mid-summer
Primula auricula 'Old Yellow Dusty Miller'	15/15cm 6/6in	yellow flowers powdered with meal; one among many named, spring-flowering border auriculas
Primula vulgaris 'Alba Plena' primrose	15/20cm 6/8in	double, white and one of many variations on the common primrose, long cherished as among the chief delights of spring
Ranunculus aconitifolius 'Flore Pleno' fair maids of France	60/45cm 2/1½ft	moisture-lover of airy beauty with exquisitely doubled, white buttercups in late spring and early summer
Scabiosa caucasica 'Clive Greaves' scabious	60/60cm 2/2ft	young plants give a long summer season of lovely mauve flowers with wavy petals
BULBS		
Fritillaria imperialis crown imperial	90/30cm 3/1ft	tall stem topped by a leafy tuft beneath which cluster drooping bells, usually brick-coloured
Hyacinthus orientalis 'Pink Pearl' hyacinth	25/15cm 10/6in	reliable pink cultivar, one of many valued for their spikes of waxy, scented flowers in spring
Lilium candidum madonna lily	150/30cm 5/1ft	sublimely beautiful; each stem carries many fragrant trumpets of pure white in early to mid-summer; best shallow-planted on alkaline soil
Narcissus pseudonarcissus obvallaris Tenby daffodil	25/15cm 10/6in	lovely little trumpet daffodil of almost uniform yellow; many other daffodils and jonquils are suitable (see page 75)
Narcissus 'Telamonius Plenus' ('Van Sion')	30/15cm 12/6in	double flowers of strong yellow in early to mid-spring
Tulipa 'Couleur Cardinal'	35/15cm 14/6in	old favourite with purple-tinged, red flowers in mid-spring; many to choose from other than those described as 'cottage tulips' (see page 76)

The rambling rose 'Albertine' remains a great favourite on account of its profuse display of wonderfully fragrant flowers of rich copper-pink. It has its drawbacks, however: it does not repeat; it is prone to mildew, especially if grown on a wall rather than in a more open position, and the petals of faded flowers turn brown but do not fall.

Trees, Shrubs and Climbers for Cottage Gardens

Unless described otherwise, the following plants are deciduous.

Name	height/spread	description
TREES AND SHRUBS		
Buxus sempervirens box	2.2/1.5m 7/5ft	slow-growing evergreen for topiary and hedging; small, glossy, dark green leaves; inconspicuous flowers
Crataegus laevigata 'Paul's Scarlet' hawthorn, may	6/5.5m 20/18ft	hedging plant or tree, sometimes lightly shaped; thick clusters of double, scarlet flowers in late spring, followed by crimson haws
Daphne mezereum mezereon	1.5/1.2m 5/4ft	naked stems thickly clustered with fragrant flowers, usually purplish-pink, from late winter to early spring; scarlet berries in autumn
Laburnum anagyroides laburnum	5.5/3.7m 18/12ft	tree, sometimes trained; dangling clusters of yellow, pea flowers in late spring; all parts of the tree are poisonous
Ligustrum ovalifolium privet	4.5/4.5m 15/15ft	semi-evergreen; rankly scented, creamy flowers in mid-summer, followed by black berries
Rosa 'Great Maiden's Blush'	1.5/1.2m 5/4ft	superb and sweetly scented old-timer with double, pearly pink flowers in mid-summer
Syringa vulgaris 'Katherine Havemeyer' lilac	3.7/3m 12/10ft	reliable example with pyramids of fragrant, semi-double, lavender-purple flowers in late spring; in other colours, from lilac to near red and white
Viburnum opulus guelder rose	3.7/3.7m 12/12ft	vigorous bush with jagged leaves that colour well in autumn; lacecap heads of heavily scented white flowers in late spring and early summer, followed by translucent red berries
CLIMBERS AND WALL SHRUBS		
Chaenomeles speciosa 'Simonii' Japanese quince	90/180cm 3/6ft	'japonicas' are usually grown as wall-trained shrubs; this is low-growing, with deep red flowers in spring; fragrant, green-yellow fruits
Clematis 'Jackmanii'	300/90cm 10/3ft	climber much loved for the mid-summer display of large, velvety, dark purple to violet flowers
Jasminum nudiflorum winter jasmine	3/3m 10/10ft	lax wall shrub, its leafless, arching stems bright with yellow flowers through winter to mid-spring
Jasminum officinale common jasmine	6/5m 20/15ftft	vigorous, twining climber with clusters of sweetly scented, white flowers in summer
Lonicera periclymenum honeysuckle, woodbine	6/6m 20/20ft	twining hedgerow scrambler loved for its scent; 'Belgica' (early Dutch) has clusters of deep pink flowers, creamy yellow inside, from late spring to early summer; 'Serotina' (late Dutch) is red-purple on the outside, white to yellow inside, from mid-summer to mid-autumn
Rosa 'Albertine'	4.5/3m 15/10ft	clusters of richly scented, loosely double copper-pink flowers in one splendid summer burst
Rosa 'Gloire de Dijon'	3.7/2.5m 12/8ft	early- and repeat-flowering climber; fragrant, buff-yellow flowers; loose and muddled petals

meaning here the men and women who grew to perfection and showed competitively plants such as auriculas and pinks. But a cottage garden that does not convey the feeling that it is cultivated with loving husbandry is a failure.

Ornamentals for cottage gardens

For many admirers of cottage gardens one of its chief appeals is its reliance on a body of familiar and reliable hardy plants. The conservatism of cottagers in the past almost certainly owed much to economic factors; they were simply too poor to chase after sensational new introductions from the four corners of the world. But the repertoire of plants long in cultivation and preserved in cottage gardens, often when neglected elsewhere, has acquired a mystique of its own.

Of the hardy perennials some of the most fascinating are double flowers or unusual colour forms, early gardeners having to make do with variety within a limited range rather than across a multitude of species and hybrids. We cannot always be sure that the cultivars we grow today are exactly the same as those written about by John Parkinson and other seventeenth-century authorities but plants such as the double white primrose (*Primula vulgaris* 'Alba Plena') have a character they would certainly recognize.

Almost as important as the perennials are a number of easy annuals and biennials that thrive in sunny, well-drained gardens, often giving a long season if regularly deadheaded.

Whatever the kind of plant, cottage gardeners of the past placed high value on those that are scented. Some old favourites, such as mignonette (*Reseda odorata*) are quite unshowy but others, including the madonna lily (*Lilium candidum*), are magnificent in any context. Unfortunately, space restrictions have meant

LEFT The common foxglove (*Digitalis purpurea*), usually biennial, has a happy knack of self-seeding freely, its tall spires making a lovely contrast to plants of looser form. Unwanted plants are easily removed. In several hybrid versions, such as that shown here, flowers are held horizontally, not drooping, and all round the stem, rather than on one side.

AUTHENTIC ANNUALS AND BIENNIALS FOR COTTAGE GARDENS

Unless described otherwise, the plants listed are summer-flowering. The hardy annuals easily grown from seed given on page 81 could be added to this list.

Name	height/spread	description
GROWN AS HARDY ANNUALS		
Consolida ambigua Imperial Series giant larkspur	120/30cm 4/1ft	tall spikes of double, spurred flowers in pink, blue or white above feathery leaves
Helianthus annuus 'Russian Giant' sunflower	300/45cm 10/1½ft	a giant among giants, yellow petals ringing a green-brown disc
Lathyrus odoratus Spencer Series sweet pea	250/30cm 8/1ft	climber with tendrils bearing sprays of pea flowers in white and many shades of pink, blue and purple,which exhale a wonderful scent
Lobularia maritima 'Snow Drift'	15/30cm 6/12in	sweet alyssum with rounded heads of tiny, white flowers in sweetly scented profusion
Malcomia maritima Virginian stock	20/8cm 8/3in	slender plant loved for the sweet scent of its flowers in pink, red, lilac or white
Papaver somniferum Peony-flowered Series	75/30cm 2½/1ft	opium poppy with large, almost blowsy, double flowers in red, pink, purple or white above grey-green leaves
Reseda odorata mignonette	30/30cm 12/12in	not showy but the heads of tiny, white flowers with orange-brown stamens are sweetly scented
Scabiosa atropurpurea Cockade Series	90/30cm 3/1ft	sweet scabious with scented, pincushion, double flowers in shades of pink, purple, red or blue
GROWN AS HALF-HARDY ANNUALS		
Alcea rosea 'Chater's Double' hollyhock	250/60cm 8/2ft	tall spikes of peony-like, double flowers, the colours including pinks, reds, yellows and white, over a base of rough leaves
Amaranthus caudatus love-lies-bleeding	120/45cm 4/1½ft	curious, red tassels up to 45cm/18in long droop against pale green foliage
Callistephus chinensis china aster	30/45cm 12/18in	bushy plants with heavy, double flowers in a wide colour range but predominantly white, blue or rose
Cosmos 'Sensation'	90/60cm 3/2ft	red, pink or white flowers up to 10cm/4in across, lightly borne over feathery foliage
Matthiola Ten-week Series stock	30/30cm 12/12in	dense spikes of heavily scented flowers above grey-green leaves, the colour range including crimson, pink, lavender, cream and white; dwarf and double varieties available
GROWN AS BIENNIALS		
Bellis perennis 'Dresden China'	15/15cm 6/6in	jaunty, spring-flowering miniature daisy studded with pink buttons
Campanula medium canterbury bell	90/30cm 3/1ft	masses of single or double bells in shades of blue, pink or white; dwarf cultivars available
Erysimum (Cheiranthus) cheiri wallflower	45/30cm 18/12in	dense spikes of velvety flowers of beguiling fragrance, often grown as warm-coloured mixtures including red-brown, yellow and crimson; dwarf kinds and separate colours available
Dianthus barbatus Monarch Series sweet william	45/30cm 18/12in	sturdy stems carry flat heads of fragrant, bicoloured flowers in combinations of pink, red, crimson or white; known as auricula-eyed
Lunaria annua honesty	75/30cm 2½/1ft	heads of lightly scented, white to deep purple flowers in spring and early summer, succeeded by papery, silver seed discs
Myosotis 'Blue Ball' forget-me-not	20/20cm 8/8in	compact, bushy plants with heads of small, deep blue flowers in spring and early summer
Viola x wittrockiana 'Majestic Giants'	20/20cm 8/8in	large pansies in a wide range of vivid colours, some prettily masked; reliably early-flowering

In old cottage gardens herbs were important as a source of remedies as well as the means to improve the flavour of what might otherwise have been a dull diet. The ornamental qualities of feverfew (here the golden-leaved form), sage, chives and many other herbs also warranted a place for them in the garden, usually not segregated but mixed among other plants.

that the coverage of scented plants here is rather cursory. The old-fashioned pinks (*Dianthus*) are represented in the chart on page 115 by only one example, but these are wonderfully fragrant plants that deserve priority in sunny gardens. Many of the scented plants listed on pages 121-5 would be fully at home in a cottage garden.

The narrow dimensions of most old cottage gardens meant that there was little room for trees and not much for shrubs. Although a few old favourites commonly found a place, including old shrub roses, more important were climbers. A modern cottage garden would not be complete without its complement of climbing or rambling roses and honeysuckle.

Useful plants

Although the balance of the modern cottage garden may have shifted in favour of ornamentals, to be authentic it must have useful plants. If there is only just room for trees and shrubs they should be apple trees and gooseberry bushes rather than ornamentals. Dwarfing rootstocks make it possible to fit an apple grown as a bush into a small garden. Another option that is space-saving and picturesque is to grow fruits as espaliers, with

USEFUL AND ORNAMENTAL HERBS

Name	height/spread	description
ANNUALS AND BIENNIALS		
angelica **Angelica archangelica**	2.2/1.5m 7/5ft	biennial with large, handsome leaves; rounded heads of small, yellow-green flowers in summer
basil, Greek **Ocimum basilicum minimum**	20/15cm 8/6in	small-leaved, tender annual of neat shape and deliciously aromatic
basil, sweet **Ocimum basilicum**	60/30cm 2/1ft	tender annual with bright green leaves of clove-like flavour; pinching out promotes bushy growth
borage **Borago officinalis**	90/30cm 3/1ft	hardy annual with dull green, hairy leaves brightened by blue, star-shaped flowers
chervil **Anthriscus cerefolium**	45/30cm 18/12in	annual or biennial with bright green, fern-like leaves; light aniseed flavour
coriander **Coriandrum sativum**	45/30cm 18/12in	hardy annual with bright green leaves like broad-leaved parsley; spicy flavour
dill **Anethum graveolens**	90/30cm 3/1ft	hardy annual making a feathery clump with thread-like, blue-green leaves; delicately aromatic
feverfew **Chrysanthemum parthenium**	45/45cm 18/18in	hardy annual with heads of small, white daisies above aromatic, lobed leaves
marjoram, sweet **Origanum majorana**	60/30cm 2/1ft	sweetly aromatic subshrub usually grown as a half-hardy annual; red-stems carry grey leaves and in summer clusters of white or pink flowers
parsley **Petroselinum crispum**	45/23cm 18/9in	biennial or annual, the curly types with serrated leaves make dense, ornamental clumps, the plain or broad-leaved types reputedly of better flavour
savory, summer **Satureja hortensis**	30/23cm 12/9in	bushy hardy annual with strongly aromatic dark green leaves; minute lilac flowers in summer
PERENNIALS AND SHRUBS		
bay **Laurus nobilis**	5.5/3.7m 18/12ft	semi-hardy evergreen shrub or tree often grown as a standard or half-standard; aromatic, mid- to dark green leaves; small cream flowers in summer
chives **Allium schoenoprasum**	25/10cm 10/4in	perennial, grassy clumps of onion-flavoured, tubular leaves topped by heads of rose-pink flowers in summer
chives, garlic **Allium tuberosum**	60/20cm 24/8in	perennial with flat-bladed leaves tasting of garlic and chives; starry, white flowers in summer
fennel **Foeniculum vulgare**	200/45cm 6½/1½ft	feathery mass of thread-like, blue-green leaves; flat heads of tiny, sulphur flowers in summer
hyssop **Hyssopus officinalis**	45/30cm 18/12in	bushy, semi-evergreen perennial with strongly aromatic leaves and spikes of purple-blue, tubular flowers from mid- summer to early autumn
marjoram, pot **Origanum onites**	30/30cm 12/12in	sprawling subshrub; red stems bear bright green leaves and whorls of mauve or white, tubular flowers in summer
mint, apple **Mentha suaveolens**	90/60cm 3/2ft	moisture-loving, invasive perennial with pale green, fragrant leaves that are softly hairy
rosemary **Rosmarinus officinalis**	1.5/1.5m 5/5ft	refreshingly aromatic evergreen shrub with narrow leaves white on the reverse; scented mauve flowers in spring and sporadically in summer
sage **Salvia officinalis**	60/90cm 2/3ft	sprawling evergreen subshrub; aromatic, grey-green leaves of velvety texture and small, tubular, violet-blue flowers in summer; purple-leaved and variegated forms available
savory, winter **Satureja montana**	30/23cm 12/9in	compact, erect, semi-evergreen perennial with small, grey-green leaves that are spicily aromatic; lavender flowers in late summer
spearmint **Mentha spicata**	60/60cm 2/2ft	moisture-loving, invasive perennial; prominently veined oval leaves strongly minty when crushed
tarragon **Artemisia dracunculus**	60/30cm 2/1ft	open perennial with narrow, grey-green leaves; French tarragon is generally considered more refined than Russian tarragon
thyme, common **Thymus vulgaris**	20/30cm- 8/12in	dwarf, evergreen shrub making a mound of aromatic, dark green leaves; clusters of mauve, tubular flowers in early summer
thyme, lemon **Thymus x citriodorus**	10/25cm 4/10in	similar to common thyme but with broader lemon-scented leaves; also silver- and gold-leaved forms

ORNAMENTAL VEGETABLES

The dimensions given provide only a rough guide to the size of plants as there can be considerable variation from one cultivar to another.

Name	height/spread	description
ANNUALS		
asparagus pea	30/15cm 12/6in	pretty pea flowers of an unusual reddish-brown are followed by winged pods, which are harvested while still young during summer
broccoli, sprouting	75/60cm 2½/2ft	immature flowerheads of purple sprouting broccoli look attractive against the blue-green leaves in spring, when they are harvested
cabbage	30/45cm 12/18in	round-head cabbages, mainly harvested in autumn and winter, make attractive rosettes of foliage, the red kinds with a distinct bloom; there are also cabbages – green, white and red or mixtures – grown specifically as ornamentals
carrot	25/15cm 10/6in	feathery foliage is ornamental at the front of borders; successional sowings give long season
cauliflower	45/75cm 1½/2½ft	the most familiar have heads of creamy curds surrounded by blue-green leaves but there are even more ornamental types with purple or green curds; many are harvested in winter but there are types suitable for other seasons
courgette, trailing types	45/180cm 1½/6ft	can be trained on supports or left to trail; fruits, green or yellow, are harvested through summer
French beans, climbing	250/30cm 8/1ft	alternatives to the dwarf kinds and looking picturesque trained up wigwams; green, yellow or purple-podded beans are harvested through summer into autumn
lettuce	20/30cm 8/12in	the most ornamental are the non-hearting kinds, often with attractive, frilly leaves tinted bronze or red; can be harvested through much of year
ruby chard	45/25cm 18/10in	form of spinach beet with red stalks and mid-ribs; grown as an annual for cropping in summer or autumn and spring
runner bean, climbing	250/30cm 8/1ft	orange-red, sometimes white, flowers followed by long beans that are harvested from mid-summer into autumn; ornamental on wigwams
sweet corn (maize)	250/60cm 8/2ft	impressive grass with strap-shaped leaves arching out from a main stem; edible cobs ripen in late summer or autumn; there are ornamental forms with variegated foliage or cobs
tomato, cordon types	120/30cm 4/1ft	clusters of red or yellow fruits ripening in late summer or autumn but success depends on good summer weather; need support
PERENNIALS		
asparagus	120/60cm 4/2ft	usually planted in beds, the young shoots being harvested in late spring; the feathery foliage is very pretty with flowers in borders
cardoon	180/90cm 6/3ft	magnificent fountain of grey foliage topped by thistly flowers; as a crop the young shoots are blanched and harvested in spring
globe artichoke	120/90cm 4/3ft	handsome clump of jagged, silvery leaves topped by thistly flowers, which are harvested in summer while still immature
seakale	60/60cm 2/2ft	large, waxy, sea-blue leaves; as a crop the blanched shoots are harvested in spring

the branches trained out horizontally in one plane, or as cordons, with trees usually trained at an angle of about 45 degrees and branches pruned back to produce fruiting spurs.

Herbs, grown now for culinary and ornamental value rather than for physic, mix happily with flowering plants. So, too, can many vegetables. Traditionalists might look askance at some of those listed on this page but they have been chosen for the modern cottage garden where the aim is often to make the vegetable patch pretty as well as useful. Almost all vegetables and herbs do best in full sun where the soil is fertile and well drained.

In modern gardens inspired by cottage models the ornamental role of useful plants is often given an emphasis that traditionalists might find excessive. However, many vegetables, including lettuces and cabbages, do make handsome foliage plants. One of the most spectacular is ruby chard, with dark, crinkled foliage and strongly coloured stems.

The scented garden

It is perfectly possible to make a grand and beautiful garden in which fragrance plays no part but it is well nigh impossible to create a garden of personal charm and intimacy without scented plants. Admittedly, the appreciation of scent is highly personal. It is not simply that the sense of smell is developed to different degrees in different people. The appeal of scents depends very heavily on associations; what triggers a sensation of warm sentiment in one person might set off an ill-defined feeling of unease in another. This variability in our reactions is not, however, sufficient reason to garden without taking any account of the fragrance of flowers or the aromatic scents of foliage, for there is fairly broad unanimity about what is most agreeable.

It is commonly said that the more highly bred a plant, the less likely it is to be well scented. There is some truth in this but it is a generalization that cannot be taken for granted. The Dutch hyacinths are among the most powerfully scented of flowers but have been bred for centuries to produce uniform, waxy, solid spikes. On the other hand, some species of plants that have undergone very little breeding have no appreciable scent. One thinks sometimes what perfection some of the campanulas or Japanese anemones would achieve if only their flowers were fragrant. Fortunately there are many scented companions that can make up for their short-coming.

It is a common complaint of modern roses that they never measure up in richness of perfume to the old roses. Frankly, it is infertile ground for debate. Some old roses are superbly fragrant (few plants of any description can match the refined, deep scent of 'Madame Isaac Pereire') but some have virtually no scent at all while many modern roses – the choice, after all,

Few roses are more ravishingly fragrant than the nineteenth-century 'Madame Isaac Pereire', which, like a number of Bourbon roses, can be grown either as a shrub or as a low climber. It more than lives up to the reputation for good scent that the old roses have acquired but others are just as disappointing as unscented modern roses.

ROSES NOTABLE FOR THEIR FRAGRANCE

In this chart bush roses are described as large- or cluster-flowered, terms that now replace hybrid tea and floribunda. Unless stated otherwise, these roses repeat, the flowers generally being borne in two main flushes.

Name	category	height/spread	description
BUSH ROSES			
R. 'Alec's Red'	large	90/60cm 3/2ft	bushy plants bear large, double blooms of deep cherry-red
R. 'Arthur Bell'	cluster	75/60cm 2½/2ft	clusters of yellow, semi-double blooms hold their colour best in cool weather; glossy foliage
R. 'Fragrant Cloud'	large	75/60cm 2½/2ft	exceptionally fragrant modern rose with masses of large, double, dusky coral flowers; dark green, glossy leaves
R. 'Fragrant Delight'	cluster	110/75cm 3½/2½ft	large, semi-double blooms of coppery salmon; young leaves tinted bronze
R. 'Paul Shirville'	large	75/75cm 2½/2½ft	double peach blooms shaded salmon-pink; glossy, dark foliage
R. 'Radox Bouquet'	cluster	90/60cm 3/2ft	bears clusters of large, individual double and rose-pink flowers; glossy leaves
R. 'Royal William'	large	110/75cm 3½/2½ft	deep crimson, classically shaped double flowers; upright growth and dark leaves
SHRUB ROSES			
R. 'Blanche Double de Coubert'	Rugosa	1.8/1.5m 6/5ft	large, semi-double flowers of dazzling white among fresh green foliage
R. 'Boule de Neige'	Bourbon	1.5/1.2m 5/4ft	sprays of double, globular blooms open white from pink-splashed buds; dark leaves
R. 'Fantin-Latour'	Centifolia	2.2/2.2m 7/7ft	among the loveliest of old roses, with double, cup-shaped blooms of soft pink; flowers profusely but only once
R. 'Königin von Dänemark'	Alba	1.5/1.2m 5/4ft	one fine burst of double, quartered, light to deep pink flowers on a lax bush with grey-green foliage
R. 'Louise Odier'	Bourbon	1.8/1.2m 6/4ft	exquisitely camellia-shaped, double pink blooms with lilac shading; good trained as a short climber
R. 'Madame Hardy'	Damask	1.5/1.2m 5/4ft	one of the choicest of old roses, with double, white flowers opening flat to reveal a green eye; flowers early but once only
R. 'Madame Isaac Pereire'	Bourbon	2.2/1.8m 7/6ft	large, double blooms of purplish-crimson with a scent to match their sumptuous splendour; vigorous and suitable as a climber
R. 'Roseraie de l'Haÿ'	Rugosa	2.2/1.8m 7/6ft	large, double, purple-red flowers, loose and opening flat to show yellow stamens; bright leaves leathery and wrinkled

LESS-FAMILIAR SCENTED PERENNIALS

Name	height/spread	description
Cosmos atrosanguineus	75/45cm 2½/1½ft	the long succession of dark maroon, single flowers in summer smell, astonishingly, of chocolate
Hemerocallis lilioasphodelus	75/45cm 2½/1½ft	refined, yellow, trumpet flowers in spring with a scent to match
Hosta 'Honeybells'	90/75cm 3/2½ft	hosta flowers are usually considered incidental to the foliage although some are of quiet beauty and fragrant; this has scented, lilac bells in late summer
Iris 'Florentina' German iris	60/30cm 2/1ft	elegant, milky white, fragrant flowers; many of the hybrid bearded irises are fragrant
Iris unguicularis	25/40cm 10/16in	flimsy, lilac, deliciously scented flowers thrust their way through grassy clumps over winter
Lysichiton camtschatcensis	90/90cm 3/3ft	bog lover with white flowers in spring, their sweet scent a contrast to the rankness of *L. americanum*
Paeonia lactiflora 'Monsieur Jules Elie'	75/60cm 2½/2ft	one of the many hybrid peonies that bear fragrant flowers in late spring or early summer; double pink
Petasites fragrans winter heliotrope	30/120cm 1/4ft	a menace except in very large landscapes but the mauve flowers in winter are beguilingly fragrant
Polygonatum odoratum	60/30cm 2/1ft	woodlander in the style of solomon's seal but with fewer flowers that are white and scented
Primula florindae	60/60cm 2/2ft	summer-flowering and moisture-loving; the fragrant, yellow bells are powdered with meal
Romneya coulteri tree poppy	180/30cm 6/1ft	large, crinkled, white poppies with a sweet scent in the second half of summer
Smilacina racemosa false spikenard	90/45cm 3/1½ft	fluffy heads of fragrant, creamy flowers are a delight in shade during late spring and early summer
Verbena bonariensis	150/60cm 5/2ft	gangling plant topped by small tufts of lavender-blue, fragrant flowers in late summer and early autumn

LESS-FAMILIAR SCENTED BULBS

Name	height/spread	description
Amaryllis bella-donna	75/30cm 2½/1ft	fragrant, pink trumpets, 3-4 per stem in autumn, appear before leaves; best on warm, sunny sites
Cardiocrinum giganteum	250/90cm 8/3ft	the massive stems of this giant lily relative carry fragrant, creamy trumpets in late summer
Crocus chrysanthus 'E.A. Bowles'	8/5cm 3/2in	honey-scented flowers, rich yellow with bronze feathering at the base in late winter
Crinum × powellii 'Album'	75/45cm 2½/1½ft	sweetly scented, funnel-shaped, white flowers over strap-shaped leaves in late summer or early autumn
Galanthus 'S. Arnott' snowdrop	20/10cm 8/4cm	early spring snowdrop with a sweet scent
Gladiolus callianthus 'Murieliae'	90/20cm 36/8in	elegant, fragrant, white flowers, blotched maroon at the centre, open in early autumn
Muscari armeniacum 'Heavenly Blue'	25/10cm 10/4in	flower spikes in spring densely clustered with blue bells; sweetly scented, as is the paler 'Cantab'
Tulipa 'Bellona'	38/20cm 15/8in	rounded, yellow flowers in mid-spring that surprise with the strength of their scent
Tulipa 'Generaal de Wet'	35/15cm 14/6in	one of the best known of the scented tulips; yellow flowers with an orange overlay in mid-spring

is staggering – have perfumes in the top rank. My own disappointment is not so much with modern roses but with many of the modern lilies (see page 78). The genus includes some superbly scented plants, some so heavily fragrant that they can be overpowering in a confined space, but there are many hybrids that have no scent at all.

Scented flowers

It is worth positioning plants carefully in the garden so that the full benefit of their fragrance can be appreciated. A few need to be treated with some caution. The mock oranges (Philadelphus) have such a heavy fragrance that its sweetness can be oppressive if planted close to an area for sitting out. Furthermore, the plant is nondescript when out of flower so it is not unfair to plant it in a position at the back of a border, where its rich perfume will benefit from being somewhat diluted.

Even plants with less heavy scents but which none the less carry well are often best tucked away. The shrubby, winter-flowering honeysuckle Lonicera x purpusii is an indifferent plant in summer but on a sombre day its penetrating scent is revivifying. The scent of the sweet box Sarcococca hookeriana digyna is another that wafts mysteriously through the winter garden but this is a low plant that is worth fitting in to a shady corner near a door.

Many winter flowers only reveal the full richness of their scent when they are picked and brought indoors, the warmth of a room allowing the fragrance to develop. This is true of wintersweet (Chimonanthus praecox) and the witch hazels (Hamamelis). Low-growing plants present a rather different problem. It is undignified and awkward crawling around to sniff the flowers of Iris unguicularis or the small honey-scented crocuses of late winter. The iris flowers are superb for picking (pull them out

RIGHT There are many viburnums that are worth growing for their scent, including the winter-flowering Viburnum x bodnantense 'Dawn'. The sweet scent of the V. carlesii, shown here, has made it a favourite spring shrub and a number of excellent selections have been named, all to some extent pink in bud and opening to white or pink flowers.

FAR RIGHT Climbers that work their way around windows and doors bring the fragrance of the garden into the house. The wisterias are vigorous twiners, all with dangling clusters of flowers that are to some degree fragrant. The best scented of the species, Wisteria sinensis, is also the most vigorous, needing strong supports on a wall or a solid pergola to clamber over.

from their grassy tufts) but unfortunately they do not last long in water. The crocus flowers are really too small to treat in this way. They are lovely to grow in small pots so that they can be examined close to and their scent appreciated.

Valuable though the scented winter flowers are, those that give the greatest pleasure are for me associated with sitting outdoors or with catching a breath of perfumed outdoor air

SHRUBS WITH SCENTED FLOWERS IN SPRING

Unless stated otherwise, the following flower in late spring, often into summer

Name	height/spread	description
Berberis x stenophylla	3/3.7m 10/12ft	arching, evergreen shrub with masses of yellow flowers; sparse showing of small, purple berries
Choisya ternata Mexican orange blossom	1.8/1.8m 6/6ft	aromatic, evergreen shrub with clusters of sweetly scented, white flowers; often repeats in autumn
Corylopsis pauciflora	2/3m 6/10ft	deciduous, woodland shrub for lime-free soils; drooping, cowslip-scented flowers in early spring
Daphne x burkwoodii 'Somerset'	1.2/1.2m 4/4ft	semi-evergreen, upright shrub with dense heads of white flowers, pink on the outside; rich scent
Daphne cneorum 'Eximia' garland flower	10/50cm 4/20in	clusters of rose-pink flowers on a prostrate, evergreen shrub exhale a delicious, pervasive scent
Osmanthus delavayi	1.8/1.8m 6/6ft	one of the loveliest early spring shrubs; white, tubular flowers among glossy, evergreen leaves exhale a delicious scent
Syringa vulgaris 'Vestale' lilac	3.7/3m 12/10ft	deciduous shrubs or small trees, with large heads of richly fragrant flowers in a wide range of colours, straddle the spring-summer divide; this bears erect pyramids of white flowers
Viburnum x burkwoodii 'Park Farm Hybrid'	2.5/3.7m 8/12ft	semi-evergreen shrub with rounded heads of waxy flowers opening white from pink buds to release a penetrating sweetness
Viburnum carlesii 'Diana'	1.5/1.5m 5/5ft	all the forms of this deciduous shrub are superbly fragrant; heads of waxy flowers open white from red buds; the foliage, bronze when young, shows good autumn colour

SHRUBS WITH SCENTED FLOWERS IN SUMMER

Name	height/spread	description
Buddleja alternifolia	5/4m 16/13ft	deciduous, arching shrub or small tree, in early summer bearing clusters of lilac-purple flowers in a fragrant cascade
Buddleja davidii 'Dartmoor' butterfly bush	3/3m 10/10ft	vigorous, deciduous shrub hard-pruned in spring to produce in late summer dense plumes of rich lilac flowers with a heady fragrance that attracts butterflies; many other cultivars available
Clerodendrum trichotomum	3/3m 10/10ft	deciduous shrub or small tree covered with small, sweetly scented, white flowers in late summer; astonishing turquoise berries follow
Elaeagnus angustifolia oleander	5/5m 16/16ft	deciduous shrub or small tree with silvery leaves; in early summer the perfume of the small, creamy yellow flowers is intoxicating; ideal for dry sites
Jasminum humile 'Revolutum'	2.5/3m 8/10ft	slightly tender, semi-evergreen shrub; clusters of sweet-scented, yellow flowers over a long season
Lavandula x intermedia 'Hidcote Giant'	90/150cm 3/5ft	most lavenders are well scented and this, with large flower spikes in mid- to late summer, is especially so
Magnolia grandiflora 'Exmouth'	6/3m 20/10ft	evergreen best grown as a wall shrub; in late summer and autumn grandiose, bowl-shaped, creamy white flowers nestle among large, leathery leaves that have a rusty felt on the underside
Myrtus communis myrtle	3/3m 10/10ft	aromatic, evergreen shrub for a sheltered position; fragrant, white flowers in mid- to late summer sometimes succeeded by purple-black fruits
Philadelphus 'Beauclerk' mock orange	2.5/1.8m 8/6ft	from a pack of richly scented, deciduous hybrids one that is super fragrant; graceful arching bush; in early summer white flowers with a purple stain

SHRUBS WITH SCENTED FLOWERS IN AUTUMN AND WINTER

Unless special conditions are mentioned, all of the plants listed will succeed in sunny positions where the soil is well drained and reasonably fertile. Shrubs for which no flowering period is given are usually at their peak in late winter but often start earlier and run on into spring.

Name	height/spread	description
Daphne odora 'Aureomarginata'	1.5/1.5m 5/5ft	glossy, evergreen shrub, the leaves edged yellow; clusters of purplish buds open to crystalline white flowers and release a voluptuous scent
Elaeagnus x ebbingei	4.5/4.5m 15/15ft	fast-growing, bushy evergreen with silvery young leaves, surprising with a lovely scent from inconspicuous flowers in autumn
Hamamelis x intermedia 'Jelena' witch hazel	3/3m 10/10ft	deciduous, the bare branches glowing in mid-winter with the massed effect of spidery flowers blending yellow and copper-red; superb autumn colour; one of several excellent hybrids
Lonicera x purpusii	1.5/1.5m 5/5ft	bushy, deciduous shrub; creamy white flowers release a pervasive, sweet scent over a long season
Mahonia japonica	2.5/3m 8/10ft	evergreen shrub with spiny foliage and sprays of lemon-yellow flowers with lily-of-the-valley scent over a long period; dark purple berries
Osmanthus heterophyllus	3/3m 10/10ft	evergreen, holly-like shrub with hidden clusters of sweetly scented, white flowers in autumn
Sarcococca confusa	1.2/1.2m 4/4ft	most of the sarcococcas, useful evergreens for shade, have inconspicuous but fragrant flowers; this has white flowers followed by black berries
Viburnum x bodnantense 'Dawn'	3/3m 10/10ft	upright, deciduous shrub providing a succession of sweetly scented, pink flowers in autumn and winter

SCENTED CLIMBERS AND WALL SHRUBS

All of the following are deciduous and climbers, except where indicated. See also the chart for climbing roses on page 19.

Name	height/spread	description
Buddleja crispa	3/2.5m 10/8ft	grey-leaved shrub with clusters of small, pale lilac flowers in late summer and early autumn
Chimonanthus praecox 'Grandiflorus' winter sweet	3/3m 10/10ft	twiggy shrub, that comes into its own in winter, with yellow flowers of deliciously spicy scent
Clematis flammula	3/2.5m 10/8ft	masses of small, creamy flowers in late summer or early autumn; grown mainly for their scent
Clematis montana 'Alexander'	12/6m 40/20ft	one of several cultivars of this vigorous clematis with scented flowers, in this case creamy white
Cytisus battandieri	4.5/3.7m 15/12ft	shrub with cylindrical clusters of yellow, pineapple-scented, pea flowers in early summer
Jasminum officinale jasmine	5/7.5m 15/25ft	breathes a sweet scent from starry, white flowers in the second half of summer
Lonicera x italica (L. x americana)	7/4.5m 23/15ft	the powerfully fragrant flowers, yellow with a red flush, are borne in the first half of summer
Lonicera periclymenum honeysuckle, woodbine	6/4.5m 20/15ft	classic scented climber: 'Belgica' (early Dutch), has purplish-red flowers fading to yellow-pink in early to mid-summer, followed by 'Serotina' (late Dutch), a darker purple
Trachelospermum jasminoides	3.7/3m 12/10ft	dark-leaved evergreen with fragrant, starry, white flowers in the second half of summer
Wisteria sinensis	25/18m 80/60ft	the most vigorous of the wisterias and with the most fragrant flowers, the mauve clusters being borne in late spring or early summer and sometimes a few blooms in late summer

Some of the modern cultivars of the tobacco plant, which are available in a range of pinks, white and green, do not have the exquisite evening scent of the fragrant, half-hardy annual *Nicotiana alata*. Those that do, such as N. 'Fragrant Cloud', are worth planting in positions where their seductive perfume can best be appreciated at night.

The leaves of aromatic plants generally have to be bruised before their scents are released. An unusual aromatic is *Houttuynia cordata* 'Chameleon', a plant worth growing for its strikingly variegated foliage. It is free-running and likes moist conditions. It is, however, so bold that it is sometimes difficult to place in the garden and is better in a container.

through an open window. Biennials and annuals such as wallflowers (*Erysimum cheiri*, syn. *Cheiranthus cheiri*) and stock (*Matthiola*) are ideal for planting under windows or near doors but for sitting-out areas almost nothing can beat the spicily scented pinks (*Dianthus*). What is more, they make a very lovely foreground to roses. A sunny seat backed by a fragrant climber or rambler surrounded by pinks and shrub roses comes close to a perfect setting for thinking about the next thing to do in the garden.

Fluctuations in the scent of flowers often take one by surprise. Many are more intense at night and in the case of some this is the only time they are detectable. The tobacco plant (*Nicotiana*) is one that waits until the evening to flood the garden with its perfumes. However, in some tobacco plants scent has been lost completely.

Aromatic plants

In most cases the scent of aromatic leaves is less obvious than that of flowers. Light bruising is needed to release the volatile oils that give a leaf its spicy or pungent perfume. This is true for many of the plants listed on page 125 and also for most of the useful and ornamental herbs described on page 118.

A herb garden can be an attractive way of corralling aromatic plants but as so many look well with other plants (and, furthermore, the herb garden can look a bit forlorn in winter) my preference is to see them dispersed throughout the garden. Ideally, the large plants should be strategically placed so that, wandering down a path, one comes across them naturally. Sometimes they need only to be brushed against lightly for them to taint hands or clothes

deliciously. The freedom with which rosemary (*Rosmarinus*) releases its scent is a very good reason for leaving a drunken specimen lurching into a pathway. Plants that only release their scent when crushed, such as the lemon-scented verbena (*Aloysia triphylla*) are best positioned near a doorway, where one's first instinct may be to take a leaf. A few of the low-growing plants, especially the thymes (*Thymus*), will tolerate a little treading and are worth planting so that they can encroach on pathways.

The scented-leaved pelargoniums really deserve a section on their own. Most have relatively small flowers but the foliage is often highly ornamental and the range of scents is astonishing. They can be grown in beds and borders and lifted annually in autumn. They are obviously, too, superb container plants.

ANNUALS AND BIENNIALS WITH SCENTED FLOWERS

The following plants thrive in sunny positions where the soil is well drained. Most flower in summer and the season can often be extended by successional sowing and regular deadheading. Where the flowering season differs, this is noted.

Name	height/spread	description
GROWN AS HARDY ANNUALS		
Centaurea moschata sweet sultan	45/20cm 18/8in	large, fragrant, thistle-like flowers in a range covering white, yellow, pink and purple
Lathyrus odoratus sweet pea	250/30cm 8/1ft	mixtures available of old kinds which, though small-flowered and in a limited colour range, are outstanding for their fragrance
Lobularia maritima (Alyssum maritimum) 'Wonderland'	15/30cm 6/12in	round heads of tiny, sweetly scented, purplish-pink flowers
Malcomia maritima Virginian stock	20/8cm 8/3in	slender plants with cross-shaped, sweetly scented flowers that are red, lilac, rose or white
Matthiola bicornis night-scented stock	38/25cm 15/10in	scrappy plants but the spikes of lilac flowers release a heavy scent at night
Reseda odorata mignonette	30/30cm 12/12in	not showy but the creamy flowers with orange-brown stamens are evocatively fragrant
Scabiosa atropurpurea sweet scabious	90/30cm 3/1ft	lightly scented, pincushion flowers in purple, crimson, pink or white
Tropaeolum majus Jewel Series	30/30cm 12/12in	dwarf, with characteristic trumpet-shaped flowers in red, yellow or orange; spicy scent
GROWN AS HALF-HARDY ANNUALS		
Brachycome iberidifolia Swan River daisy	45/45cm 18/18in	pretty, lightly scented, daisy flowers, mainly blue but also in mauve, pink, purple or white
Cleome hassleriana (C. spinosa)	120/45cm 4/1½ft	large, rounded heads of fragrant, spidery flowers that are white with a pink flush
Heliotropium arborescens 'Marine'	60/60cm 2/2ft	large heads of deep violet-blue flowers drenching the air about them with a powerful scent
Matthiola East Lothian Series	30/30cm 12/12in	relatively dwarf and often grown as biennials; spikes of heavily scented, single or double flowers in pink, red, purple, yellow or white
Matthiola Ten-week Series	30/30cm 12/12in	wide range of size and colour but all having dense spikes of deliciously fragrant flowers
Nicotiana 'Fragrant Cloud'	90/30cm 3/1ft	some tobacco plants disappoint but this has a powerful evening fragrance
GROWN AS BIENNIALS		
Calomeria amaranthoides (Humea elegans) incense plant	180/90cm 6/3ft	cascades of incense-scented, tiny, pink, brownish-red or crimson flowers
Dianthus barbatus Monarch Series sweet william	45/30cm 18/12in	flat heads of fragrant, bicoloured (auricula-eyed) flowers in white and shades of pink, red or crimson in early to mid-summer
Erysimum (Cheiranthus) cheiri Fair Lady Series wallflower	45/38cm 18/15in	in spring and early summer spikes of velvety flowers with a mellow scent to match; available in a mixture of soft colours including apricot, cream, salmon and mahogany
Matthiola Brompton Series	45/30cm 18/12in	best as biennials, the dense spikes of heavily scented, single or double flowers available in white and shades of pink, red or yellow
Papaver nudicaule Iceland poppy	60/30cm 2/1ft	tissue-paper poppies on tall, hairy stems in a wide colour range; highly individual scent

AROMATIC PLANTS

Unless special conditions are mentioned, all the plants listed will succeed in sunny positions where the soil is well drained and reasonably fertile. In addition to these plants, many herbs (see page 118) are strongly aromatic and highly ornamental.

Name	height/spread	description
HARDY BROAD-LEAVED SHRUBS		
Artemisia arborescens 'Faith Raven'	120/90cm 4/3ft	evergreen and fairly hardy with finely dissected silvery leaves; small, yellow flowers in summer and autumn; all artemisias are aromatic
Choisya ternata Mexican orange blossom	1.8/1.8m 6/6ft	year-round, 3-part leaves of luxuriant, glossy, green, aromatic when crushed, and fragrant, white flowers in spring and autumn
Eucalyptus gunnii	22/4.5m 70/15ft	fast-growing, evergreen tree with creamy bark and white flowers in summer; often coppiced for blue-green or silver juvenile foliage
Helichrysum italicum serotinum curry plant	15/15cm 6/6in	an evergreen pungently aromatic in hot, dry positions and making a low dome of silvery grey; bright yellow flowers in summer
Lavandula angustifolia 'Twickel Purple' lavender	60/90cm 2/3ft	silver-grey foliage year round and purple flowers provide a lovely combination of homely scents
Myrtus communis myrtle	3/3m 10/10ft	deliciously aromatic evergreen for a sheltered position; fragrant, white flowers in mid- to late summer followed by purplish berries
Perovskia atriplicifolia Russian sage	120/90cm 4/3ft	deciduous subshrub with grey-green leaves smelling of sage; spikes of violet-blue flowers in late summer and autumn
Santolina chamaecyparissus cotton lavender	60/60cm 2/2ft	silver-grey, feathery hummocks invite touch; yellow, button flowers in mid-summer
TENDER BROAD-LEAVED SHRUBS		
Aloysia triphylla (Lippia citriodora) lemon-scented verbena	3/3m 10/10ft	deciduous shrub with mauve flowers that count for little but the leaves release a delicious lemon scent when crushed
Pelargonium 'Chocolate Peppermint'	75/75cm 2½/2½ft	evergreen subshrub with strongly mint-scented large leaves; these are 3-lobed with a heavy brown blotch in the centre
Pelargonium 'Prince of Orange'	60/45cm 2/1½ft	unmistakably orange-scented leaves; pale purple flowers have dark veining
Prostanthera rotundifolia mint bush	2.2/2.2m 7/7ft	the tiny evergreen leaves are deliciously minty and the bush is smothered in spring or early summer with purplish flowers
HERBACEOUS PERENNIALS		
Calamintha nepeta	30/30cm 12/12in	deliciously minty foliage and masses of tiny, mauve flowers in late summer and autumn
Geranium macrorrhizum	38/45cm 15/18in	easy-going semi-evergreen with pink flowers in early summer and slightly sticky, aromatic leaves, which take on reddish tints in autumn
Houttuynia cordata 'Chameleon'	10/60cm 4/24in	heart-shaped leaves with bold red and yellow splashes on green and pleasantly orange-like scent when crushed; white flowers in summer
Monarda didyma 'Croftway Pink' bee balm, Oswego tea	90/45cm 3/1½ft	in late summer whorls of pink flowers are carried over a clump of aromatic foliage; cultivars available in pinks, reds and white
Nepeta 'Six Hills Giant'	75/45cm 2½/1½ft	large version of catmint with spikes of lavender-blue flowers in summer

Formal gardens

In the often heated exchanges between proponents of formal and informal gardening, it is commonly overlooked that artifice plays a part in garden-making of all kinds. Some process of ordering and selection inevitably takes place in setting aside a privileged piece of ground within which selected plants are grown. What gives the formal garden its distinctive character is the blatant relish with which that order is imposed. Hedges and walls make clear boundaries to the garden or divisions within it. Paths form axes that divide the space into considered proportions. The eye is pulled to focal points that may be anything from a statue or fountain to a specimen tree. The deliberate use of rhythmic repetition reasserts the formal way the components of the garden are arranged. This may simply be the pairing of potted plants either side of a gateway but can be elaborated in much more complex patterning that includes knot gardens and parterres, with bedding plants making regular designs within clipped edging.

Inspiration from the past

Those favouring formal gardens often turn to the past, deliberately intending to create a replica or evocation of a garden from a period when formality was the norm. Landscaping on the megalomanic scale of Louis XIV's garden designer Le Nôtre can be ruled out but details in the grand French manner, such as a *parterre de broderie*, the pattern composed of scrolled lines of clipped box, could easily feature within quite a small garden. More common as a source of inspiration are Dutch gardens of the seventeenth century, in which walls and hedges enclose simple oblong beds divided by straight paths, with accents, often in the form of topiary, emphasizing the garden's structure. It should be

Cropping of the kitchen garden often leaves it looking disordered. The addition of formal elements that provide continuity can help to enhance it as a decorative component of the larger garden. Box hedging and topiary have been used here. Fruit trees trained as espaliers or cordons can also be used to impose a formal structure.

TREES AND SHRUBS OF A NATURALLY REGULAR SHAPE

Trees and shrubs of narrowly upright or compact, rounded growth are useful in formal schemes as focal points or, when planted at regular intervals, to form avenues.

Name	height/spread	description
EVERGREEN		
Chamaecyparis lawsoniana 'Witzeliana' Lawson's cypress	4.5/1.2m 15/4ft	slender conifer making a vivid green, narrow column
Hebe cupressoides 'Boughton Dome'	30/60cm 1/2ft	slow-growing shrub making a tight dome; a few blue-tinged white flowers in summer
Ilex aquifolium 'Handsworth New Silver' holly	6/3m 20/10ft	makes a dense column of dark green, lit by creamy variegation; red berries are borne freely
Juniperus chinensis 'Keteleeri' Chinese juniper	12/4m 40/13ft	dense, grey-green columnar conifer with aromatic foliage
Juniperus communis 'Compressa'	60/15cm 24/6in	dense, narrow, grey-green column that has become a platitude of rock gardens but could be used more imaginatively
Picea glauca albertiana 'Conica'	150/90cm 5/3ft	dwarf, dense conifer making a solid, grass-green cone
Prunus lusitanica 'Myrtifolia' Portugal laurel	5/3m 16/10ft	small-leaved form making a dense cone of glossy foliage
Taxus baccata 'Fastigiata' Irish yew	4.5/3m 15/10ft	conifer making an impressive, dark green column with an irregular summit
DECIDUOUS		
Acer rubrum 'Scanlon' Canadian maple	15/4.5m 50/15ft	columnar growth, especially when young, and brilliant autumn colour
Carpinus betulus 'Fastigiata' hornbeam	10/5m 33/16ft	young trees have a sharply defined, oval outline; good foliage colour in autumn
Malus tschonoskii	12/6m 40/20ft	narrowly conical when young; white blossom with a pink tinge followed by green-yellow crab apples with a purple tinge; foliage colours brilliantly in autumn
Prunus 'Spire'	7.5/2.5m 25/8ft	columnar then vase-shaped flowering cherry with soft pink flowers; bronze-tinted young leaves and brilliant autumn colour
Pyrus calleryana 'Chanticleer'	12/3m 40/10ft	narrowly conical tree with sprays of white flowers in spring; leaves turn purple or maroon in autumn and are long lasting
Sorbus x thuringiaca 'Fastigiata'	12/4.5m 40/15ft	the dense growth of upright branches creates a distinctive oval head; white flowers in late spring followed by scarlet fruits

remembered, however, that the venerable charm of a garden in a historic mould does not exhaust the potential for formal organization of space, and that the layout of a small garden need not rely on the rather unadventurous geometry found in seventeenth-century gardens in the Dutch manner.

The role of plants

One factor that counts against the formal garden in some eyes is that it often draws on a very small repertoire of plants. The case is generally overstated because, as some of the finest gardens of this century show, it is possible to combine rich planting with a very firm overall structure. For example, many of the herbaceous perennials, shrubs, roses, bulbs and annuals listed on pages 44-85 can easily be accommodated in beds and borders, perhaps edged with low hedges, that are part of a formal layout. It is true, however, that a handsome formal garden might draw on a very small range of plants and if architectural boundaries are used, there may be no need for hedging plants such as those described on page 11.

The charts included in this section are intended to cover quite specific requirements in formal gardens. The rhythm of an avenue is one of the most telling features in a formal garden, with paired plants – or sculpture – flanking a path or view at regular intervals. What first comes to mind when we think of this device are trees marching across a landscape but an avenue can consist of rows of potted plants lining a path. In a small garden there may not be space for anything more but in gardens of moderate size there could be room for avenues of compact trees or shrubs. Those of a regular shape, such as the examples given in the chart on the left, are especially useful.

Small-leaved evergreens, such as box (*Buxus sempervirens*) and yew (*Taxus baccata*) are needed for topiary of detailed design. The hollies are too large in the leaf for such work but make good bold shapes. The variegation of *Ilex x altaclarensis* 'Golden King', used here, helps to give the traditional form a curious liveliness.

PLANTS FOR TRAINING AS STANDARDS

Although for display purposes the following might be placed outdoors, their formative training needs to be done under glass.

Name	description
Argyranthemum (Chrysanthemum) frutescens Paris daisy	subshrub often grown as an annual but can be trained on a clear stem up to 90cm/3ft high; white daisies over grey-green foliage all summer and under glass almost all year
Dendranthema (Chrysanthemum) 'Salmon Margaret'	example of a vigorous, spray florists' chrysanthemum suitable for training on a clear stem 45-75cm/1½-2½ft high; reflexed flowers of salmon-pink in autumn
Fuchsia 'Snowcap'	suitably vigorous hybrid; semi-double red with a white bell beneath, which can be trained on a clear stem up to 90cm/3ft high; also suitable: 'Annabel', double with pink-tinged, creamy flowers and 'Mrs Lovell Swisher', with small, pink and red flowers; long summer and autumn season
Heliotropium arborescens heliotrope	useful in bedding or containers on a clear stem of about 60cm/2ft; heads of very fragrant, dark blue flowers in summer
Pelargonium 'Flower of Spring'	example of a vigorous zonal pelargonium that can be trained on a clear stem about 60-90cm/2-3ft high; white-variegated leaves and single, red flowers
Solenostemon (Coleus blumei) 'Pineapple Beauty'	one of the most suitable cultivars for training on a clear stem to 1.2m/4ft, making a mophead of yellow leaves blotched red-brown near the base

TREES AND SHRUBS FOR TOPIARY

With the exception of *Crataegus monogyna*, the following plants are evergreen. These plants are best kept trimmed within the range of heights given.

Name	height	trim	description
Buxus sempervirens common box	30-150cm 1-5ft	x1 late sum. to early aut.	classic evergreen, suitable for detailed work
Crataegus monogyna hawthorn	2.5-4.5m 8-15ft	x1 late sum. to early spr.	deciduous and only suitable for simple, strong shapes
Cupressus sempervirens Italian cypress	1.8-4.5m 6-15ft	x1 sum.	frost-tender conifer much used in southern Europe
Ilex x altaclarensis	1.5-4.5m 5-15ft	x 1 mid- to late sum.	variegated female holly and other forms suitable for simple shapes
Ilex aquifolium common holly	1.5-4.5m 5-15ft	x1 mid- to late sum.	suitable for large shapes; variegated forms can be used for bright effects
Juniperus communis common juniper	90-250cm 3-8ft	x1 sum.	conifer now little used but can be trimmed to simple shapes
Laurus nobilis sweet bay	1.2-3m 4-10ft	x2 sum.	large-leaved but suitable for mopheads and similar shapes
Ligustrum ovalifolium 'Aureum' golden privet	90-250cm 3-8ft	x3 late spr. to early aut.	this and the less interesting plain-leaved form are fast-growing and only hold shape if regularly trimmed
Lonicera nitida 'Baggesen's Gold'	60-150cm 2-5ft	x3 late spr. to early aut.	this and the plain-leaved form need frequent trimming
Phillyrea angustifolia	90-180cm 3-6ft	x1 late spr.	formerly much used but needs a sheltered position
Prunus lusitanica Portugal laurel	1.5-3.7m 5-12ft	x 1 sum.	large leaves but splendid for bold shapes
Taxus baccata yew	1.5-3.7m 5-12ft	x1 sum.	fine-textured conifer superb for architectural and more detailed topiary

Topiary and other forms of hard pruning and training are often associated exclusively with gardens of traditional layout. Beautiful though these gardens can be, it is refreshing to see traditional techniques applied in a garden of original design, as in this sloping site. The variety of the components in such a small area is in itself part of the appeal.

Plants that can be trained as low standards are particularly useful as accents in smaller gardens. The plants listed on page 128 are all to some extent tender and should not be put outdoors until all risk of frost is past. They are particularly attractive used as 'dot' plants in bedding schemes or paired, flanking doors or seats.

Using topiary

In the past, many trees and shrubs were considered suitable for trimming and training into artificial decorative shapes but in modern gardens, box (*Buxus sempervirens*) and yew (*Taxus baccata*) are used almost exclusively. These have the advantage of tolerating close clipping. Their slow rate of growth might infuriate impatient gardeners but as mature specimens they hold their shape with a minimum of trimming, once or twice a year in the summer is usually enough.

The simplest way to make a topiary shape is to build it up gradually by training and clipping. Even at an early stage close clipping is advisable as this will stimulate dense growth. For a bird shape, train stems in the required direction for head and tail extensions by tying them to a firmly secured bamboo cane. Alternatively, plant a young specimen inside a framework, clipping any growths that extend beyond the frame as the plant develops. This has the advantage of providing a shape from the outset.

Choice of shape is very much a matter of personal taste. The whimsicality that looks delightful in a cottage garden can look out of place in a more severe setting but there is room for experimenting with less conventional geometric shapes than are commonly used.

To encourage vigorous growth on young specimens feed generously and apply an organic mulch. Older specimens should be fed sparingly, otherwise they will make excessive growth.

Woodland gardens

On the face of it, woodland gardening seems an absurdly optimistic enterprise for all but those embarrassed by the amount of land at their disposal. On quite a small scale, however, it is possible to capture the essence of 'natural' woodland, using as a core even as few as one or two trees.

The most characteristic feature of old deciduous woodland is that its vegetation is ordered vertically. The topmost tier is formed by dignified large trees. Provided the foliage canopy they create is not too dense, beneath it thrives a tier of smaller trees and shrubs that are reasonably tolerant of shade, some needing the light shelter that the canopy provides. On the woodland floor is yet another layer of vegetation, consisting mainly of bulbs and perennials that make active growth and flower in winter and spring, before the deciduous canopy is fully developed. Along with these there are plants of the woodland margins and glades, preferring generally higher light levels, that flower in the summer months. To make a convincing woodland garden these three layers all need to be represented and to be grouped with the nonchalant informality that is so appealing in wild woodland.

Trees & shrubs

There must be merit points and an enormous amount of personal satisfaction for those who create woodland from scratch. It is, however, a long-term project that involves land clearance, the planting of shelter belts and, after the planting of the trees that are to form the canopy, a wait before planting the shrubs, perennials and bulbs that are to form the lower tiers.

If you are lucky enough to have a fragment of real woodland, you might well be content to leave its beauty ungardened, except perhaps to

Natural woodland has a layered arrangement, with a canopy arching over a tier of shrubs and a floor consisting largely of perennials, ferns and bulbs. The tall, wild foxgloves (*Digitalis purpurea*) and climbers make natural links between the different layers. In an artificial woodland plants must seem to have found their own way to the site.

SMALL TREES AND LARGE SHRUBS TO MAKE A DECIDUOUS CANOPY

The following are suitable for planting at the edge of woodland comprised of large trees, or as part of a small clump that conveys the impression of woodland. Most can be grown as shrubs or trees; those described as trees naturally develop a single main stem. Other possibilities can be found in the list of maples on page 132, and among the deciduous trees and larger shrubs suitable for acid soils on page 105.

Name	height/spread	description
Betula pendula weeping birch	7.5/3.7m 25/12ft	a familiar tree but attractive for its silvery bark, light structure and trembling foliage
Betula utilis jacquemontii	7.5/3.7m 25/12ft	dazzling white stems make this beautiful as a specimen but it is just as lovely among other trees and shrubs
Cornus controversa 'Variegata'	7.5/6m 25/20ft	tiered arrangement of branches is highlighted by white variegated foliage
Cornus florida 'Cherokee Chief' flowering dogwood	4.5/6m 15/20ft	in early summer insignificant flowers are made showy by the surrounding rose-red bracts; the foliage, coppery in spring, colours richly in autumn
Cornus kousa chinensis	6/4.5m 20/15ft	dominating in early summer when the petal-like, white bracts surround insignificant flowers; good foliage colour in autumn and sometimes strawberry-like fruit
Davidia involucrata pocket-handkerchief tree	7.5/5m 25/16ft	insignificant flowers in late spring but the handkerchief bracts that surround them make this an unusual and beautiful tree
Dipelta floribunda	4.5/3m 15/10ft	open growth shows the peeling, light brown bark; the tubular, fragrant flowers are very pale pink with a yellow throat
Disanthus cercidifolius	3/3m 10/10ft	tiny purplish flowers in autumn are inconspicuous but the foliage colours to brilliant red and crimson; for light shade in moist, lime-free soil
Hamamelis x **intermedia** 'Diane'	4.5/4.5m 15/15ft	fragrant, orange-red flowers light up the branches in winter and the foliage glows in autumn; one of several good hybrids
Hamamelis mollis Chinese witch hazel	3.7/3.7m 12/12ft	scent of spidery, yellow flowers carries far in mid- to late winter; the large leaves turn butter-yellow in autumn
Magnolia x **loebneri** 'Leonard Messel'	7.5/6m 25/20ft	floppy, many petalled flowers that cover bare branches in mid-spring are pale pink and fragrant
Magnolia sieboldii	6/7.5m 20/25ft	fragrant, creamy flowers borne with leaves during summer cup the claret stamens and decorative, pink seed capsules; for lime-free soil
Magnolia x **soulangeana** 'Brozzoni'	7.5/6m 25/20ft	one of the triumphs of spring when covered in tulip-shaped, purplish-tinged white flowers
Malus hupehensis Hupeh crab	7.5/6m 25/20ft	crab apple of upright growth with fragrant, white blossom opening from pink buds in late spring; large crops of yellow fruits with a red tinge
Nyssa sinensis	9/7.5m 30/25ft	an alternative to the much larger *N. sylvatica*; pointed leaves, purplish when young, turn green and then glowing reds in autumn
Prunus incisa Fuji cherry	4.5/3.7m 15/12ft	pink buds and single, white flowers create a mass of pink-tinged blossom in early spring; the foliage usually colours well in autumn
Sorbus cashmiriana	4.5/3m 15/10ft	shrub or tree with a head of light foliage; clusters of pink-tinged white flowers in early summer followed by conspicuous white berries
Viburnum plicatum 'Lanarth'	3.7/3.7m 12/12ft	tiered branches laden with flat heads of tiny flowers surrounded by large, sterile, white florets in early summer; good foliage colour in autumn

MAPLES (ACER)

Most maples, including all in this highly selective list, are deciduous. Although their flowers are relatively inconspicuous, maples are an important group of ornamental trees and shrubs on account of their foliage. Some also have bark and twigs of considerable ornamental value and here these have been grouped separately, as have those with variegated foliage.

Name	height/spread	description
A. cappadocicum 'Aureum' Cappadocian maple	20/15m 65/50ft	tree with light green leaves, bright yellow when young and tinted yellow in autumn
A. japonicum 'Aconitifolium'	6/3m 20/10ft	bushy tree; purple flowers, large for a maple, in mid-spring; long-fingered, elegantly cut leaves colouring crimson in autumn
A. japonicum 'Vitifolium'	6/3m 20/10ft	fan-shaped leaves with 10-12 serrated lobes; autumn tints are red, orange and purple
A. palmatum atropurpureum Japanese maple	5/3m 16/10ft	usually a shrub making a mound of bronzy purple in summer and dark crimson in autumn
A. palmatum dissectum Japanese maple	1.1/1.5m 3½/5ft	shrub with finely cut, light green leaves, a lovely contrast to the bronze forms
A. palmatum 'Heptalobum Elegans' Japanese maple	6/6m 20/20ft	shrub or small tree with large leaves, usually with 7 lobes and prettily toothed edges; crimson in autumn
A. platanoides 'Crimson King' Norway maple	15/12m 50/40ft	tree with 5-lobed, reddish-purple leaves, brighter in autumn
A. rubrum 'October Glory' red maple	20/10m 65/33ft	tree with numerous tiny, red flowers on bare branches in spring; leaves, with 3 or 5 lobes, turn from dark green to rich red in autumn
A. saccharinum silver maple	25/15m 80/50ft	fast-growing tree, the silver on the underside of the fingered leaves giving a lively effect in wind; good autumn tints
A. shirasawanum aureum (A. japonicum aureum)	6/3m 20/10ft	slow-growing with soft yellow leaves that may scorch in sun; leaves turn crimson in autumn

VARIEGATED FOLIAGE

Name	height/spread	description
A. negundo 'Elegans' box elder	15/8m 50/26ft	fast-growing tree, the leaves consisting usually of 3-5 leaflets edged with bright yellow
A. negundo 'Variegatum' box elder	15/8m 50/26ft	similar to the above but the variegation is white, with a pink tinge at first; tends to revert
A. platanoides 'Drummondii' Norway maple	15/12m 50/40ft	eye-catching tree, especially in early summer when the contrast of green and the white edge of the leaves is fresh; tendency to revert
A. pseudoplatanus 'Brilliantissimum'	7.5/7.5m 25/25ft	slow-growing sycamore, the foliage making a lovely progression of colour from pink to pale greenish-yellow and then dark green

ORNAMENTAL BARK AND TWIGS

Name	height/spread	description
A. capillipes snake-bark maple	9/9m 30/30ft	small tree with the trunk and older branches striped green and white while the young growths are coral-red; brilliant autumn colour
A. griseum paper-bark maple	6/3.7m 20/12ft	small tree with shavings of old bark curling back to reveal an orange-brown under-bark; 3-lobed leaves colour richly in autumn
A. palmatum 'Sango-kaku' ('Senkaki') coral bark maple	4.5/3.7m 15/12ft	shrub or small tree with coral-pink shoots; leaves turn soft yellow in autumn
A. pensylvanicum snake-bark maple	6/4.5m 20/15ft	small tree with young stems striped green and white; yellow leaves in autumn

RHODODENDRONS AND AZALEAS (RHODODENDRON)

In this chart azaleas are distinguished from rhododendrons.

Name	height/spread	flowering season	description
EVERGREEN 3-6m/10-20ft			
R. 'Blue Peter'	3.7/3.7m 12/12ft	early sum.	frilled flowers in lavender and purple
R. 'Loderi King George'	3.7/3.7m 12/12ft	late spr.	large heads of wonderfully fragrant, pale pink flowers, darker in bud
R. 'Sappho'	3.7/3.7m 12/12ft	late spr. to early sum.	mauve buds open to white flowers with a near-black blotch
EVERGREEN 1.5-3m/5-10ft			
R. cinnabarinum	3/3m 10/10ft	late spr.	young foliage blue-green, against which droop clusters of waxy, orange-red flowers
R. 'Elizabeth'	1.5/1.5m 5/5ft	mid-spr.	leafy dome studded with clusters of trumpet-shaped flowers of brilliant red
R. 'Gomer Waterer'	3/3m 10/10ft	early sum.	large, leathery leaves; clusters of funnel-shaped, white flowers, edged pale mauve with a mustard basal blotch
R. 'Hinodegiri'	1.5/1.5m 5/5ft	late spr.	azalea with masses of small, crimson flowers with a deeper coloured throat
R. 'Hydon Hunter'	1.5/1.5m 5/5ft	late spr. or early sum.	tidy shrub with pink flowers, red at the rim and spotted orange inside
R. moupinense	1.5/1.8m 5/6ft	late win. to early spr.	rounded; loose bunches of fragrant, pink or white flowers, sometimes spotted red
R. orbiculare	3/3m 10/10ft	late spr.	dome-shaped shrub; rounded leaves and loose clusters of blue-tinged, pink flowers
R. 'Temple Belle'	2.2/2.2m 7/7ft	mid- to late spr.	rounded leaves, grey-green beneath; loose clusters of bell-shaped, pink flowers
R. williamsianum	1.8/1.8m 6/6ft	mid-spr.	loose clusters of red buds fading to soft pink flowers; leaves bronze when young
EVERGREEN LESS THAN 1.5m/5ft			
R. 'Cilpinense'	90/90cm 3/3ft	early spr.	rounded bush; bell-shaped, blush-pink flowers open from deeper coloured buds
R. 'Curlew'	30/30cm 12/12in	late spr.	relatively large, yellow flowers prettily marked greenish-brown
R. 'Dora Amateis'	60/60cm 2/2ft	late spr.	many small white flowers tinged with pink and marked with green over glossy foliage
R. 'Ptarmigan'	30/75cm 1/2½ft	early to mid-spr.	sun-loving and making a mound of small, white flowers
R. yakushimanum	90/150cm 3/5ft	late spr. to early sum.	leaves silvery when young and with buff felt on the underside; rounded flowerheads, pink in bud, fade to white
DECIDUOUS AZALEAS			
R. 'Gibraltar'	1.5/1.5m 5/5ft	late spr. to early sum.	crinkly, orange flowers open from dark red buds; good autumn colour
R. luteum	1.5/2.5m 5/8ft	late spr.	heavily scented, yellow flowers and the autumn foliage colours richly
R. 'Narcissiflorum'	1.5/2.5m 5/8ft	late spr. to early sum.	twiggy shrub with double, soft yellow blooms; bronze autumn foliage
R. 'Strawberry Ice'	1.5/2.5m 5/8ft	late spr.	translucent pink flowers flushed deeper pink and with yellow in the throat

ABOVE Although their flowers are generally insignificant, maples (*Acer*) are among the most beautiful of shrubs and trees and they are ideal for acid woodlands. Many have foliage that colours spectacularly in autumn but the bronze and purple of several forms of *A. japonicum* are highly ornamental throughout the growing season.

Rhododendrons and azaleas, all belonging to the genus *Rhododendron*, are the most important group of evergreen trees and shrubs for woodland conditions. Almost all demand an acid soil. Here a rhododendron walk is lined with naturalized candelabra primulas.

thin crowded branches in order to maintain the reasonable light levels that benefit many of the plants of the bottom storey. It is, however, the ideal setting for native and exotic woodlanders, for which it is worth making considerable efforts to eradicate vigorous weedy plants such as brambles. Many of the small trees and large shrubs listed on page 131 can be planted at the margins or to form an understorey beneath a high canopy. To these can be added the shade-tolerant shrubs listed on pages 33, 90 and 91 and, provided the soil conditions are suitable, many of the trees and shrubs that are classic plants for acid soils (see page 105). Two outstanding genera of woodland ornamentals, the maples (*Acer*) and rhododendrons, warrant separate treatment (see page 132). The maples have a well-justified reputation for providing some of the most brilliant foliage colours of

autumn but the genus also includes plants of very varied ornamental qualities, with some that are remarkable for the patterning of their bark.

The rhododendrons (azaleas belong to the same genus) are lime-haters but in a class of their own among flowering evergreens. They do not always show to best advantage in the collections of them made by their zealots; after what is sometimes an outrageously vivid flowering peak they can lapse into a lugubrious sobriety that palls before the next flowering season. However, what really counts against massed use of rhododendrons is that their dense foliage prevents light from reaching any bulbs or perennials beneath them. To my mind they are best interplanted with deciduous shrubs.

Keeping the planting in scale is important when establishing the shrubby understorey. An allusion to a woodland garden can be

beautifully created under the canopy of one or two old orchard trees but in such a situation just a few shrubs of low to medium height are needed as a background to a planting that is dominated by perennials and bulbs.

Perennials & bulbs
Ground-cover plants (see page 41) and free-spreading bulbs such as the English bluebell (*Hyacinthoides non-scripta*), grape hyacinth (*Muscari armeniacum*) and star of Bethlehem (*Ornithogalum umbellatum*) are legitimate woodlanders. There are, however, many other choicer plants that revel in woodland conditions. An informal planting from those listed on pages 134 and 135 could be the making of a garden of artless charm. To these can be added the daffodils and most of the other bulbs for naturalizing listed on page 36, the short-growing daffodils

Herbaceous Perennials for Woodland Conditions

Name	height/spread	flowering season	description
Actaea alba white baneberry	90/45cm 3/1½ft	late sum.	finely cut leaves and fluffy, white flowers that are less exciting than the poisonous, white berries on red stems
Arisaema candidissimum	30/45cm 12/18in	early sum.	the arum flower, with a hooded, white spathe with pale pink stripes, emerges before the distinctive, 3-lobed leaves
Cimicifuga simplex 'White Pearl'	120/60cm 4/2ft	early aut.	well-poised plant with white, bottle-brush flowers followed by attractive green seedheads
Corydalis flexuosa	20/25cm 8/10in	late spr. to early sum.	a plant warranting the fuss made at its recent reintroduction; pretty foliage and spurred flowers in shades of blue
Dicentra 'Langtrees'	30/30cm 12/12in	late spr. to early sum	blue-grey, ferny foliage of exceptional beauty and above it arching sprays of cream and pink flowers
Digitalis lutea	60/30cm 2/1ft	early sum.	reasonably perennial foxglove with tall spires of narrow, yellow flowers
Dodecatheon meadia shooting star	30/30cm 12/12in	late spr. to early sum.	heads of purple-pink flowers with swept-back petals resembling a little shower of darts
Gentiana asclepiadea	60/45cm 2/1½ft	mid- to late sum.	the willow gentian is a graceful plant, its arching stems carrying paired blue trumpets
Helleborus orientalis Lenten rose	60/45cm 2/1½ft	late win. to eary spr.	usually evergreen with saucer-shaped flowers from greeny yellow to darkest plum, often prettily speckled
Hepatica nobilis	10/25cm 4/10in	late win. to mid-spr.	available in various forms, the blue single with anemone-like flowers as lovely as any
Hosta 'Snowden'	75/60cm 2½/2ft	late sum.	any number to choose from; impressive clump of pointed sage-green leaves and white flowers valuable in their season
Kirengeshoma palmata	90/60cm 3/2ft	early aut.	aristocratic in every detail and especially in the cool yellow, waxy flowers dangling from dark stems
Meconopsis betonicifolia Himalayan blue poppy	120/45cm 4/1½ft	early sum.	tends to be short-lived but the wonder of its blue poppies always excites; for lime-free soil
Meconopsis quintuplinervia harebell poppy	25/30cm 10/12in	late spr. to early sum.	sublime when arching stems carry nodding flowers of lavender-blue over a mat of bristly foliage
Primula vulgaris	15/25cm 6/10in	early to mid-spr.	familiar but a plant of rare beauty making tuffets of pale yellow flowers with darker centres
Thalictrum delavayi 'Album'	150/60cm 5/2ft	early to late sum.	all forms are suitable, this with its sprays of minute, white flowers is effervescent
Trillium grandiflorum	40/30cm 16/12in	mid-spr.	the wake robin represents a group of distinguished plants; the 3-petalled flowers are pure white, then tinged pink
Uvularia grandiflora	60/25cm 24/10in	late spr.	yellow bells with twisting petals dangle elegantly from arching stems
FERNS			
Adiantum pedatum	45/30cm 18/12in	none	black, wiry stems and foliage resembling that of the tender maidenhair fern
Asplenium scolopendrium hart's tongue fern	30/30cm 12/12in	none	makes a clump of evergreen, strap-shaped fronds with a wavy edge
Athyrium filix-femina lady fern	60/60cm 2/2ft	none	deciduous but beautifully lacy and fresh green in spring and summer
Dryopteris erythrosora	50/40cm 20/16in	none	usually deciduous outdoors, the young fronds emerging rusty red before turning green
Polystichum setiferum soft shield fern	75/90cm 2½/3ft	none	evergreen and tolerant but at its luxuriant best in moist conditions

on page 75 and the shade-tolerant perennials on page 93. Some of the most distinguished from among these plants, including spring bulbs, Lenten roses (*Helleborus orientalis*) and the trilliums, are over by early summer but there are plants for all seasons. The lilies (see also page 78) are especially useful in summer, doing best where the flowers, rising above a shaded base, get a reasonable amount of sun during the day.

Too much emphasis on foliage plants such as hostas can turn a woodland garden into a collection that seems to be deliberately labour-saving. It is often forgotten, though, how attractive in a pallid sort of way many hostas can be when they flower in summer. For autumn refinement almost nothing can beat *Kirengeshoma palmata* but colchicums and *Cyclamen hederifolium* are much above the common run in quality.

It has to be admitted that some trees, such as birches (*Betula*), are shallow-rooted and mop up a lot of surface moisture. Most perennials and bulbs will benefit, therefore, from the ground being mulched with well-rotted leafmould.

LEFT Two bulbous plants that can develop into large colonies under a deciduous canopy are *Crocus tommasinianus* and the green-ruffed winter aconite, *Eranthis hyemalis*. The crocus is very variable in colour, some forms being a deep purple.

FAR LEFT Many small bulbs that flower early thrive under a deciduous canopy. The first of the snowdrops coincide with the winter-flowering *Cyclamen coum*, which has magenta, pink or white flowers. There are forms with beautifully silvered foliage. This cyclamen makes an ideal successor to the splendid autumn-flowering *C. hederifolium*.

BULBS FOR UNDER TREES

The bulbs listed below do best in part-shade created by deciduous trees, especially in a glade-like setting. Many of the bulbs recommended for naturalizing on page 36 are also well suited to woodland conditions.

Name	height/spread	flowering season	description
Anemone nemorosa 'Robinsoniana' wood anemone	20/15in 8/6in	early to mid-spr.	large, lavender-blue flowers; good form of a plant that naturalizes readily
Cardiocrinum giganteum	250/90cm 8/3ft	mid- to late sum.	magnificent giant of the lily family with a massive stem bearing drooping trumpets that are creamy and fragrant
Colchicum 'The Giant'	20/20cm 8/8in	early to mid-aut.	most colchicums are suitable; this is large, with white-centred, lilac-mauve flowers
Crocus tommasinianus 'Whitewell Purple'	10/8cm 4/3in	late win.	spreads freely; purplish-mauve flowers, silvery inside
Cyclamen coum	10/10cm 4/4in	mid- to late win.	carmine, pink or white flowers; foliage sometimes silvered; *C. hederifolium* and *C. purpurascens* also suitable
Erythronium californicum 'White Beauty'	20/15cm 8/6in	late spr.	prettily reflexed flowers are white with red-brown markings near the centre; lightly mottled leaves
Galanthus plicatus byzantinus	10/10cm 4/4in	early spr.	broad, greyish leaves are folded back at the margins; green marks at the base and tip of inner segments; most snowdrops are suitable
Lilium canadense	150/25cm 60/10in	early to mid-sum.	lily of exceptional elegance for lime-free soils; a candelabrum of pendulous, orange or yellow flowers with the tips turned back
Lilium martagon album	120/25cm 48/10in	mid-sum.	turk's-cap lily; pendulous flowers with rolled-back petals, especially lovely in the white form
Lilium pardalinum panther lily	150/30cm 5/1ft	mid-sum.	tall stem bears numerous orange-red turk's-cap lilies, heavily spotted with purple or brown; enjoys moist soil but not lime
Scilla bifolia	20/10cm 8/4in	late win. to early spr.	lax stems bear starry, purplish-blue flowers; like *S. siberica* tolerates part-shade
Tulipa sylvestris	40/20cm 16/8in	mid-spr.	nodding buds open to erect, yellow flowers with greenish interior; does not need lifting

The cyclamen-like flowers of the shooting star *Dodecatheon meadia* are usually a pinkish-purple but the white form *album* is, if anything, lovelier. The shooting stars are hardy perennials of the primula family from North America. All do well in woodland gardens, liking moist, leafy soils and thriving in light shade.

Patios & Terraces

Changes in life style and attitudes over the last fifty years have influenced decisively the design of gardens. More and more of us live in towns or their suburban periphery where the premium on space means that most of us have comparatively small gardens. We do not automatically think of the garden as a potential source of food for the household, as cottage gardeners in the past would have done, even when we are not well off. Rather we want a garden to be beautiful in so far as this is consistent with our focus on leisure. Today we expect to relax in our gardens, not to labour in them. We are happiest when part or all of a garden can be used as an outdoor room and for that we need space for furniture and preferably a surface that wears and looks well with a minimum of maintenance.

In the patio and terrace gardens that exemplify this relaxed life style planting is very often not the dominant element. None the less plants are needed and they have a special value when they are labour-saving, reliable and ornamental over a long season. Fortunately there are many accommodating plants that go along with this approach to the garden.

The room outdoors has become an increasingly important feature of gardens. Planting in containers allows for alterations to the arrangement of space and makes it possible to decorate with foliage and flowering plants even where there is a hard surface. Here shaped bays (*Laurus nobilis*) create a formal frame, which is carried through in the white planting of Paris daisies (*Argyranthemum frutescens*), hydrangeas and busy lizzies (*Impatiens*).

Framework plants

There is often something comical about patios and terraces that are planted exclusively with low-growing plants. Even in these paved areas of the garden, woody plants, including climbers, that provide an enduring framework are invaluable – but good judgement is needed to get the scale right.

Trees

Large, even medium-sized trees do not go well with patios and terraces. In hot, sunny weather their shade near the house may be welcome but they exaggerate the gloom of dull days, especially where they rob rooms of daylight. Also, the roots of some trees can pose a serious threat to the foundations of a house, especially one built on clay soil, where shrinkage in periods of drought, exacerbated by thirsty trees taking up what moisture is available, may lead to subsidence. Not as serious but sometimes troublesome is the way in which extending roots cause paving to heave.

There are, however, a few neat trees, most usually grown as standards (with clear trunks to a given height), that can be fitted in to quite small gardens. Trees almost invariably do best planted in the open ground but most of those listed on page 139 could be grown in large containers in a soil-based compost. Trees often stand up well to life in containers provided they are watered sufficiently during dry spells and fed annually with a slow-release compost. In spring the top layer of compost, to a depth of about 15cm/6in, should be removed and replaced with fresh compost.

Climbers

Climbers and wall shrubs are even more important than trees for making a patio or terrace area seem clothed. The house walls

Specially built containers have made it possible to create this impressive terrace garden well above street level. Planting on a scale that includes trees and climbers on a pergola should not be undertaken without carefully considering the load-bearing strength of the floor, the way plants are to be irrigated and drainage for excess water.

SMALL TREES FOR PATIOS

Name	height/spread	description
Caragana arborescens 'Pendula'	1.8/1.8m 6/6ft	deciduous; when grafted makes a small, weeping tree with yellow, pea flowers in early summer
Cotoneaster salicifolius 'Pendulus' **(C.** 'Hybridus Pendulus'**)**	3/1.8m 10/6ft	prostrate unless grafted to make a small, weeping evergreen; white flowers in early summer are followed by red berries
Elaeagnus 'Quicksilver' oleaster	3.7/3.7m 12/12ft	deciduous foliage, willow-like and silvery; tiny, scented flowers in early summer; can be shaped
Laurus nobilis sweet bay	5.5/3.7m 18/12ft	aromatic evergreen that can be maintained as a mophead standard at a suitable height
Magnolia stellata 'Rosea'	3/2.5m 10/8ft	deciduous with starry, fragrant flowers, faint pink then white
Malus floribunda Japanese crab	4.5/3.7m 15/12ft	deciduous with a densely branched head covered in pink and white blossom in late spring, followed by yellow fruit
Prunus lusitanica Portugal laurel	4.5/3.7m 15/12ft	dense evergreen that tolerates shaping; scented flowers in summer, the fruits that follow turning from red to black
Salix caprea 'Kilmarnock' goat willow	2.5/1.5m 8/5ft	deciduous shrub grafted to make a weeping standard; silver catkins in spring

TIDY CLIMBERS FOR PATIOS

Name	height/spread	description
Beriberidopsis corallina coral plant	3.7/2.5m 12/8ft	evergreen twiner for a sheltered site with conspicuous clusters of deep red flowers in summer and early autumn
Clematis 'Alba Luxurians'	3.7/1.8m 12/6ft	deciduous twiner, like other *C. viticella* hybrids and cultivars, flowering in late summer and early autumn; small, white flowers with a mauve flush
Clematis alpina 'Frances Rivis'	1.8/1.5m 6/5ft	deciduous twiner with nodding, pale blue flowers in spring
Jasminum officinale jasmine	6/4.5m 20/15ft	evergreen twiner with sweetly scented, white flowers in summer
Lonicera x **italica** **(L**. x **americana)**	7/4.5m 23/15ft	deciduous, twining honeysuckle with very fragrant, yellow flowers, flushed red, in early summer
Passiflora caerulea passion flower	4.5/2.2m 15/7ft	semi-evergreen twiner with unusual blue-and-white flowers in summer
Trachelospermum jasminoides	3.7/3m 12/10ft	evergreen twiner with fragrant, creamy flowers from mid- to late summer
Vitis vinifera 'Purpurea' claret vine	6/3m 20/10ft	deciduous climber with tendrils; this highly ornamental grape has claret-red foliage in summer that colours richly in autumn

SHRUBS FOR PATIOS

Most of the following can be grown in containers, making smaller plants than they do in the open garden. The dimensions given are for mature plants in containers.

Name	height/spread	description
EVERGREEN		
Buxus sempervirens box	150/90cm 5/3ft	bushy plant with glossy, dark green leaves, ideal for small-scale topiary
Camellia x williamsii 'Anticipation'	1.8/1.2m 6/4ft	one among many good cultivars with glossy foliage and flowering through winter to mid-spring; double, deep pink flowers
Choisya ternata Mexican orange blossom	1.5/1.8m 5/6ft	rounded plant with aromatic, glossy leaves and clusters of fragrant, orange-blossom-like white flowers in mid- to late spring and again in autumn
Erica carnea 'Myretoun Ruby' heather	30/35cm 12/14in	among dwarf shrubs the heathers excel; this example is a mass of deep red flowers in winter and spring
Euonymus fortunei 'Silver Queen'	90/90cm 3/3ft	insignificant flowers but the white edge to the dark green leaves looks lively all year
Fargesia (Arundinaria) nitida	3/1.2m 10/4ft	bamboo with sprays of small leaves carried on arching, purplish stems
Fatsia japonica 'Variegata'	1.8/1.5m 6/5ft	large, fingered leaves of glossy green with irregular creamy variegation; sprays of round flowerheads in autumn sometimes followed by black fruits
Gaultheria (Pernettya) mucronata	1.2/1.2m 4/4ft	several cultivars have colourful, round berries set in glossy foliage; 'Mulberry Wine' has wine-red berries; use lime-free compost
Laurus nobilis sweet bay	2.5/1.8m 8/6ft	tree or shrub with glossy, aromatic, dark green leaves easily kept to the required height; makes handsome standards or simple topiary shapes
Pieris japonica 'Scarlett O'Hara'	1.8/1.8m 6/6ft	one of several good forms, all needing lime-free compost; bronze-red shoots and young leaves become dark green; sprays of white flowers in spring
Pinus mugo 'Gnom' mountain pine	1.2/1.2m 4/4ft	gnarled and slow-growing shrubby conifer with bright to dark green foliage and brown cones
Rhododendron yakushimanum	90/150cm 3/5ft	dome of deep green leaves, silvery when young and brown-felted beneath; pink buds open to funnel-shaped flowers that fade to white; use lime-free compost
Skimmia japonica reevesiana	75/75cm 2½/2½ft	makes an aromatic, dark green mound with clusters of fragrant, white flowers in spring followed by red berries if a male plant nearby; use lime-free compost
DECIDUOUS		
Acer palmatum dissectum	90/150cm 3/5ft	rounded, almost weeping bush with deeply divided, green leaves that colour splendidly in autumn; many others to choose from
Ficus carica	1.8/1.5m 6/5ft	impressive hand-like leaves; root restriction encourages the development of fruit
Fuchsia magellanica 'Versicolor'	1.5/1.2m 5/4ft	leaves blending grey, cream and rose-pink complement perfectly the small, dangling, red flowers
Hydrangea macrophylla 'Madame Emile Mouillère'	1.2/1.2m 4/4ft	one of many good mopheads, in this the dense cluster of white flowers in mid- to late summer fading to pale pink; prefers partial shade
Hydrangea serrata 'Bluebird'	90/90cm 3/3ft	lacecap flowers in mid- to late summer, the small, violet-blue, fertile flowers ringed by pale pink, lilac or blue florets; purplish autumn foliage

The choice of container can do much to enhance the ornamental value of a plant. Here the large fluted jar complements a specimen of *Fatsia japonica*. This is an excellent evergreen choice for a container in a shady corner, the glossiness of the fingered leaves catching the light. There is also a good variegated form with irregular cream markings on the edge.

themselves are often the most important of the supports available. But there may also be panels of trellis separating one area of the garden from another or a pergola that is intended to create relatively light shade. The climbers listed on page 139 are useful in a limited space because they are not too vigorous or, as in the case of *Vitis vinifera* 'Purpurea', will take systematic pruning that limits growth.

Many other climbers listed in this book (see, for example, pages 14-16) might also be suitable for planting on patios and terraces. Especially useful on shady surfaces are the ivies (page 21) but for an intimate, sunny garden the climbing and rambling roses (pages 19 and 20) and scented climbers (page 123) provide the extra dimension of fragrance that can lift a garden out of the ordinary.

Few plants do better in containers than pelargoniums. They are usually remarkably tolerant of drought, most flower over a very long season, some have outstandingly beautiful foliage and there is a tremendous range of flower colour and shape to choose from. Roses are more problematic but some of the patio and ground-cover roses have proved very successful in large containers.

Roses (*Rosa*) for Patios and Terraces

Unless mention is made of fragrance, the following patio and miniature roses have little or no scent.

Name	height/spread	description
PATIO		
R. 'Angela Rippon'	45/30cm 18/12in	bushy rose with clusters of lightly scented, small, double blooms of salmon-pink
R. 'Festival'	60/60cm 2/2ft	luxuriant foliage and numerous clusters of large, double, crimson-scarlet blooms with a silvery reverse
R. 'Gentle Touch'	40/40cm 16/16in	bushy and dark-leaved with clusters of lightly scented, double blooms that are pale pink
R. 'Little Bo-Peep'	30/50cm 12/20in	dense, low growth and crowded clusters of small, semi-double, pale pink blooms
R. 'Mandarin'	40/40cm 16/16in	bushy rose with dark, glossy foliage; double, deep pink flowers with an orange-yellow centre
R. 'Perestroika'	45/45cm 18/18in	clusters of double, bright yellow flowers over dark, bronze-green foliage
R. 'Queen Mother'	40/60cm 16/24in	spreading bushy rose with clusters of lightly scented, soft pink, semi-double blooms over dark, glossy foliage
R. 'Sweet Dream'	40/35cm 16/14in	leafy, upright grower with large clusters of double, often quartered, apricot blooms with a light scent
MINIATURE		
R. 'Baby Masquerade'	45/40cm 18/16in	twiggy growth with deep green foliage and clusters of lightly scented flowers combining pink, red and yellow
R. 'Colibre'	30/30cm 12/12in	upright grower with small, double blooms of red-tinted yellow
R. 'Gold Pin'	25/25cm 10/10in	vigorous and bearing a profusion of fragrant, golden flowers
R. 'Para Ti' ('Pour Toi')	30/25cm 12/10in	upright grower with dark foliage bearing clusters of small, semi-double, creamy white blooms

Shrubs

Many of the shrubs suitable for beds and borders (see pages 54-63) are also suitable for the relatively small scale of beds surrounding patio and terrace gardens. Some of them, as well as the plants listed on page 140, make excellent subjects for container planting (see also pages 146-53). Although growing in containers comes into its own in parts of the garden where the surface is paved or concreted, it is an option to consider elsewhere, too. A well-chosen container planted with a handsome specimen can make an arresting focal point anywhere in the garden, the container helping to define the plant and giving it extra height.

Bush and shrub roses have already been covered fairly fully (see pages 64-71) but two categories of roses – patio and miniature – have almost been tailor-made for a modern style of gardening. In effect, the patio roses are simply low-growing, cluster-flowered bush roses (floribundas) and the miniatures even smaller and twiggier versions. The use of the terms frankly owes a great deal to the way roses are marketed and the distinction between the two groups is rather blurred. As a general rule roses are not ideal plants for containers but the patio and miniature roses do very much better than most. This is worth remembering because in the open garden, unless skilfully grouped and perhaps grown in a raised bed that lifts them nearer eye level, they often make little impact.

All shrubs, including roses, that are grown in containers should be planted in a soil-based compost. Renew the top layer of compost annually before applying a slow-release fertilizer.

Raised beds & paving

Raised beds are not exclusively features of patios and terraces but they tend to look best set in paved areas. On a lawn they look oddly abrupt unless they have a surround of paving, which will also simplify mowing.

There is no single category of plants that has a territorial claim on raised beds; provided the growing conditions are suitable many of the plants suggested earlier for beds and borders (see pages 43-85) can be successfully planted in them. However, they are particularly suitable for growing a wide range of rock garden plants and dwarf bulbs, plants that go together well because they are of the same scale and because, too, so many like an open position and free-draining soil. The raised level of the bed allows these plants to be appreciated and it means that it is relatively simple to ensure free drainage.

Preparing a raised bed

The walls of a raised bed should be about 60cm/2ft high and can be constructed of a wide range of materials, including brick, stone or wooden railway sleepers. Beds much more than 1.5m/5ft across are difficult to weed and maintain. A layer of broken brick or similar material about 8cm/3in deep in the bottom of the bed will help drainage. Use upturned turves as a barrier between this drainage layer and the compost. A suitable compost consists of three parts (by volume) of loam, one part leafmould or garden compost and one part sharp sand. A few well-placed large rocks bedded in the compost will suggest the natural environment of the plants to be grown and provide the cool root-run that suits many of them well. The filled raised bed should be watered and then allowed to settle before being planted. Some topping up with spare compost may be necessary.

Autumn is a good time to plant, although almost any time is suitable provided the ground is not frozen. In summer, plants will need watering until they are established. A top-dressing of stone chippings gives an attractive finish, helps to conserve moisture and discourages the growth of weeds.

LEFT The easy alpines suggested in the list on this page are well known. There are many less familiar rock garden plants, such as *Anemone x lesseri*, that are not difficult to grow in the sort of well-drained conditions that can be created in a raised bed. Choicer kinds should be kept well away from those, such as aubrietas, that make smothering growth.

FAR LEFT The pasque flower (*Pulsatilla vulgaris*) is beautiful in all its parts. The leaves have a ferny delicacy, and much of the plant, including the flower buds and the seedheads, is covered in silky hairs. This spring-flowering perennial, of which there are some good named forms, does well in a raised bed.

EASY PERENNIAL ALPINES

The plants in this chart generally require full sun and well-drained soil but in other respects are not unduly demanding. They are particularly suitable for growing in raised beds combined with dwarf bulbs.

Name	height/spread	description
Achillea x lewisii 'King Edward'	10/25cm 4/10in	over a long summer season heads of pale primrose flowers over a base of grey-green ferny leaves
Anacyclus pyrethrum depressus	8/30cm 3/12in	white, daisy flowers with a red reverse to the petals borne profusely in summer
Arabis alpina caucasica 'Flore Pleno'	20/30cm 8/12in	in late spring stems of fragrant, double, white flowers over evergreen foliage
Armeria juniperifolia 'Bevan's Variety'	8/15cm 3/6in	tiny thrift, its evergreen hummock studded in late spring and early summer with round heads of pink flowers
Artemisia schmidtiana	8/20cm 3/8in	pretty, silver hummock of silky, finely cut foliage; insignificant flowers
Aubrieta 'Doctor Mules'	8/30cm 3/12in	there are numerous aubrietas, evergreen and smothered in flowers in spring; the large flowers of this example are double and rich purple
Aurinia saxatilis citrina (Alyssum saxatile 'Citrinum'**)**	25/30cm 10/12in	sprawling evergreen smothered with cool, lemon-yellow flowers in late spring and early summer
Campanula 'Birch Hybrid'	10/30cm 4/12in	one among many good alpine bellflowers; an evergreen with deep violet flowers in summer
Campanula carpatica 'Bressingham White'	15/15cm 6/6in	pure white flowers that are cup-shaped and of a very clean outline stand out boldly in summer
Dianthus 'Little Jock'	10/10cm 4/4in	clump of evergreen, grassy foliage studded in summer with dark-eyed, pink flowers that have a spicy scent
Gentiana septemfida	25/30cm 10/12in	tufted plant with deep blue, upward-facing, trumpet flowers in late summer and early autumn
Geranium cinereum 'Ballerina'	20/30cm 8/12in	grey-green leaves and appealing flowers for weeks in summer, the lilac colouring improved by purple veining
Iberis sempervirens 'Weisser Zwerg'	10/30cm 4/12in	sometimes known as 'Little Gem'; evergreen with dark foliage smothered in late spring and early summer by rounded heads of white flowers
Origanum 'Kent Beauty'	20/30cm 8/12in	aromatic plant of great beauty in summer when green bracts, tinged bright pink, surround pink flowers
Phlox 'Chattahoochee'	20/30cm 8/12in	sprawler which throughout summer and into autumn is bright with red-centred, lilac flowers
Phlox douglasii 'Boothman's Variety'	8/20cm 3/8in	evergreen mat covered in late spring and early summer with flat lilac flowers, each with a purple ring around the eye
Pulsatilla vulgaris pasque flower	20/20cm 8/8in	plant of seductive silkiness, in late spring nodding flowers, mainly in shades of purple, red or white, with a yellow central boss; pretty, feathery seedheads
Saxifraga 'Wetterhorn'	5/30cm 2/12in	mat of slightly hoary foliage obscured in early spring by cupped flowers of intense red; prefers some shade
Sedum spathulifolium 'Cape Blanco'	8/30cm 3/12in	rosettes of fleshy, grey-green leaves with purple tinting are the main attraction; heads of starry, yellow flowers in summer
Viola 'Ardross Gem'	13/20cm 5/8cm	an example from a wide range of neat plants; small, blue flowers with a gilt finish in early summer

CHOICE DWARF BULBS

The following are not difficult to grow in sunny positions where the soil is well drained, and are ideal for raised beds and sinks.

Name	height	description
Chionodoxa sardensis	15cm/6in	arresting in the first half of spring with little sprays of bright blue, white-centred flowers
Crocus ancyrensis	8cm/3in	vivid in winter, each corm producing numerous starry flowers of deep orange-yellow
Crocus corsicus	8cm/3in	deep lilac goblets in early to mid-spring, the outside buff with heavy purple feathering
Crocus goulimyi	13cm/5in	beautifully formed autumn-flowering species; lavender goblets with slender, pale stems
Crocus sieberi 'Hubert Edelsten'	8cm/3in	eye-catching in late winter or early spring; gold-throated pale lilac with bands of purple and white
Cyclamen coum	10cm/4in	dumpy flowers in winter or early spring are magenta, pink or white; all forms worth growing, especially those with pewter or silvery leaves
Eranthis hyemalis 'Guinea Gold' winter aconite	10cm/4in	a late winter prize; conspicuous green ruff surrounds globular, deep yellow, fragrant flowers; foliage sometimes bronzed
Fritillaria michailovskyi	20cm/8in	in mid- to late spring 1-3 purplish-brown bells with a band of bright yellow round the rim
Galanthus reginae-olgae	13cm/5in	like the common snowdrop except it flowers in autumn
Ipheion 'Rolf Fiedler'	15cm/6in	an enamelled beauty for early to mid-spring; star-shaped flowers of clear azure over grassy leaves
Iris danfordiae	10cm/4in	stubby species flowering in mid- to late winter, its yellow flowers nicely spotted with green
Iris 'J. S. Dijt'	15cm/6in	one of many named Reticulata irises; scented, reddish-purple flowers in late winter
Iris 'Katharine Hodgkin'	13cm/5in	a gem for late winter or early spring, unusual for its combination of sea-green, blue and yellow
Muscari botryoides 'Album'	15cm/6in	pyramidal spike of pearly white, fragrant flowers in mid-spring
Muscari tubergenianum	15cm/6in	striking in early to mid-spring with clustered flower spikes, the top pale blue, bright blue lower down
Narcissus minor 'Cedric Morris'	23cm/9in	daffodil that astonishes with its little trumpets as early as mid-winter
Oxalis adenophylla	10cm/4in	beautifully furled, pink flowers show among grey-green foliage in late spring; not invasive
Puschkinia scilloides libanotica	10cm/4in	in early spring produces arching sprays of pale blue flowers with darker pencilling on the petals
Scilla mischtschenkoana (S. tubergeniana)	15cm/6in	lovely in late winter or early spring with lax sprays of pale blue flowers with a dark stripe
Tulipa linifolia	15cm/6in	late spring miniature; dull red flowers with a silky interior of flaming scarlet

PLANTS FOR CREVICES IN PAVING

Except where noted, the following plants thrive in sun where the soil is free-draining.

Name	height/spread	description
Acaena microphylla	5/15cm 2/6in	compact mats year-round of bronze-green foliage covered in summer with reddish, spiny burrs
Antennaria dioica 'Rubra'	8/45cm 3/18in	in summer fluffy heads of pink flowers are borne over a semi-evergreen mat of silver-grey, woolly leaves
Arenaria montana	10/40cm 4/16in	in late spring and early summer saucer-shaped flowers of glistening white obscure rich green foliage
Aubrieta 'Silberrand'	8/30cm 3/12in	a creamy edge to the leaves gives this example interest year-round; blue flowers in spring and early summer
Campanula cochleariifolia	10/30cm 4/12in	invasive but beautiful with blue, bell flowers on wiry stems in the second half of summer
Dianthus 'Pike's Pink'	10/15cm 4/6in	many neat pinks are suitable; this has large, semi-double, pink flowers over spiky, grey-green foliage in summer
Erinus alpinus	8/15cm 3/6in	low hummocks studded in summer with starry, pink flowers
Geranium cinereum subcaulescens	15/30cm 6/12in	makes a tuft of deeply divided, soft leaves and throughout summer produces purple-magenta flowers with a dark centre
Helianthemum 'Amy Baring'	10/25cm 4/10cm	compact example from a useful group of evergreens available in a wide colour range that flower profusely in summer; this has apricot-yellow flowers
Mentha requienii Corsican mint	1/30cm ½/12in	tiny, apple-green leaves, peppermint-scented when crushed; pale lavender flowers in summer; best in part-shade with a moist run
Persicaria affinis (Polygonum affine) 'Donald Lowndes'	15/30cm 6/12in	vigorous, mat-forming evergreen bearing dense spikes of small, red flowers that pale to pink
Pratia pedunculata	1/30cm ½/12in	creeping evergreen with masses of star-shaped, blue or blue-purple flowers in summer; for moist sites
Raoulia australis	1/25cm ½/10in	evergreen making a dense, grey-green mat stained yellow by tiny flowers in spring
Saponaria 'Bressingham'	5/30cm 2/12in	in mid-summer bright pink flowers cover a close mat of narrow leaves
Sempervivum tectorum	10/15cm 4/6in	evergreen succulent rosettes sometimes coloured deep red; in summer starry, purplish-red flowers are carried on stems 30cm/12in high
Sisyrinchium idahoense (S. bellum)	13/10cm 5/4in	makes a semi-evergreen, grassy tuft with a long succession of blue or violet-blue flowers in summer and autumn

Rock garden plants & dwarf bulbs

The true alpines have a reputation, far from universally justified, for being difficult plants. Beware starting with them, however; it is not that you are doomed to failure but you will be flirting with one of the most addictive specialist areas of gardening. In the more general run of rock garden plants, compact perennials and shrubs that are mostly natives of open hillsides and rough terrain, many are easy-going and dependable ornamentals. Useful supplements to the list on page 143 could include one or two dwarf conifers such as *Picea mariana* 'Nana'.

Many of the dwarf bulbs listed on page 74 and the short-growing daffodils on page 75 can be mixed with these low-growing shrubs and compact perennials. Numerous less familiar bulbs, including those listed on page 144, are no more trouble than those that are better known. Some easy rock garden plants might swamp these bulbs, which are best kept away from *Arabis*, *Aubrieta*, *Aurinia*, *Iberis* and their like.

The compact plants recommended here for raised beds can also be grown in rock gardens, troughs and sinks. The rock garden, however, is not a feature for a patio or terrace and the raised bed has several advantages over it. It is more readily integrated than the rock garden, which often appears as a conspicuously unnatural feature, despite deliberate efforts at imitating an alpine environment.

Many rock garden plants have a knack for making the most of tiny pockets of soil trapped between and under stones, some surviving on a thin diet and little moisture. The plants listed in the second chart on page 144 will soften the effect of paving by running between the slabs or making compact tufts or domes. Their effect is out of proportion to their diminutive scale for they manage to give a garden an established air.

ABOVE Coincidences are as telling in small raised beds as they are in a large border. Here Reticulata irises of violet-blue poke through the trailing grey-green stems of the curious *Euphorbia myrsinites*. Lime-green is already showing in the terminal rosette, which will soon open to reveal tiny flowers cupped in bracts of the same colour.

LEFT The starry flowers of *Pratia pedunculata*, an evergreen perennial, are borne in summer over a low, creeping mat of foliage. This is an attractive plant to grow among paving but only does well where the soil is reasonably moist.

Container gardens

On many patios and terraces there are no beds and borders. If you want plants – and most of us are glad of the way they civilize the area near a house – then they have to be grown in containers. This is not, as some would have us believe, an inferior form of gardening but one with its own rewards and challenges. There are plants for every season and there is an added interest in matching these to containers and grouping containers effectively. It should not be thought that the only place for containers is near the house. They can be used to make focal points in many places but on patios and terraces they take on a special value.

Choosing containers

The range of purpose-made containers is vast and there is great variety in the materials with which they are made. Traditional, unglazed terracotta pots remain popular, their simple forms and sympathetic colouring providing a standard against which many other containers are measured. They are porous, and the compost in them dries out more quickly than in non-porous containers, such as those made of plastic. Like the more stylish glazed earthenware pots, they may crack in frosty weather and they are very easily chipped or broken.

Other traditional materials for containers include stone, wood and metal. Although very beautiful, the weight of a large stone container makes it difficult to move. Wooden half barrels make excellent large containers for shrubs or

The most popular bulbs for the open garden and containers in late spring are tulips. The availability of separate colours in a wide colour range makes it possible to ring the changes from year to year. There is a reasonable range, too, in the winter-flowering pansies, remarkably hardy and often blooming into summer if regularly deadheaded.

BULBS FOR CONTAINERS

These bulbs are listed within each seasonal division according to the sequence in which they flower and not alphabetically. Lilies are best placed with their base in shade and the flowers in sun, while tuberous begonias do best in part-shade. Other plants listed thrive in full sun.

Name	height/spread	description
LATE WINTER AND EARLY SPRING		
Narcissus 'Tête-à-Tête'	15/10cm 6/4in	starting in late winter and long-lasting; usually 2 small, yellow trumpets per stem
Crocus vernus 'Vanguard' Dutch crocus	13/8cm 5/3in	the first of the large-flowered crocus; silvery outer petals clasp the inner, lilac petals
Crocus 'Yellow Hammer' Dutch crocus	13/8cm 5/3in	several golden goblets per corm
Narcissus 'February Gold'	25/10cm 10/4in	its season is early spring, not late winter as its name suggests but the yellow trumpets with swept-back petals are long-lasting
Crocus 'Jeanne d'Arc' Dutch crocus	13/8cm 5/3in	very large white goblets lit by orange stigmata
Tulipa 'Johann Strauss'	25/15cm 10/6in	creamy yellow flowers, white inside and with a vivid red mark outside; boldly mottled leaves
Narcissus 'Jack Snipe'	20/10cm 8/4in	breezy look with cream petals swept back from a short, yellow trumpet
MID-SPRING		
Tulipa 'Red Emperor' ('Madame Lefeber')	40/15cm 16/6in	spectacular large flowers of sheeny scarlet with yellow-margined black basal blotches
Tulipa 'Apricot Beauty'	40/15cm 16/6in	soft apricot and cream colouring is a beautiful alternative to the many bright tulips; superb planted with forget-me-nots
Narcissus 'Minnow'	20/8cm 8/3in	3-4 neat flowers per stem, lemon-cupped and with cream petals
Tulipa 'Diana'	35/15cm 14/6in	globular white flowers on sturdy stems
Tulipa 'Peach Blossom'	30/15cm 12/6in	well-shaped, double flowers of rich pink
Tulipa praestans 'Fusilier'	20/10cm 8/4in	more lax than many tulips with 2-4 vermilion flowers per stem
Tulipa 'Douglas Bader'	45/15cm 18/6in	creamy pink with darker streaks
Narcissus 'Yellow Cheerfulness'	50/10cm 20/4in	4-6 muddle-centred, soft yellow flowers per stem; well scented
LATE SPRING		
Tulipa marjoletii	23/8cm 9/3in	slender stems carry creamy flowers with a purplish-red tinge on the outside
Hyacinthus orientalis 'Orange Boven' hyacinth	23/15cm 9/6in	spikes of fragrant, peachy pink flowers, a softer colour than most hyacinths
Hyacinthus orientalis 'Delft Blue' hyacinth	25/15cm 10/6in	large spikes of light blue flowers that are heavily fragrant
Tulipa 'Carnaval de Nice'	40/15cm 16/6in	cupped, double flowers, the white petals striped red, over variegated leaves
Tulipa 'Shirley'	60/15cm 24/6in	white flowers with a finely feathered purple edge
Muscari comosum 'Plumosum' feather hyacinth	30/10cm 12/4in	a curiosity, with feathery plumes of violet threads
Hyacinthus orientalis 'Carnegie' hyacinth	23/15cm 9/6in	spikes packed with pure white, fragrant flowers
EARLY SUMMER		
Lilium 'Enchantment'	90/15cm 36/6in	upward-facing, orange-red flowers with black spots
Begonia x tuberhybrida 'Masquerade' tuberous begonia	75/75cm 2½/2½ft	example of a group of tender tubers with large, white, camellia-like, double flowers
Lilium 'Connecticut King'	120/20cm 4ft/8in	upward-facing flowers of yellow
Lilium 'Côte d'Azur'	35/15cm 14/6in	upward-facing, pink flowers with brown spotting in the centre
MID-SUMMER		
Lilium regale Album Group	150/20cm 5ft/8in	superb heads of fragrant, white trumpets with a faint yellow tinge
Lilium 'Pink Perfection'	120/20cm 4ft/8in	deep pink to purple trumpets with a powerful scent
Lilium 'African Queen'	120/20cm 4ft/8in	heavily scented, soft orange trumpets
Tigridia pavonia tiger flower	50/20cm 20/8in	succession of eye-catching flowers, each lasting a day, until autumn; 3 large petals, usually red, yellow or white, radiating from a spotted centre
Lilium 'Casa Blanca'	120/20cm 4ft/8in	fragrant, white trumpets opening flat to show a warty surface and yellow midrib to petals
LATE SUMMER AND EARLY AUTUMN		
Lilium 'Elvin's Son'	30/10cm 12/4in	dwarf with upward-facing, yellow flowers
Gladiolus callianthus 'Murieliae'	90/20cm 3ft/8in	sweetly scented, white flowers with maroon centres
Lilium auratum platyphyllum	120/20cm 4ft/8in	large, white flowers with a central yellow band to the petals and crimson spots; heavily scented

TRAILING PLANTS WITH ORNAMENTAL FLOWERS

The plants listed here may not be true annuals but are often treated as such. However, some, including diascia, fuchsia, lotus and pelargonium, are worth overwintering. All have a long flowering season in summer and into autumn. Regular deadheading will help to ensure continuity of bloom.

Name	height/spread	description
Begonia x **tuberhybrida** 'Apricot Cascade'	90/90cm 3/3ft	tuberous begonia with double, orange-apricot flowers dangling on slender stems below emerald-green leaves
Bidens ferulifolia	30/90cm 1/3ft	throws out lax stems with finely cut leaves and prodigious quantities of yellow flowers resembling tiny, honey-scented dahlias
Convolvulus sabatius	8/45cm 3/18in	slender stems carry grey-green, oval leaves and exquisite, funnel-shaped flowers of purplish-blue
Diascia rigescens	23/40cm 9/16in	lax stems bear erect spikes crowded with spurred, salmon-pink flowers
Fuchsia 'Marinka'	1.8/1.8m 6/6ft	one of many trailing fuchsias; this has crimson-ribbed, dark leaves and masses of 2-toned, red flowers dangling from arching stems
Lobelia erinus 'Sapphire'	15/25cm 6/10in	trailing lobelias are commonplace but make free-flowering, easy companions for other plants; this example has masses of white-eyed, sapphire-blue flowers
Lotus berthelotii	30/90cm 1/3ft	beautiful for the cascade of silvery, needle-like foliage as well as for the clusters of scarlet, parrot-bill flowers in mid-summer
Pelargonium 'L'Elégante'	60/60cm 2/2ft	one of many ivy-leaved pelargoniums with trailing but brittle stems and attractive foliage; this has creamy variegation, sometimes stained red, and semi-double, pale mauve flowers
Petunia Cascade Series	30/60cm 1/2ft	loose-limbed plants with masses of soft-textured, wavy-edged trumpets in a colour range including reds, pinks, blues and white
Scaevola aemula 'Blue Fan'	30/90cm 1/3ft	stems trail stiffly before turning up to display terminal spikes of fan-shaped, purplish-blue flowers
Tropaeolum majus Gleam Series	30/40cm 12/16in	short-stemmed trailer with double, scarlet, yellow or orange flowers and attractive circular leaves
Verbena 'Silver Anne'	8/30cm 3/12in	many verbenas carry dense heads of flowers in mauve, red, pink or white on low, spreading growth; the flowers of this are in shifting shades of pink

RIGHT Plants of trailing growth help to unify a planting with its container. Here a vivid petunia has been juxtaposed with an excellent grey-leaved trailer, *Plecostachys serpyllifolia*, and *Scaevola aemula* 'Blue Fan', an introduction that has proved an exceptionally useful container plant. This is a combination that will remain attractive throughout summer and into autumn.

ANNUAL CLIMBERS FOR CONTAINERS

Although many of the following plants are not true annuals, all of them can be treated as such. Those that are half-hardy are best started under glass in spring but should not be planted out until the risk of frost is over.

Name	height/spread	description
Cobaea scandens cathedral bell, cup and saucer plant	3.7/2.5m 12/8ft	climbs using tendrils; bell-shaped, purple flowers, greenish-white in the case of 'Alba', in summer
Eccremocarpus scaber Chilean glory vine	3/1.2m 10/4ft	evergreen with tendrils, often grown as a half-hardy annual; orange-red flowers in summer, followed by inflated seed pods
Ipomoea purpurea morning glory	370/90cm 12/3ft	half-hardy twiner with trumpet-shaped, purple or blue-purple flowers in summer and early autumn
Lathyrus odoratus sweet pea	250/30cm 8/1ft	hardy annual with tendrils; sprays of deliciously fragrant, pea flowers in summer; a good range of single colours available and also mixtures; there are also short-growing varieties
Rhodochiton atrosanguineum	3/1.2m 10/4ft	evergreen twiner often grown as a half-hardy annual; long-tubed, red-purple, bell flowers in summer
Thunbergia alata black-eyed susan	300/90cm 10/3ft	half-hardy twiner for a sheltered position, orange-yellow flowers with dark brown centres in summer
Tropaeolum majus nasturtium	250/90cm 8/3ft	climbing selections available with fast-growing lax stems and spurred, orange or yellow flowers in summer
Tropaeolum peregrinum (T. canariense) canary creeper	3.7/1.5m 12/5ft	fast-growing as a half-hardy annual, with lobed, grey-green leaves and fringed, yellow flowers in the second half of summer

mixed plantings, and wood can also be used to make much more formal tubs. Treating wood with a preservative that is not harmful to plants (not creosote) will greatly extend its life. Metal is less commonly used, although it is possible to get copies of Victorian cast-iron urns and pots.

Many gardeners have a prejudice against purpose-made containers of synthetic materials such as plastic, fibreglass and concrete. Useful and attractive containers can, however, be made from all these materials – they are often least successful aesthetically when they are attempting to imitate traditional materials.

What all the purpose-made containers have in common is a capacity to hold a reasonable quantity of a growing medium while letting excess water drain away. For those with a flair for improvisation there is no shortage of alternative receptacles that can be adapted for the growing of plants. On the grand scale there are copper urns but also effective are simple domestic items such as baskets lined with plastic or old buckets furnished with drainage holes. Using improvised containers with imagination and discretion can help to give a garden a highly individual character.

Useful categories of plants

If you have a mind to it, you can make practically anything grow in a container. Undoubtedly, though, some plants are more tolerant of root restriction than others and produce a much more satisfying ornamental effect than other plants might do.

For our purposes bulbs are an exceptionally useful group of plants, offering a tremendous range in colour, form and size and with a large number performing superbly when grown in containers. So magnificent are the main spring bulbs that others are sometimes neglected. On

BELOW *Bidens ferulifolia* flings out slender stems that bear bright yellow flowers like miniature single dahlias that only frosts will bring to an end. It is a perfect addition to brighten a white scheme such as this, which includes petunias, Paris daisies (*Argyranthemum frutescens*) and the cream foliage of *Helichrysum petiolare* 'Limelight'.

page 147 a selection of bulbs is listed according to their flowering sequence. To this list could be added many small bulbs that flower in late winter or early spring which are exquisite grown in shallow pots (see pages 74 and 144). The best of the daffodils to supplement this list are the short-growing kinds listed on page 75 but for additional tulips and lilies almost all from pages 76 and 78 are suitable.

In many container plantings the most prominent components are flowering plants but they would often fail to make the effect they do were it not for the support of good foliage.

Some of the most useful foliage plants grown as annuals are listed on page 150 and to these I would also add the scented-leaved pelargoniums (see page 125). A number of good perennials (see page 151), some of which are much more familiar as plants in the open garden than they are as container plants, can also form a useful supplement. Although widely used, the small-leaved ivies (*Hedera helix*) are so beautiful and versatile that their popularity has not spoiled the pleasure they give (see also page 21).

The trailing habit of ivies and some other foliage plants is one of their most attractive

characteristics. Just as valuable for softening the edge of containers are many flowering plants that have lax or cascading growth. They are particularly good in mixed plantings, some such as *Bidens* and *Scaevola* creating an irregular fringe of pretty flowers orbiting the main planting.

Both of these flower for months and by rights should feature in the chart on page 148 of invaluable plants that flower in summer over a very long season. Most plants listed represent familiar flowers, some of which deserve to be much more fully covered in this book. For some of these, fuchsias and pelargoniums in

TEN UNUSUAL CHOICES FOR CONTAINERS

Name	height/spread	description
Angelica archangelica angelica	2.2/1.5m 7/5ft	biennial aromatic herb, with an impressively branched framework supporting broad, divided leaves; in mid- to late summer their mid-green mass is topped by large yellow-green flowerheads
Clematis 'Madame Julia Correvon'	3/3m 10/10ft	wine-red, propeller flowers borne freely between mid-summer and early autumn; one of many clematis suitable for trailing from a capacious, tall container best stood in shade
Corydalis flexuosa 'Père David'	20/25cm 8/10in	magically beautiful perennial for sun or part-shade with finely cut foliage above which dangle sprays of spurred, blue flowers in spring and early summer, sometimes repeating later
Gladiolus callianthus 'Murieliae'	90/15cm 36/6in	6-12 corms in a large pot make an exquisitely scented feature in late summer or early autumn, the purple-centred, white flowers arching out elegantly above sword-like leaves
Hakonechloa macra 'Alboaurea'	30/60cm 1/2ft	deciduous perennial grass best in part-shade; makes a soft clump of laxly arching leaves, mainly cream and yellow but with hints of bronze
Hemerocallis 'Stella de Oro' day lily	50/45cm 20/18in	perennial with grassy leaves, wonderfully fresh when emerging; bell-shaped, yellow flowers from mid-summer to early autumn
Hosta fortunei aureomarginata	75/75cm 2½/2½ft	large, heart-shaped leaves, mid-green with an irregular creamy margin, make an impressive clump through summer into autumn in sun or part-shade; spikes of violet flowers in summer
Hydrangea quercifolia 'Snow Queen' oak-leaved hydrangea	1.5/1.5m 5/5ft	deciduous shrub suitable for sun or shade but best with its roots in shade; highly ornamental, large, oak leaves colour well in autumn; between mid-summer and early autumn conspicuous heads of white flowers gradually take on a pink tinge
Polystichum setiferum Divisilobum Group soft shield fern	1.2/1.5m 4/5ft	moisture- and shade-loving evergreen fern with large, very finely cut fronds that are erect when young but later form a prostrate rosette
Trifolium repens 'Purpurascens'		carpeting perennial clover with green-rimmed, chocolate leaves; lovely alone in a low container or as an edging to other plants

ANNUAL FOLIAGE PLANTS FOR CONTAINERS

Included in this list are some tender shrubby and perennial plants that are usually grown as annuals. Nasturtiums are true hardy annuals and ornamental cabbages, although biennial, are usually treated as hardy annuals. The remaining plants in this list, or cuttings from them, can be overwintered but are often discarded at the end of summer.

Name	height/spread	description
Brassica oleracea ornamental cabbage	40/40cm 16/16in	large rosettes of thick, crinkled leaves, usually combining red, pink or white with green, superb in autumn and winter
Helichrysum petiolare	45/150cm 1½/5ft	deservedly popular for its stiffly trailing stems clothed with felted, heart-shaped leaves of soft grey
Helichrysum petiolare 'Limelight'	30/90cm 1/3ft	a version of the above with leaves of cooling yellowish-green
Helichrysum petiolare 'Variegatum'	30/90cm 1/3ft	creamy yellow variegated leaves
Pelargonium 'Lady Plymouth'	60/50cm 24/20in	the strongly aromatic leaves are sage-green with cream variegation and deeply cut; clusters of small, white flowers in summer
Plecostachys serpyllifolia	30/45cm 12/18in	like a small-leaved version of *Helichrysum petiolare*
Plectranthus madagascariensis 'Variegated Mintleaf' **(P. coleoides** 'Variegatus')	60/60cm 2/2ft	bushy plant with greyish-green leaves that have a serrated white edge
Senecio cineraria (S. maritimus) 'Silver Dust'	30/30cm 12/12in	deeply cut, hairy, silver-grey leaves; the yellow, summer flowers are best removed
Solenostemon (Coleus blumei) Wizard Series	45/30cm 18/12in	tender plants with nettle-like leaves illuminated by astonishing combinations of green, yellow, red and maroon
Tradescantia fluminensis 'Quicksilver' wandering Jew	5/60cm 2/24in	trailing houseplant happy outdoors in summer; the leaves, striped green and white, are wrapped round the stems; occasional clusters of tiny, white flowers
Tropaeolum majus 'Alaska' nasturtium	30/30cm 12/12in	rounded leaves beautifully variegated green and white; red or yellow, trumpet flowers throughout summer

particular, I am relying on individual gardeners choosing according to their own personal taste from the vast range of cultivars on offer.

To heighten the appeal of the familiar it is worth container-gardening with some less usual plants. A short selection is given on this page and to these could be added fast-growing climbers such as those listed on page 148. Wigwams for support can themselves add to the appeal of these highly ornamental plants.

Potting composts

The many commercially prepared potting composts available, which should be sterile and contain a well-balanced mixture of nutrients, fall into two main groups. Those that are loam-based are generally prepared according to standard formulae, usually those devised by the John Innes Horticultural Institute. The John Innes composts come in various strengths. No. 2 is a general-purpose compost that suits a wide

RIGHT Differences of scale in container-grown plants can be combined with staging to dress a paved courtyard effectively with plants. There is a risk in using plants lavishly as in this scheme that the overall effect becomes bitty. A few large accents are needed and in this courtyard they are provided by the magnificent cannas. Even if they do not flower, these are superb foliage plants.

BELOW Despite having beautiful foliage and long-lasting seedheads, grasses are rarely used in container gardening. Here tufts of *Pennisetum alopecuroides* rise above a base made by a dark purple *Ricinus communis* and the grey-leaved *Helichrysum petiolare*.

PERENNIAL FOLIAGE PLANTS FOR CONTAINERS

The following plants will usually survive winters outdoors.

Name	height/spread	description
Glechoma hederacea 'Variegata' variegated ground ivy	15/90cm 6/36in	carpeting evergreen trailing marbled green-and-white leaves with a scalloped edge
Hakonechloa macra 'Aureola'	45/60cm 1½/2ft	one of several suitable grasses; the leaves striped yellow and green later turn a bronzy red
Hedera helix 'Adam' ivy	20/90cm 8/36in	small-leaved ivies, many of them variegated, will make swags of foliage spilling over the edge of containers; this is greyish with an irregular cream edge
Heuchera micrantha diversifolia 'Palace Purple'	45/45cm 18/18in	evergreen with heart-shaped leaves, irregularly cut, of bronzy purple with a pink reverse; sprays of tiny, white flowers in summer
Heuchera 'Snow Storm'	40/40cm 16/16in	evergreen, best in part-shade, making clumps of near white leaves speckled green; cerise flowers in summer
Hosta sieboldiana elegans	90/90cm 3/3ft	large hostas make splendid pot-grown plants; magnificent puckered, blue-green leaves
Houttuynia cordata 'Chameleon'	10/60cm 4/24in	aromatic perennial, the leaves vividly stained yellow and red
Lysimachia nummularia 'Aurea' creeping Jenny, moneywort	5/50cm 2/20in	evergreen perennial with creeping and trailing stems carrying rounded, yellow leaves and in summer cup-shaped, bright yellow flowers
Phormium 'Bronze Baby'	60/60cm 2/2ft	year-round clumps of strap-shaped, wine-red leaves; occasionally stems of reddish flowers in summer
Tolmiea menziesii 'Taff's Gold' pick-a-back plant	45/30cm 18/12in	forms dense pile of maple-like leaves speckled green and pale yellow with new plants forming on old leaves; good in sun or part-shade

ABOVE A pink-tinged, pot-grown osteospermum seems stained with the vivid colouring of *Geranium x riversleaianum* 'Russell Prichard'. Osteospermums produce their flowers over a long summer season but need sun. Container-grown plants can often be integrated successfully with larger schemes.

LEFT A constantly changing patio garden can be made by regrouping containers as plants come into their season. An abutilon and white and blue agapanthus top an organic arrangement of pots centred on a generous planting of petunias. Other plants include the trailing *Scaevola aemula* and cherry pie (*Heliotropium*).

range of container plants but No. 3 is appropriate for large shrubs and vigorous growers. Ericaceous composts, generally loam-based, are made up without chalk and are suitable for plants requiring acid soils such as rhododendrons and camellias.

Peat, coir fibre and bark are used as the bulky component of soil-less composts. Because of concern at the depletion of peat reserves there is a shift away from using peat-based composts but other materials have yet to prove themselves. Soil-less composts have the advantage of being light and clean to handle but are less successful at providing large plants with an anchor and, when they are used, plants must be fed regularly.

FLOWERS GIVING A LONG SUMMER SEASON

All of the plants in this chart are suitable for growing in containers. Regular deadheading will in many cases extend their long flowering season. Although the tender plants are sometimes discarded at the end of the flowering season, plants or cuttings can usually be overwintered successfully.

Name	height/spread	description
HARDY ANNUALS		
Calendula officinalis 'Gitana' pot marigold	30/30cm 12/12in	dwarf example of an aromatic hardy annual; double, daisy flowers from cream to orange
Tropaeolum majus 'Strawberries and Cream' nasturtium	30/30cm 12/12in	many selections are available of these trumpet-shaped and spurred flowers, mainly as mixtures in shades of yellow to dark crimson; this is a semi-double, light yellow with crimson blotches
GROWN AS HALF-HARDY ANNUALS		
Ageratum houstonianum 'Blue Danube'	15/15cm 6/6in	dwarf example with fluffy clusters of lavender-blue, pompon flowers; colour range includes mauve, pink and white
Antirrhinum Monarch Series snapdragon	40/30cm 16/12in	rust-resistant with familiar snapdragon flowers on erect stems, usually available in bright separate colours; others have flared, double or ruffled flowers
Begonia x carrierei (B. semperflorens) 'Organdy'	15/15cm 6/6in	fibrous-rooted begonia with glistening, pink, red or white flowers against waxy, bronze-green foliage
Brachycome iberidifolia Swan River daisy	45/45cm 18/18in	finely cut foliage with small, fragrant daisies, usually blue but also pink, purple or white
Heliotropium 'Princess Marina' heliotrope	60/60cm 2/2ft	shrubby plant with dark, corrugated leaves and large heads of violet-purple flowers with a rich scent that carries far
Impatiens New Guinea Hybrids	60/60cm 2/2ft	large-flowered busy lizzies; in some the colours are of such startling vivacity that they may jar with the red, bronze or yellow variegation of the glossy leaves
Impatiens Super Elfin Series busy lizzie	15/15cm 6/6in	large, spurred flowers in a mixture of vibrant colours open flat, nearly hiding the foliage
Lobelia erinus 'Mrs Clibran Improved'	10/10cm 4/4in	slender, tufted plants producing small, fan-shaped flowers with wanton profusion; this example is white-eyed and bright blue
Nicotiana Domino Series tobacco plant	30/30cm 12/12in	sticky plants with flowers, mainly in white, lime, pink or red, consisting of a narrow tube and starry mouth; this is compact
Petunia Cloud Series	30/30cm 12/12in	example of large-flowered petunias with floppy blooms of satiny texture in a wide colour range; may be spotted by rain
Petunia Resisto Series	30/30cm 12/12in	single, trumpet flowers, available in separate bright colours, are small but borne profusely and stand up well to wet weather
Salvia splendens Cleopatra Series	30/30cm 12/12in	the usual form has dense spikes of searing scarlet; this series includes less violent colours
Tagetes erecta Inca Series African marigold	30/30cm 12/12in	the numerous *T. erecta* hybrids have aromatic, feathery foliage and large, double flowers in yellow or orange; dwarf with large flowers
Tagetes patula 'Cinnabar' French marigold	30/30cm 12/12in	one of many single and double cultivars with yellow to brown-crimson, daisy flowers over aromatic, feathery foliage; this is single with orange-centred, rust-red flowers
Verbena 'Peaches and Cream'	25/30cm 10/12in	most of the invaluable verbenas are in the pink and red to blue, lilac and white colour range; the flowerheads of this are unusual in their combination of apricot, orange, yellow and cream
Viola 'Padparadja' pansy	15/15cm 6/6in	from a superb range of single and mixed colours, often with a contrasting eye or mask; this is an intense orange
TENDER SHRUBS, PERENNIALS AND TUBERS		
Argyranthemum 'Jamaica Primrose'	60/45cm 2/1½ft	soft yellow, daisy flowers over grey-green foliage
Begonia 'Roy Hartley'	75/75cm 2½/2½ft	salmon-pink example from the many tuberous begonias with sumptuous, camellia-like flowers
Felicia amelloides 'Santa Anita' blue marguerite	45/45cm 18/18in	shrubby plant with a long succession of yellow-centred, blue daisies
Fuchsia 'Annabel'	90/75cm 3/2½ft	one of many hybrids, these shrubs typically produce numerous dangling, skirted flowers, often bicoloured, in this case double and creamy with a pink tinge
Fuchsia 'Thalia'	90/90cm 3/3ft	unusual fuchsia with dangling clusters of slender, tubular, orange-red flowers against velvety, green-maroon foliage
Gazania 'Daybreak'	20/20cm 8/8in	large, daisy-like flowers in shades of orange, yellow, pink, bronze or white, carried above narrow grey-backed leaves; unlike those of most gazanias, the flowers remain open in dull weather
Osteospermum 'Whirligig'	60/45cm 2/1½ft	among a group of ardent sun-loving daisies, this is unusual for the spoon shape and the slate-blue reverse of the white rays
Pelargonium 'Dale Queen'	30/23cm 12/9in	zonal pelargoniums, singles and doubles, offer a wide choice in flower and leaf colour; this is a single with salmon-pink flowers
Pelargonium 'Lord Bute'	50/38cm 20/15in	regal pelargonium, a group with showy, rich-coloured and often frilled flowers; this is purplish-black with a wine edge

Routine care

Plants in containers require much the same care as plants in the open garden but as their roots are restricted they rely almost entirely on the gardener for water. Even rain is commonly shed by foliage outside the container. Plants should be watered liberally, so that the compost is well wetted, before they show signs of stress. During hot summer weather, especially if there is wind, this may mean watering more than once a day.

The use of slow-release fertilizers combined with compost at planting reduces greatly the need to feed plants during the growing season but some supplementary feeding is useful during the growing season, especially when free-flowering bedding plants are grown in soil-less composts. Shrubs that are kept in containers for several years can be repotted from time to time. However, many long-term plantings can be kept going for several years by replacing the top 5-8cm/2-3in of the old compost with fresh compost annually in spring. To keep plants looking well groomed, cut back straggly growth and remove faded flowers.

List of Charts

Index

Acknowledgments

The author gratefully acknowledges the assistance of many people in the making of this book. At the risk of causing offence to those not mentioned by name, he would like to thank the following: Jerry Harpur, whose photographs were his inspiration, and the permanent and freelance staff of Conran Octopus who have been involved in the book's production, especially Alistair Plumb and Helen Ridge.

The photographer and publishers would like to thank the following garden designers and owners for allowing them to photograph their gardens:

1 Deidre Capron; 2 Saling Hall, Essex; 4-6 Barnsley House, Gloucestershire; 8-9 Stone House Cottage, Stone, Hereford & Worcester; 10-11 Pengymill, Essex; 13 The Old Rectory, Sudborough, Northamptonshire; 14 right Designer: Judith Sharpe; 17 above Designer: Simon Fraser; 17 below left Fudlers Hall, Mashbury, Essex; 17 below right Rodmarton Manor, Gloucestershire; 18 Stellenberg, Cape Town; 19 below David Austin Roses; 19 above Lower Hall, Worfield, Shropshire; 20 Broughton Castle, Oxfordshire; 22 and 23 below Designer: Arabella Lennox-Boyd; 24 East Lambrook Manor, Somerset; 25 Designer: Beth Chatto; 26-7 The Old Coach House, Oxfordshire; 30 Park Farm, Great Waltham, Essex; 31 Saling Hall, Essex; 33 below Designer: Mrs Jim Hudson; 34 Designer: Mirabel Osler; 35 Chenies Manor, Oxfordshire; 36-7 Designer: Beth Chatto; 38 Royal Rose Society, St. Albans; 39 Designers: Oehme and van Sweden Associates, Washington D.C.; 40 Burford House, Oxfordshire; 41 above Designer: Bruce Kelly; 41 below Rofford Manor, Oxfordshire; Designer: Michael Balston; 42-3 The Priory, Kemerton, Hereford & Worcester; 44-5 The Old Rectory, Burghfield, Berkshire; 47 below Designer: Sheila Chapman;

47 above Jenkyn Place, Surrey; 49 below Abbot's Ripton Hall, Cambridgeshire; 49 above Designers: Peter Wooster and Gary Keim; 50 Fudler's Hall, Mashbury, Essex; 51 The Old Rectory, Burghfield, Berkshire; 53 below Park Farm, Essex; 54 Coton Manor, Northamptonshire; 57 left Kettle Hill, Blakeney, Norfolk; Designer: Mark Rumary; 57 right Rofford Manor, Oxfordshire; Designer: Michael Balston; 59 Great Dixter, Sussex; 60-1 Kettle Hill, Blakeney, Norfolk; Designer: Mark Rumary; 62 The Dingle, Welshpool, Dyfed; 63 Cambridge University Botanic Gardens; 64-5 Manor House, Birlingham, Hereford & Worcester; 65 The Old Rectory, South Lopham, Norfolk; 66 Manor House, Birlingham, Hereford & Worcester; 67 Powis Castle Gardens, Powys; 68 David Austin Roses; 69 above David Austin Roses; 69 below David Austin Roses; 71 below Royal Rose Society, St. Albans; 72-3 Chenies Manor, Buckinghamshire; 75 above Barnsley House, Gloucestershire; 75 below Designer: Susan Whittington; 76 below Designer: Jenny Robinson; 76-7 above Herterton House, Cambo, Northamptonshire; 77 above Barnsley House, Gloucestershire; 79 above Designer: Beth Chatto; 79 below The Old Rectory, Sudborough, Northamptonshire; 80-1 Tintinhull House, Somerset; 82 Designer: Gunilla Pickard; 84-5 House of Pitmuies, Guthrie-by-Forfar; 86-7 Designer: Beth Chatto; 88-9 Designer: Bruce Kelly; 91 right Pengymill, Essex; 91 below Designer: John Plummer; 91 above Pengymill, Essex; 92 right Designer: Beth Chatto; 92 left Designer: Sheila McQueen; 94-5 Chelsea Physic Garden, London; 96 Hestercombe, Taunton, Somerset; 97 Designer: Beth Chatto; 98-9 above Wakehurst Place, Sussex; 99 above Designer: Beth Chatto; 99 below Designers: Oehme and van Sweden Associates, Washington D.C.; Carol Rosenberg; 101 Bank House, Borwick, Lancashire;

105 Savill Garden, Windsor; 106-7 Designer: Bruce Kelly; 109-11 above Designer: Beth Chatto: 111 below Rofford Manor, Oxfordshire; Designer: Michael Balston; 112-13 Hatfield House, Hertfordshire; 114-15 Designer: Peter Place; 115 right Designer: Peter Partridge; 116 above Broughton Castle, Oxfordshire; 116 below Stellenberg, Cape Town; 118 left Designer: Helen Yemm; 119 right Designer: Frank Cabot; 120 Designer: Deborah Kellaway; 123 right Little Lodge, Thames Ditton; 124 right Designer: Beth Chatto; 124 left Hadspen House, Castle Cary, Somerset; 126-7 Old Rectory, Sudborough, Northamptonshire; 128 Barnsley House; 129 Designer: Sonny Garcia; 130-1 Designers: Joe Eck and Wayne Winterrowd, Vermont; 132-3 above The Old Rectory, Burghfield, Berkshire; 133 below Designer: Beth Chatto; 133 above right The Old Rectory, Burghfield, Berkshire; 135 right Arbigland, Dumfries; 135 left Sun House, Long Melford, Suffolk; 136-7 Designer: Simon Fraser; 138-9 Designer: Edwina von Gal; 140 Designers: Nick and Pam Coote; 141 Designer: Chris Rosmini, Los Angeles; 142 left Designer: Beth Chatto; 142 right Designer: Beth Chatto; 145 above The Old Rectory, Burghfield, Berkshire; 146 Designers: Arabella Lennox-Boyd and Michael Balston; 149 right Designers: Peter Wooster and Gary Keim; 149 right The Old Rectory, Burghfield, Berkshire; 151 below Designer: Wesley Rouse, Washington, Connecticut; 151 above Designers: Nick and Pam Coote; 152 left Designer: Anne Alexander-Sinclair; 152 right Designer: Ryl Nowell.

The author and publisher also thank Jackie Matthews, Kate Bell, Barbara Haynes, Marcus Harpur, Barbara Nash and Janet Smy.

Index compiled by Indexing Specialists, Hove, East Sussex BN3 2DJ.